Salvation Manual

Topical Exegesis of the Book of Genesis - Volume 1

Johnny, Nsikan Effiong

Grosvenor House
Publishing Limited

This book is published by
Grosvenor House Publishing Ltd
Link House
140 The Broadway, Tolworth, Surrey, KT6 7HT.
www.grosvenorhousepublishing.co.uk

This book is a commentary on the Bible and non-Biblical
illustrations used are works of fiction. Any resemblance to
people or events, past or present, is purely coincidental.

A CIP record for this book
is available from the British Library

Paperback ISBN 978-1-80381-046-1
Hardback ISBN 978-1-80381-111-6
eBook ISBN 978-1-80381-084-3

www.smni.org

TABLE OF CONTENTS

TABLE OF CONTENTS

FOREWORD

The purpose of God, to reach humanity with the message of salvation, has not diminished across generations. He entrusts that eternal assignment to men who are willing and available. The author of *Salvation Manual: Topical Exegesis*, Nsikan E. Johnny, was challenged in a service, at which his pastor demanded to know how many times members of the congregation read the whole Bible. One person answered, saying "twenty-plus". That incident planted in him the hunger for the word of God, which led him to design ways to read and understand the Bible. The Lord at several instances kept pointing him to these facts: the primary purpose of the Bible is to unfold the salvation of humanity through Christ; the doctrine of salvation is foundational to every subject in the word of God; and each subject must be interpreted in the light of salvation through Christ. The author's unwavering dislike of wrong biblical teachings, either deliberately for selfish motives or out of ignorance, is unparalleled.

It has been my pleasure to know Nsikan E. Johnny for quite some time in a friendship that has gone from mere acquaintance to being co-labourers in ministry. His vision to reach out to people with the truth relating to salvation led him to organise Bible studies which he taught at his office. Later, he sponsored a Bible quiz programme on radio in Akwa Ibom State, Nigeria. In 2015, the vision expanded to a national level through the Bible 'Answer and Win' programme on social media and its accompanying blog site, which he presided over to transform lives. However, the vision has not stopped; it keeps growing, which is evident in this book, all in a bid to promote the message of salvation to the ends of the earth.

The subject of salvation resonates through the book's pages. The book is eternally valuable, scripturally based, doctrinally sound and reflects God's will about salvation, which is beneficial for all ages. It is given with prayers to positively change the erroneous trend concerning Bible truth and salvation. This remarkable work instructs and illustrates the importance of the Bible as a manual for our lives. It helps unlock salvation principles that will benefit both preachers and teachers of the word and all who would live a Christ-like life. It is shaped with one thought in mind: to help people understand God's word with an *emphasis on salvation*. The book is well written, informative and an eye-opener for Christians who want to know God for themselves. It implores Christians to study the Bible from the angle of salvation, which will protect them from possible errors of wrong teachings.

A big thanks to the author for writing this much-needed manual. Through the help of the Holy Spirit, I believe this piece of work will help people return to the narrow path, now that the door of mercy is still open. I recommend this book to you, fellow pilgrims; it shall serve as a guide through this world back to our heavenly home.

Revd B. Agbor Anayo
Bristol, UK.

PREFACE

Precious things in the world are hard to come by, and sometimes when found they are highly priced. Salvation is more precious than anything else and is not without a cost or price. Christ paid the price through His death and He admonishes us to carry our cross and follow Him. This entails responsibility on our part to obtain this gift of salvation. If a man finds a jewel of inestimable value, will he not sell all he has to enable him to purchase it? The gift of salvation is something we should go all out to obtain, with all that is in us and all we have.

This book is written and published chiefly with a view to enlightening many. In defence of that which is true and with a desire to correct the many erroneous teachings spreading through the church, I think of this book as a valuable companion for all genuine seekers journeying through life. My soul's salvation and the salvation of others have always driven me to create avenues and systems to spread the gospel. Lying deep in my heart, the great commission demanded by the Saviour has become not only a purpose but a passion for continuing my Master's work and making known to the world the burden placed in my heart by the Holy Spirit.

The scripture says that faith comes by hearing and hearing by the word of God (Romans 10:17). But what happens when the word is not correctly taught, or correctly taught but not completely broken down and hence not properly understood? So much has gone wrong among sincere seekers of God due to a lack of understanding of the scriptures. That is why we have preachers, called and empowered by the Holy Spirit, to teach the word and ensure mankind find their way back to God. However, many still teach wrongly due to many factors. As such, souls are endangered and instead of being saved they proceed to hell. Against this backdrop, *Salvation Manual: Topical Exegesis* is born – it is a series of topical commentaries on each book of the Bible that explains vital biblical subjects with the emphasis on salvation.

Knowledge is power, but nothing is as powerful as the right knowledge of the word of God. All those who find the Bible hard to understand or who have questions should try reading this book. Assuredly, all your doubts and confusion will be cleared. If you are ready to make sacrifices towards the salvation of your soul, *Salvation Manual: Topical Exegesis* is for you. If you desire to understand God and His works by following His word, *Salvation Manual: Topical Exegesis* is the guide. With this book, the messages in the Bible are explained with their right application. The Bible contains the word of God and this book details the right and practical application of the word to ensure the salvation of our souls.

INTRODUCTION

Much of man's foremost quest in life has often revolved around the needs that affect his survival and ensure his relevance. From a tender age to the winter of his life, he devises plans and spares no effort in attaining these goals. However, in his ephemeral pursuits man often ignores attention to matters with eternal value.

Ask a man without eyes about his greatest need and he will most likely tell you he wants to see. Quiz some people who have had to endure penury on what they desire most and they will most certainly tell you they want riches. While these desires in and of themselves are not wrong, they do not rank as man's prime need or what is most essential for us. Man's greatest need has never been the food that satiates his hunger, the building that gives him shelter, the status that makes him relevant or anything that caters to his physical needs. The salvation of our souls constitutes the greatest need and should occupy the top echelon of our priorities. The words of Jesus, "seek first the kingdom of God", strikes at the core of what should be our life's goal. It entails prioritising the salvation of our soul over anything else in the world. It is what we should long for, strive for and live for. The words in this book have been written to help you achieve a precious and priceless gift – salvation – that will make your existence in this world a meaningful one.

Salvation Manual: Topical Exegesis of the Book of Genesis Vol. 1 expounds on what has been written in the book of Genesis Chapter 1 to 25, though relevant references are taken from other books of the Bible. The lessons you will learn are drawn partly from the context of the scriptures, the express commands of God and from the lives and experiences of several biblical characters. We examine the strengths and flaws, successes and failures of some biblical characters and extract valuable lessons that will guide us on the journey through life. While we can scan through the Bible and get a general understanding of the stories within these chapters, this book will draw your attention to vital lessons we may not have noticed. Remember that every scripture is given by God and is useful for teaching, reproof, correction and training in righteousness (2 Timothy 3:16).

The phrase 'emphasis on salvation' reverberates through the pages of this book. This concept portrays how we are to approach the study of God's word – focusing our minds on how the word of God will help us grow intimately in our relationship with God, a relationship that will culminate in a glorious eternal destination with God.

In this book, the questions we have always wondered about, the issues that often bother us, and the problems we have painstakingly sought solutions to are accurately addressed. One of the many mysteries that has intrigued the minds of mankind is the origin of God. Many wonder how and when the Creator of the universe came into existence. Several theories and opinions have been offered to explain this phenomenon. While some have their basis in the scripture, others have been drawn from outside it. From the information provided in the Bible, it will be explained to you whether God has an origin or not. Another question that has boggled the minds of many is whether drinking alcohol is approved or condemned by God. Tithing has also been a topic of contention, with opinions varying among believers. *Salvation Manual: Topical Exegesis of the Book of Genesis Vol. 1* provides answers to these questions and many others that have posed a challenge to people.

Many people also wonder why the world is in so much disarray; they wonder why God created the things that cause diseases and natural disasters in the world. The answer to these questions in this book will clarify these grey areas for you and strengthen your faith in God. Also, regardless of their social and economic status, many people have often wondered what their purpose in life is. From God's assignment to the first man, before sin came into the picture, man's purpose on earth is addressed. This purpose is drawn from a focal point and projected to every man's life on earth. Understanding and adhering to this lesson will help you live a purposeful and fulfilled life, no matter what your field of endeavour.

Also detailed in this book is God's awesomeness, which is expressed in the magnificent creation of the world. His love for those who fear Him is demonstrated by His guidance, protection and provision. Other information you will learn about God is His providence, His abhorrence for sin, the equity in His justice system, His faithfulness in keeping to His promise and His relentless pursuit of restoring His broken relationship with man.

In this book you will also discover God's expectations of the way man should conduct himself and relate to his fellow man. Since man was fashioned in God's image, he is expected to replicate God's nature of holiness. There is no other option in this expectation, nor is there an allowance for compromise. Everything you need to know to fulfil this divine mandate is contained in this book. If you desire to stand out in a world filled with temptations and sin, the information provided in this book will help you live a distinguished life. Through the context of the scriptures and the lives of various biblical heroes, you will learn what it means to be blameless, what true circumcision is, how to overcome temptations and live a consecrated life. Also provided in this book are the indispensable elements – the word of God and prayer, that will help us attain and sustain holiness in our Christian walk. God's expectation is that we live above sin, but peradventure we fall into sin; what should our reaction be? From the lives of those who walked before us we will learn the attitude we should exhibit when we err. We will learn how we can grow in intimacy with God by communing with Him and how valuable the word of God – the Bible – is if we study it with an *emphasis on salvation* and obey it without reservation.

This manual will guide us as we journey through this world as pilgrims. In it, you will see how we are to demonstrate love towards our fellow man and how we are to react to those who offend us. Disunity has played a crucial role in the inability of a group to work together to achieve a common goal. From this book you will learn the power of unity as an indispensable tool for success.

Another aspect of our existence that is spotlighted in this book is family. If you desire marital guidance you will come across vital information to help you. Other family-related matters such as impartial parental love, our attitude to parental misconduct, how to handle strife within the family, the relevance of parental blessing in marriage and putting your house in order before your demise have been comprehensively discussed to broaden your understanding. The ideal qualities to look out for in your choice of spouse and God's design for marriage is also adequately communicated.

As you read this book, you will encounter other subjects that can help you live a purposeful life in this world. One reality man experiences daily is coming face to face with life's various challenges. From the lives of biblical characters, you will gain insight into the right attitude to display when engulfed in adversity. You will learn to acknowledge God as the source behind whatever feat you attain, whatever good is bestowed on you, whatever blessing you are enjoying and, most importantly, the salvation of your soul. Zooming into the life of one man – Abraham, through whom God kickstarted His plan to restore man to Himself, you will learn principles and truth that will challenge you in your walk with God. Thriving in this world can also be made possible by learning about certain pivotal principles such as contentment, giving and faith.

Since our soul's salvation remains the apogee for us, it behoves us to place primacy on what will help us achieve that. Therefore, you will find in this book a compendium of writings encompassing human experiences that will guide you in reaching that goal and living the kind of life that God expects.

CHAPTER 1

TOPIC 1: ORIGIN OF GOD

GENESIS 1:1

Some children stood by the side of the road that passed through their village gazing curiously at the horizons on both sides:

"Look, that village (mentioning a village name) is the beginning of the world, and that village (mentioning the name of another village on the other side of the road) is the end of the world," one boy said, jumping, as he tried to look beyond the hill.

"The sky touches the earth in those villages...."

"That's not true, how do you know?" his friend retorted. "I hear there are other villages beyond."

"There are no other villages," the first boy insisted, "the rest is the sky...." (Johnny, 2022.)

The argument remained unsettled until exposure through education and travelling gave them the understanding that the earth is spherical and does not have a definite beginning or end.

Man, by nature, is an inquisitive being. The quest to satisfy this curiosity has led to discoveries, inventions and innovations in diverse spheres of life, which has brought man from the primitive way of life of ancient man to the civilised way of life of the modern man.

In Genesis 1:1, it is recorded that *"In the beginning God created the heavens and the earth."* (NHEB.) This scripture solves the puzzle of how the universe came into existence by pointing to the Creator – God – but leaves a question often raised by people: "If our existence originated from God, how did God originate?" Often, people who do not believe in God raise this question, intending to ridicule the Bible in their bid to defend their assertions. Some others ask this question out of sheer curiosity, just like those children attempting to find a definite beginning or end of the earth.

However, with the right knowledge of God's word, personal experiences with God and spiritual maturity, we get to know that curiosity that seeks explanations to the origin of the existence of God does not lead to the knowledge that is sought, not because the correct theories and correlations have not been applied, but because they do not exist.

A common argument from sceptics and atheists is that if all things need a cause then God must also be a result of a cause (the principle of causality). God is the Creator that was not created; He is self-existent.

The words 'in the beginning' in the first chapter of the book of Genesis refer to the beginning of creation but not the beginning of God. God exists out of time. Before the world came into existence, God was in existence.

The origin of His existence is a mystery that man can never understand. We can see throughout the scriptures that there is no attempt to prove the origin of God but, about His existence, it is revealed that:

- He is the origin of everything that now is, as seen in Genesis Chapter 1.
- He is everlasting: *"Before the mountains were brought forth, before you had formed the earth and the world, even from everlasting to everlasting, you are God."* (Psalm 90:2 NHEB.)

- He is the Creator and Upholder of everything, maintaining everything He created by His word *"and upholding all things by the word of his power…"* (Hebrews 1:3 NHEB).

The plans of God for us are for good, to prosper us, to give us a future and hope, but not to harm us. To this end, He has given us all the information we need. Whatever has been revealed to man by God was meant for man's consumption and to be passed down to his descendants, but there are certain things which God keeps to Himself; He calls them "the secret things". Deuteronomy 29:29 says, *"The secret things belong to the LORD our God; but the things that are revealed belong to us and to our children forever, that we may do all the words of this law."* (NHEB.)

Apart from God revealing Himself to man individually or in groups, He has not left man without evidence of His existence in all of creation so that no one will be excused for denying His existence. *"because what can be known about God is plain to them, because God has shown it to them. [20] For since the creation of the world his invisible attributes, his eternal power and divine nature, have been clearly seen, being understood from what has been made. So they are without excuse."* (Romans 1:19–20 NHEB.)

God has given His word – the Bible – as a manual and the Holy Spirit as a guide and teacher to help us through the journey of life. In His word lies sufficient information about His person for us to live peaceably and to prevent us from getting involved in vain thoughts and actions that may put our souls at risk of condemnation, for everyone will give an account of the choices they made while on earth.

At the end of this life, we will have a clearer understanding of the things that were once mysteries to us. *"For now we see in a mirror, dimly, but then face to face. Now I know in part, but then I will know fully, even as I was also fully known."* (1 Corinthians 13:12 NHEB.)

Our priority should not be to search for the origin of God; rather, it should be to live our lives in obedience to the instructions of God to transcend this life to glory.

TOPIC 2: SUMMARY OF CREATION

GENESIS 1:3–31

The awesomeness of God's person, the unfathomable depth of His power, the immeasurable length of His wisdom, and the strength of His aesthetic creativity were abundantly demonstrated in the creation of the universe.

The Bible records that God created the universe in six days and rested on the seventh. Everything was created to serve a purpose. The creation story tells us more about who God is. He is a God of order, pattern, system and details. We can observe the symmetry of the six days of creation: the first three days for forming and the next three days for filling. The first three days of creation could be regarded as the preparation of the foundation for what was to come. This was designed as the base to support everything that was to be laid upon the earth.

On the first day, God made light. He separated the light from darkness calling the light 'day' and the darkness 'night'. On the fourth day He created the sun to give light to the earth in the day, the moon to illuminate the earth at night. He also made the stars. God placed them all in the firmaments to serve as signs for days and nights and seasons.

On the second day, God made the space between the waters of the heavens and the waters of the earth, leaving sufficient room for every creature He would later create that would not live in water. In line with His aesthetic master-plan, God structured the atmosphere – the temperature, air pressure, wind conditions and other factors that come to bear in keeping the clouds at the roof of the troposphere.

They are perfectly designed to be the way they are, leaving a clear atmosphere for the earth's inhabitants, free from the turbulence characteristic of the roof of the troposphere where the clouds dwell.

On the third day, God gathered the waters into the various natural water bodies we see today, and dry land appeared. After that, God made the vegetation and placed it on the land He had created on the same day. On the fifth day, God made the aquatic creatures and the birds. Finally, on the sixth day, He made the terrestrial creatures, including man, who would occupy the earth He had created. All that God had created was for His pleasure, and He was pleased with it all.

God's signature on His creations is undeniably evident, from the simplest to the most complex forms of matter, the intra-dependence between the earthly creatures and their interdependence with the celestial bodies. Everything we see around us is proof of the magnificent artistry of God.

It is a pitiable thing that man had deviated from worship of the Creator to worship of the created things such as the sun, moon, stars, trees, seas, mountains, animals, crafts of his own hands. By so doing, he debased himself from the place of authority that God had intended for him. God intends for man to know Him and not to act rebelliously by ascribing the glory that is due to Him to someone else or something else. This is why He has revealed the history of creation to us through the Bible.

Everything we know now or will know in the future is made by Him, and without Him, nothing that exists now existed. John 1:3 says, *"All things were made through him, and apart from him nothing was made that has been made."* (NHEB.) God created all things and holds everything together by His word. His word is also the power by which He saves men unto Himself. We are to draw closer to God, our Creator, for He is the source of life to all creation. Colossians 1:16–17 says, *"For by him all things were created, in the heavens and on the earth, things visible and things invisible, whether thrones or dominions or rulers or powers; all things have been created by him and for him. [17]He is before all things, and in him all things are held together."* (NHEB.)

TOPIC 3: EVERYTHING GOD CREATED WAS GOOD

GENESIS 1:31

The beauty and the quality of God's creation are captured in the assertive and affirmative remark in Genesis 1:31 that all God created is good. Each creation met His preconceived standard and specifications, which creates a visible demonstration of God's magnificence and perfection.

If God's plan is for the good of mankind and everything He made was good, why does it feel like there are certain things we would have wished were not in existence, such as natural disasters, diseases and pestilence? Where did it all go wrong? Why is the world in so much disarray?

The answer is this: man disobeyed the instructions of God and brought sin into the world. Sin separates man from God, who is holy and despises iniquity. Separation from God means separation from the source that gives life and sustains all creation, and the result of such separation is disastrous. The curse that accompanied man's sin against God had its toll on the entire creation because man was created to lord over God's creations. The entire creation went into disarray due to man's sin. The pains of childbirth came to be, the elements of suffering became part of man's life and death came to be. Romans 8:20, 22 says, *"For the creation was subjected to vanity, not of its own will... [22]For we know that the whole creation groans and travails in pain together until now."* (NHEB.) Natural disasters, diseases, pestilence and the like also came into existence.

The sinful nature, now inherent in man, also caused him to misuse many good things God had created and called good. Some of this misuse includes:

6

- Drug abuse – from the misuse of plants that are meant to be of medicinal value, such as marijuana and coca.
- Idolatry – resulting from the worship of created things instead of the Creator.
- Sexual immorality – getting involved in diverse sexual acts against the will of God for mankind.
- The invention of weapons – using the wisdom and resources God has given to mankind to create instruments of destruction.

The list goes on and on.

By this misuse of God's creations, man wraps himself more and more in the web of troubles he has created for himself. This is evident in the wicked, immoral, disaster-prone and rebellious world we now live in.

By the sin of the first man, Adam, the self-destruct button of the earth was triggered. Although man continued to deviate farther and farther from God as he increased in rebellion and wickedness, God, in His love, did not leave man to his peril. He prepared a salvation plan to restore man to Himself, to the place of glory and dominion He had created him for.

The salvation plan of God for man who was doomed for death was completed on the death and resurrection of Jesus Christ: *"For God so loved the world that he gave his only Son, so that whoever believes in him will not perish, but have everlasting life."* (John 3:16 NHEB.) The way the world turned out was due to sin and the remedy to sin is Christ. The result of this salvation brought by Christ will culminate in a world where there is no pain, sorrow, anguish or pestilence. It will be a beautiful world of paradise filled with peace, joy and happiness. This is the hope of all who fall under the umbrella of Christ's redemption and salvation. *"And he will wipe away every tear from their eyes, and death will be no more, nor will there be mourning, nor crying, nor pain, anymore, for the first things have passed away."* (Revelation 21:4 NHEB.)

By his inherent sinful nature man has also misused the gospel of God's grace, which is meant to give him another chance to make it right with God, as an excuse for sin.

Many are quick to point fingers at God as the reason for the unpleasant situations they are facing, but that is not true. Man brought predicament upon himself by his choices and brings more predicaments upon himself by the choices he continues to make. It would be more profitable to see where we got it wrong and retrace our steps to the Creator by accepting His offer of salvation and living in complete obedience to His words. God despises sin, and, as such, we cannot be partakers of His salvation if we continue living the sinful life that He seeks to restore us from. Although God desires to restore man to Himself, His salvation is only for those who will come to Him in obedience and humility.

TOPIC 4: GREAT IS OUR GOD

GENESIS 1:3–31

Men naturally give honour and reverence to other men who have completed remarkable feats. What level of honour should then be ascribed to the greatest Architect, Artist and Creator of this magnificent world? Simply, unlimited honour and gratitude! *"Worthy are you, our Lord and God, to receive the glory, the honor, and the power, for you created all things, and because of your desire they existed, and were created."* (Revelation 4:11 NHEB.) Since all creation is of God, then all glory and honour must be to Him. The fascination and the grandeur of His creation, the attention to detail, the complexity and creativity is purely breath-taking.

When you see the creation in its beauty, the wisdom one derives from it is that such an organised system can only proceed from a great God; it cannot be a result of an accident. Such perfection and magnificence cannot proceed from mediocrity but from One who is excellent in wisdom and power.

By attentively considering creation's vastness, complexity, beauty and order, we can conceive a sense of the awesomeness of God. The stupendous works of God, His creative acts, painstaking orderliness, and innumerable creatures with their dynamism of operations are all indisputable proofs of His exclusive greatness. God's greatness, no doubt, is indescribable and unsearchable. Psalm 145:3 says, *"Great is the LORD, and greatly to be praised. His greatness is unsearchable."* (NHEB.)

The limited information available to humankind about God's great personality and creative works can only give us a glimpse of God's greatness through His communicable attributes and visible awesome works.

God commanded the sky to appear colourfully; obediently, it manifested. He spoke to the waters, and they properly repositioned together in the assigned place so that dry land could appear; then He commanded the aquatic creatures of various species into existence. This was followed by the creation of birds to fly in the firmament; of course, this was not before He created the beautiful and radiant firmament. He also commanded the terrestrial creatures to come into existence. The sun, moon and stars are all His creative works. He specially formed man out of the dust, according to His image for fellowship and to show forth His glory.

The greatness of God is evident in the whole work of creation. Words alone cannot describe the greatness of God. His handiworks are expressions of His glory and grandeur. Psalm 19:1 says, *"The heavens declare the glory of God. The expanse shows his handiwork."* (NHEB.) The heavens declare His glory just by their existence; we who were created in His image ought to intentionally express His glory in praises and adoration.

God's penchant for perfection is unsurmountable; everything He created was excellent, without any error, and there has been no need to modify the creation. His creation of the universe is out of love; no one prayed to Him or begged Him to do it. More so, it is essential to note that God's word has always been and will always be His tool for getting things done. God created everything by His word: *"For by him all things were created, in the heavens and on the earth, things visible and things invisible, whether thrones or dominions or rulers or powers; all things have been created by him and for him."* (Colossians 1:16 NHEB.) *"All things were made through him, and apart from him nothing was made that has been made."* (John 1:3 NHEB.) God has not stopped using His word in His dealings with man, moulding and shaping our lives for His glory.

In creative arts, a work of art is not only a transmission of an artist's imagination but also, through their work, one can have a peep into the artist's intrinsic qualities, such as their passion and beliefs. Take a second look at the creation and you will see a God who is passionately in love with the human race whom He had in mind as He created the world. You will feel His heartbeat and believe that He is currently preparing a more magnificent place for those who love Him. Look at His creation to convince you that He loves you, and let that motivate you to open your heart to Him.

Conclusively, God's awesome attributes and His creative works give a good description of His greatness. Indeed, great is our God.

TOPIC 5: UNITY OF PURPOSE IN CREATION

GENESIS 1:26

God said, "Let us make man in our image." This statement denotes a plurality of persons involved in the intended action, and what other plurality can be deduced other than the trinity? At creation, these Persons worked together to ensure that the purpose of creation was achieved. God used an expression He did not deploy beforehand. The lesson on the need for unity displayed by God in creation in the above passage is vital for consideration.

God is omnipotent, yet He displayed the attitude and character of a team player. The character is not a result of any weakness or deficiency but out of fullness, strength and complete sufficiency. With the divine teamwork at creation, God showed us the power and necessity of teamwork. John 1:1–3 expounds on teamwork and the unity of the personalities of the team. *"In the beginning was the Word, and the Word was with God, and the Word was God. ²He was in the beginning with God. ³All things were made through him, and apart from him nothing was made that has been made."* (NHEB.) This shows unity and the place of the Word (Jesus Christ) in creation. Genesis 1:2 mentions another personality of the trinity at creation. It says: *"God's Spirit was hovering over the surface of the waters."* (NHEB.) At God's word, the creation came into being through the power of the Spirit of God.

Jesus desires to see us walking in unity just as it exists between Him, the Holy Spirit and the Father. So He prayed *"that they may be one, even as we are one"* (John 17:22 NHEB). Unity erases tension, hatred and backbiting; it conquers conflicts and confronts challenges. Conspiracy and other vices hardly thrive where unity reigns. Psalm 133:1–3 says, *"See how good and how pleasant it is for brothers to live together in unity. ²It is like the precious oil on the head, that ran down on the beard, even Aaron's beard; that came down on the edge of his robes; ³like the dew of Hermon, that comes down on the hills of Zion: for there the LORD gives the blessing, even life forevermore."* (NHEB.)

Disunity is a crucial factor in the dysfunctionality of most broken families. In a functional home in which the man is the head of the household he does not work alone to achieve the family goals. He provides emotionally and materially for his household and is expected to provide protection, comfort and general direction for the family. In a traditional arrangement such as this, the woman, as the wife and mother, provides support and co-leadership.

At work, we are not expected to work in isolation. Whether as bosses or subordinates, employers or employees we should understand that we are part of the units and systems that make up the organisation.

The problem with many people and why unity seems to be a tall order is the mindset that if one is not the head, one does not find satisfaction. People fail to consider that each component is pivotal to the success of an endeavour, no matter how small a contribution it may seem. It is also expedient that heads acknowledge those under them who are instrumental in achieving the set goals, as a matter of courtesy and encouragement. For example, after a successful surgical operation, non-medical personnel usually give credit to the head surgeon. However, the head surgeon's expertise would not lead to a successful operation without nurses, anesthesiologists and other professionals. Many specialists work together to make sure that the surgery is successful. People outside may accord accolades to the head surgeon. However, the head surgeon knows he had many other team members who contributed to the surgery.

Unity among people has been quite a challenge, and more so among the Body of Christ. The devil and the world have been fighting that unity and causing division even among those speaking one language and sharing the same faith. Unity of purpose among the Body of Christ is a necessity. While we work at our different divine purposes as individuals, let us all remember that each of us is a part of God's universal purpose. This purpose is the reconciliation of the world back to Himself. God wants to fulfil this purpose through the Body of Christ. *"For as the body is one, and has many members, and all the members of the body, being many, are one body; so also is Christ."* (1 Corinthians 12:12 NHEB.)

As Christians we must strive to reproduce unity of purpose in our little way, even with non-Christians, as long as it does not go against God's word. We would need to leave this world before we can avoid working with unbelievers. 1 Corinthians 5:9–10 says, *"I wrote to you in my letter to have no company with sexual sinners; ¹⁰yet not at all meaning with the sexual sinners of this world, or with the covetous and extortioners, or with idolaters; for then you would have to leave the world."* (NHEB.) Unity may not mean sameness, but we must look more at what keeps us together than what divides us. We must learn how to tolerate one another's weaknesses. Unity must be shown in our relationship with God and our relationship with fellow humans. This level of unity is achievable by our unconditional love for God and His word.

TOPIC 6: MAN: THE IMAGE OF GOD

GENESIS 1:26–28

Man was created in God's image and likeness, possessing certain spiritual and moral attributes of God, unlike any other creature. Man was created in perfect righteousness, having no knowledge of sin.

Apparently God created other things in preparation for man's arrival – the crown of His creation. As God's image, man would be a reflection of God with the capability to exhibit certain communicable attributes of God such as love, righteousness, knowledge, dominion and peace. However, he would be unable to express and manifest God's specific incommunicable attributes such as omnipotence, invincibility, omnipresence, omniscience and sovereignty, to mention but a few.

Man is not God totally in human form, for that will amount to making man equal to God. Rather, God formed man – male and female – in His own image. Man was specifically created to have fellowship with God and show forth God's praises, not to live for himself. Revelation 4:11 says, *"Worthy are you, our Lord and God, to receive the glory, the honor, and the power, for you created all things, and because of your desire they existed, and were created."* (NHEB.)

Additionally, God bestowed upon man the divine ability to exercise dominion over every created thing for his benefit and to the glory and praises of God, who graciously endowed him with such exceptional attributes among all the creatures. It is an absolute privilege for man to receive such a rare and apex honour, to be created in God's image. Therefore, fulfilling our God-given purpose here on earth to glorify God should continually constitute our priority. Man's desire must always be to please God in all things, as His ambassador on earth.

God created us to know, love and mirror Him. In His image and likeness, He fashioned man for everlasting companionship. He places a high priority on companionship and fellowship. We should be reminded that God was never alone. God does not necessarily need our fellowship to exist. *"The God who made the world and all things in it, he, being Lord of heaven and earth, does not dwell in temples made with hands, ²⁵ neither is he served by human hands, as though he needed anything, seeing he himself gives to all life and breath, and all things."* (Acts 17:24–25 NHEB.) God does not need a relationship with us in any way to improve who He is, but to improve who we are. He desires to have us share in the fountain of His love, and we need fellowship with Him. In Psalm 73:25, Asaph calls out, *"Who do I have in heaven? There is no one on earth who I desire besides you."* (NHEB.)

At creation, man was a combination of both the physical and the spiritual. He was made from dust and bore the breath of God – physically, flesh and blood, and inwardly, carrying God's spirit. He was to exist on earth but bear the authority of heaven. He was to represent God on earth, ensuring that the will of God prevails on earth as it prevails in heaven. The first man was very much like God, and God entrusted him with overseeing His creation. While God ruled in heaven, Adam was to rule on earth, for he was a replica of God on earth. Psalm 115:16 says, *"The heavens are the heavens of the LORD; but the earth has he given to the children of men."* (NHEB.)

Before the fall of man, Adam and Eve had a perfect connection with God. Their hearts, souls and minds were in absolute sync with God's thoughts, will and desires. Their holiness measured up to God's standard. The fear and shame that made them run when they heard the voice of God in the cool of the day was not there. However, after the fall, the fellowship with God was adversely affected. Fear, shame and the nakedness caused by sin made them run from God.

Today we see the human race not fully expressing that image of God. Instead of divine love, self-centredness, lust and hate are manifest in the natural man. Sin came in and corrupted the holy attribute. Fear and shame, which were not part of God's image, found their way into man due to sin. The consequences of sin gave Satan the legal ground to rule over mankind and the world.

However, God did not leave man without a salvation plan. Right from Eden, God began a movement that would culminate in the coming of Jesus Christ. God was interested in restoring that image of the lost human race. Even today, God is still interested in bringing those not yet saved into His kingdom.

God's eternal purpose in creating man in His image will not be achieved in man unless he accepts Jesus Christ, who came to restore the fellowship and dominion that was lost through the fall of man. After the death of Jesus, every man is faced with the opportunity, like Adam, to make a choice – whether to obey God, walk in that fellowship and experience a restoration of God's image or disobey God and miss that fellowship with Him. Today, man's eternal condemnation will not be because Adam fell; it will be because he refuses Christ's offer of salvation.

CHAPTER 2

TOPIC 1: GOD RESTED

GENESIS 2:2–3

Is it not baffling to read of God, whom the scriptures say neither faints nor is weary, neither sleeps nor slumbers, but rests only after creating? It is recorded that He made everything within six days and on the seventh day rested from all His works. In the previous verses, we are made to know about the perfectness of everything He made; after each work was done, He observed and saw that it was good.

Rest is required due to exhaustion or stress; thus, this begs the question, was the work so exhausting that God had to rest after it? The answer is no. He had completed everything about creation; the world was perfectly arranged and shaped. Everything was done, and God rested from creating. This does not mean God has been resting since that time, folding His hands and letting His creation exist without His influence. We see that God is still working as Jesus said in John 5:17: *"My Father is still working, so I am working, too."* (NHEB.) In the verses in context, in Genesis 2:2–3, God's rest does not denote relaxation due to tiredness but rather a cessation from the work of creation.

There are lessons from God's rest that are worthy of note. Man has been given the responsibility to rule over other creatures and exercise his creative ability to make new things useful for himself from what God has already created. In this case, he needs rest, time and again, because his work continues until he finally leaves this earth in death.

Human beings were not designed to work tirelessly and continuously without relaxation. We should not be busy to such an extent that we trivialise the importance of creating time to rest our bodies and minds. When we rest, we become refreshed and reinvigorated. Not only does resting increase our efficiency and productivity levels, but it is also essential to our health. Stressing ourselves beyond limits is detrimental to our overall wellbeing. Anxiety and apprehension over future uncertainties can make a man slave to work, making no room for his body to relax. Work is good; we can provide for ourselves through it, but it becomes destructive to our wellbeing when work gives no room for rest. We ought to learn the art of creating time to rest our bodies.

In Exodus 20:8–11, as part of the Ten Commandments handed to them by God, the Israelites were instructed to keep the seventh day holy and rest on that day. *"Remember the Sabbath day, to keep it holy. ⁹Six days you may labor and do all your work, ¹⁰but the seventh day is a Sabbath to the LORD your God. You must not do any work, you, nor your son, nor your daughter, your male servant, nor your female servant, nor your livestock, nor your stranger who is within your gates; ¹¹for in six days the LORD made heaven and earth, the sea, and all that is in them, and rested the seventh day; therefore the LORD blessed the seventh day, and made it holy."* (NHEB.) Let us note that the Sabbath rest is symbolic, for it is a foreshadow of the rest found in Christ. *"Therefore do not let anyone judge you in eating, or in drinking, or with respect to a feast day or a new moon or a Sabbath day, ¹⁷which are a shadow of the things to come; but the body is Christ's."* (Colossians 2:16–17 NHEB.) The seventh or Sabbath day was a pointer to God's eternal rest. The book of Hebrews did not fail to enlighten us on this subject. *"There remains therefore a Sabbath rest for the people of God. ¹⁰For he who has entered into his rest has himself also rested from his works, as God did from his. ¹¹Let us therefore give diligence to enter into that rest, lest anyone fall after the same example of disobedience."* (Hebrews 4:9–11 NHEB.)

There is an eternal rest which God has prepared for His people, those whose faith in Him is revealed by their lifestyle of complete obedience. This kind of rest is one of the soul rather than the body. It is a complete cessation of life's toils and sorrows – freedom from trials, temptations and all forms of struggle against the flesh. Those who attain this rest will be fully united with the Lord in perfect love and harmony at the end of time.

Since there is a rest from life's struggles we must unceasingly work for God, with the hope of resting when our time is over. Jesus said in John 9:4, *"We must work the works of him who sent me, while it is day. The night is coming, when no one can work."* (NHEB.) There is rest after our work on earth is done; as such, we should not give up on the work at any time in our Christian journey. We must set our minds on completing the work before us, the race we are to run, knowing we shall rest in eternal bliss with God after this world. For this reason, our lives must be filled with activities aimed at ensuring our soul's salvation and bringing souls to salvation. Our lifestyle must be carefully structured to influence lives for God, for after death there is no more repentance.

To obtain eternal rest, each of us must come to the Lord Jesus of our own free will. The Lord implores us, *"Come to me, all you who labor and are heavily burdened, and I will give you rest."* (Matthew 11:28 NHEB.) Only Jesus can lead us to this rest, for He is the way. We must all believe in Him and submit ourselves to His Lordship, follow His example and live by His word. In this world, the rest Jesus promises is not the absence of temptations or trials but solace and hope that He is with us, helping us live above sin till the end of time. We are given the grace to fight off fleshly desires and live righteously through the Holy Spirit. The culmination of the rest Jesus offers to us will be at the end of this life. However, we should continue in the work of righteousness and discipleship as Jesus exemplified in His ministry to enter with joy into the eternal rest.

TOPIC 2: DIVINE PROVISION

GENESIS 2:8–18

It is not an exaggeration to say that God's provision for man is a perfect expression of His unconditional love and goodness. God did not place Adam in a barren land or a wilderness; He planted a garden and put him there. God understood man's need even before it became a reality to man. Everything man needed was provided by God before his existence, so man required nothing that God had not created or provided.

God specially created the plants to meet man's needs. The trees bearing different fruits grew in the garden as food sources and for other uses. Natural resources such as gold, pearl and onyx were also provided. He provided water by channelling a river to pass through the garden to keep the plants and trees continuously flourishing and fruitful. The river parted into four to irrigate the garden. God made sure that Adam never lacked any good thing.

God's love for His children is evident throughout the scriptures; out of His boundless treasures He looks on His children with care and provides for their needs. There is nothing we need that He cannot give to us. Thus, we need to put our trust in Him. From age to age, He has shown Himself faithful to those who believe in Him.

Many examples in the Bible portray this love and provision. Just as God provided for Adam's needs in the garden, God also fed the Israelites throughout their journey in the wilderness after they left Egypt. Exodus 16:13 says, *"It happened at evening that quail came up and covered the camp; and in the morning the dew lay around the camp."* (NHEB.) They were to go out each day to gather as much food as required for that day and gather twice as much on the day before the Sabbath, so that they could rest on the Sabbath day. God did this to teach them to depend on Him for their daily needs. He also ensured that their clothes did not wear out throughout their journey. *"I have led you forty years in the wilderness: your clothes have not grown old on you, and your shoes have not grown old on your feet."* (Deuteronomy 29:5 NHEB.)

God is the same and never changes; this implies there is nothing He did for His servants in the Bible that He cannot still do for us today provided we walk faithfully in His commandments. He who feeds the birds of the air and the beasts of the fields is not only capable but more than willing to meet the needs of His children. Rather than fret, we need to trust in Him, for He will never forsake us. *"Therefore I tell you, do not be anxious about your life, what you will eat or what you will drink; or about your body, what you will wear. Is not life more than food, and the body more than clothing? ²⁶See the birds of the sky, that they do not sow, neither do they reap, nor gather into barns, and your heavenly Father feeds them. Are you not of much more value than they? ²⁷And which of you, by being anxious, can add one cubit to his height?"* (Matthew 6:25–27 NHEB.)

Often, the means and manner by which God meets our needs may not be in ways we expect, and the provision might not come at the time we expect; the challenge becomes recognising His provision when it comes. We must also note that divine provision does not endorse materialism, greed or indolence. *"You ask, and do not receive, because you ask with wrong motives, so that you may spend it for your pleasures."* (James 4:3 NHEB.)

God is not committed to meeting our hearts' desires, which are born out of selfishness, materialism, covetousness and the like. He will only respond to our requests as much as they align with His will. *"This is the boldness which we have toward him, that, if we ask anything according to his will, he listens to us. ¹⁵And if we know that he listens to us, whatever we ask, we know that we have the petitions which we have asked of him."* (1 John 5:14–15 NHEB.)

God might not give us all we want, but that does not mean we are not loved by Him. As believers, we must add contentment to our godliness, for this is great gain. We should bear in mind that we did not bring anything into this world and, certainly, we are not taking anything out of it. 1 Timothy 6:6–10 says, *"But godliness with contentment is great gain. ⁷For we brought nothing into the world, so neither can we carry anything out. ⁸But having food and clothing, we will be content with that. ⁹But those who are determined to be rich fall into a temptation and a snare and many foolish and harmful lusts, such as plunge people into ruin and destruction. ¹⁰For the love of money is a root of all kinds of evil. Some have been led astray from the faith in their greed, and have pierced themselves through with many sorrows."* (NHEB.) If God denies us anything in this life, we ought to trust that His will is best for us.

Finally, we can only get the best of life and secure our eternity with Christ if we establish the right priorities within our hearts. Trusting in God's provision does not mean we should not seek our daily needs and desires; it is usually through the labour of our hands that God blesses us. However, going against God's word is not the path we should take in getting those needs. Our actions ought to be guided by God's word. Our greatest need in life is the kingdom of God. When this is prioritised in all our endeavours, God will meet our needs according to His will and timing. *"But seek first the kingdom of God and his righteousness, and all these things will be given to you as well."* (Matthew 6:33 NHEB.)

TOPIC 3: TENDING THE GARDEN

GENESIS 2:15

A man once asked his teenage son: "Between doing the dishes and playing football, which one takes more energy?"

The son responded: "Playing football."

"Then why do you grumble each time you are asked to do dishes but are quite excited when it's time to play?" (Johnny, 2022.)

A child's disposition towards work is a reflection of what humans generally think of it. Naturally speaking, most people would not like to work except when it brings immediate financial benefits.

Some people mistake a place of bliss to mean where all forms of work cease; Eden proved that notion wrong. No place on earth can be compared to Eden in serenity; it was constantly filled with God's love. Yet, God kept Adam physically and mentally occupied. We may ask: for what reason would God tell Adam to tend the garden? Beautiful things, when not well cared for, could become ugly over time. Proper management is not initiated when there is a problem but to prevent problems and maintain the original status of a thing.

After completing His assignment of setting up God's kingdom on earth, Jesus emphasised the need for believers to tend His vineyard. Just as God gave Adam the responsibility of tending Eden, He has also given us the responsibility of caring for the souls of men for what He purposed – their salvation. That responsibility is what should occupy us until such a time that we render the account of our stewardship to God. Matthew 28:18–20 says, *"Jesus came to them and spoke to them, saying, 'All authority has been given to me in heaven and on earth. ¹⁹Therefore go, and make disciples of all nations, baptising them in the name of the Father and of the Son and of the Holy Spirit, ²⁰teaching them to obey all things that I commanded you. And look, I am with you every day, even to the end of the age.'"* (NHEB.)

In crop farming, certain operations are carried out, from the time the first shoot shows up to harvest time. This set of activities is collectively called tending. The main aim of tending is to improve and achieve a good-quality yield. There would be cutting off some outgrown branches, watering, mulching and adding more earth to give the plants strength; this reflects man's part in the work of salvation. The work of salvation has both divine and human aspects. God had designed and delivered the salvation package; however, believers have roles in the process. These roles range from gospel seed sowing, which is witnessing in words and deeds, to pruning, which involves teaching, rebuking and correcting the souls won into the kingdom. Tending God's garden makes us responsible to God, not only as our Father but also as our Master. We should see this assignment as a service to God and have a consciousness that God will demand our account of stewardship.

At about the point of His departure, Jesus engaged Peter to tend His sheep. To Adam, it was the garden; to Peter, it was the sheep – humans. *"He said to him the third time, "Simon, son of John, do you have affection for me?" Peter was grieved because he asked him the third time, "Do you have affection for me?" He said to him, "Lord, you know everything. You know that I have affection for you." Jesus said to him, "Feed my sheep.""* (John 21:17 NHEB.)

This particular meeting was unique, and it was a specific commission of Peter to take care of the just founded Body of Christ. To do the job of tending the flock, one needs the critical virtue of love. Jesus probed into Peter's devotion to Him, and it is relevant to us today.

We cannot effectively and acceptably do something for God without love. We love God's sheep because we love God; we love God because He first loved us. For us to tend and nurture the flocks of God under our care, we should love and not behave like hirelings; we should love as Jesus loved and became friends with us even while we were at enmity with Him. Believers are demanded by God to love fellow humans. If we say we love God and it does not translate to loving one another, we deceive ourselves.

Also, tending involves safeguarding the sheep against heresies, false teachers and other things that could threaten the salvation of their souls. Paul admonished the elders of the Ephesian church concerning Christ's sheep, saying, *"Take heed, therefore, to yourselves, and to all the flock, in which the Holy Spirit has made you overseers, to shepherd the church of God which he purchased with his own blood. [29]For I know that after my departure, vicious wolves will enter in among you, not sparing the flock. ³⁰Men will arise from among your own selves, speaking perverse things, to draw away the disciples after them. ³¹Therefore watch, remembering that for a period of three years I did not cease to admonish everyone night and day with tears."* (Acts 20:28–31 NHEB.)

The wolves Paul warned the Ephesian elders against were the teachers of wrong doctrines. Safeguarding the flock against such wolves would mean teaching, correcting and admonishing the people with God's word, which is the divinely provided manual for the tending exercise. The Bible is the manual to which we should point the sheep. Feeding God's sheep and guiding and grooming them cannot be possible without the word of God. Such responsibility requires that the shepherd be well acquainted with the word of God and be sensitive to the Holy Spirit.

Tending the sheep of God demands sacrifice; a good shepherd does not prioritise his welfare over the welfare of the flock. Paul admonishes in 1 Corinthians 10:24: *"Let no one seek his own, but his neighbor's good."* (NHEB.) Greatness is about serving others and looking after their happiness; life is meaningless if we are self-absorbed or selfish.

The sacrifice in tending the flock of God demands the ultimate price. Our Chief Shepherd said the following concerning Himself: *"¹¹I am the good shepherd. The good shepherd lays down his life for the sheep. ¹⁵even as the Father knows me, and I know the Father. I lay down my life for the sheep. ¹⁷Therefore the Father loves me, because I lay down my life, that I may take it again."* (John 10:11, 15, 17 NHEB.) As shepherds tending Christ's flock, we should not hold our lives too dear to us that we would not be willing to lay them down if circumstances demand. Many shepherds of God's flock have had to lay down their lives in the process of tending the flock. This does not mean we should go about seeking opportunities to die; instead, we should live in such a way that we would not be afraid of death in the service of the Lord. Jesus said,

"For whoever wants to save his life will lose it; and whoever will lose his life for my sake and the sake of the Good News will save it." (Mark 8:35 NHEB.)

God's anger will be great on shepherds who refuse to tend the flock or who do the work deceitfully. During the time of Ezekiel, God was angry with the leaders for not tending His sheep under their care appropriately. Ezekiel 34:6–10 says, *"'My sheep wandered through all the mountains, and on every high hill: yes, my sheep were scattered on all the surface of the earth; and there was none who searched or sought.' ⁷Therefore, you shepherds, hear the word of the LORD: ⁸'As I live,' says the Lord GOD, 'surely because my sheep became a prey, and my sheep became food to all the animals of the field, because there was no shepherd, neither did my shepherds search for my sheep, but the shepherds fed themselves, and didn't feed my sheep'; ⁹therefore, you shepherds, hear the word of the LORD: ¹⁰Thus says the Lord GOD: 'Look, I am against the shepherds; and I will require my sheep at their hand, and cause them to cease from feeding the sheep; neither shall the shepherds feed themselves any more; and I will deliver my sheep from their mouth, that they may not be food for them.'"* (NHEB.) In caring for and watching over people, you pay attention, and, with your optimal zeal, see that their needs are met and their problems solved. Human beings are made up of the physical and spiritual; tending humans entails looking out for the spiritual and physical needs and aiming to meet them to the best of our abilities. God has placed a demand on everyone to care and watch out for one another's welfare.

Tending God's garden extends beyond the Body of Christ; it also involves responding positively, within our capacity and God's grace, to the yearning of humanity. Coming to the world and leaving it the same is purpose unfulfilled no matter how long you live. Likewise, being a Christian and having no influence on people is a purposeless living. A fulfilled life is marked with a positive effect on people; it can be said that by a person's presence or existence, what would have gone wrong is contained or made right while ugly circumstances are made beautiful. We should not pass through the earth, enjoy its fruits and do nothing to help humanity; we are to give back by earnestly striving to make it better. Making the world better is all-encompassing; it involves both the spiritual and physical aspects. The journey to living a fulfilled life and positively impacting the world starts with us living for others' good, not only that of ourselves.

We have prayed for God's mercy for the sinner, which is good; we have preached the gospel, which is wonderful; but the physical aspect should also be attended to. There is a need to ask God for wisdom to tackle humanity's physical problems, such as diseases, hunger and other besetting issues. Remember, solving humanity's physical needs should go together with the message of salvation. We have the duty of tending the world. "Coming out from among them", as stated in 2 Corinthians 6:17, is forsaking their way of life; it does not mean we should escape or seclude ourselves from the world. Imagine, as a believer, that all you care about is your life and yours alone; you want to make heaven by all means, and so you cut off relationships with people and seclude yourself from the world to avoid temptation. How then shall you fulfil God's purpose of tending the garden of souls? Know that all nations of the earth lie in the scope of the garden of God. We are to be God's instruments with which He would fulfil His purpose concerning His creation.

When the sun finally sets in death, wealth amassed would be useless and properties obtained would not count. The things that will last through eternity are the records and the rewards of the good we have done and the mark we leave on the sands of time. *"But when the Son of Man comes in his glory, and all the angels with him, then he will sit on the throne of his glory. [32]Before him all the nations will be gathered, and he will separate them one from another, as a shepherd separates the sheep from the goats. [33]He will set the sheep on his right hand, but the goats on the left. [34]Then the King will tell those on his right hand, 'Come, blessed of my Father, inherit the kingdom prepared for you from the foundation of the world; [35]for I was hungry, and you gave me food to eat. I was* *thirsty, and you gave me drink. I was a stranger, and you took me in. ³⁶I was naked, and you clothed me. I was sick, and you visited me. I was in prison, and you came to me.' ³⁷Then the righteous will answer him, saying, 'Lord, when did we see you hungry, and feed you; or thirsty, and give you a drink? ³⁸When did we see you as a stranger, and take you in; or naked, and clothe you? ³⁹When did we see you sick, or in prison, and come to you?' ⁴⁰The King will answer them, 'Truly I tell you, inasmuch as you did it to one of the least of these my brothers, you did it to me.'"* (Matthew 25:31–40 NHEB.)

TOPIC 4: WORK: GOD'S WILL FOR MANKIND

GENESIS 2:15, 19–20

The natural and abundant provision for man came with a responsibility. We see man saddled with a purpose immediately after he was created. God had created the earth and work needed to be done in it, which man was commissioned to do. Judging logically, God did not need to structure the world in this manner. By His power, He could have created us to simply live in luxury and enjoy all of His creation without ever having to put in any work. That, however, was not God's will for how He intended man to exist on earth. There are indeed two sublime lessons we can derive from the responsibility given to man by God.

Firstly, Adam's responsibility to tend and keep the garden in which he resided reveals what man's disposition towards his environment should be. Man is a steward of God's creation, and as such ought to nurture and preserve it. Man is supposed to manage the natural resources available to him, be friendly to the ecosystem in all his endeavours, and make his environment more habitable.

Secondly, Adam's responsibility to tend and keep the garden reveals that working is not a punishment but God's will for mankind. The notion that God's will for Adam before the fall was to be roaming indolently about the garden is unfounded. Ever before man sinned human beings were meant to work. Thus, work was not a result of sin. Though sin changed the nature of our work and our response to it, work itself is not a curse and even though work became toil, God instituted and purposed work for His entire creation.

We must understand that working is in the character of God and that even though He does not need to work, He is ever busy. Jesus said, *"My Father is still working, so I am working, too."* (John 5:17 NHEB.) If our Father in heaven is not lazy we have no excuse to be. This is why Christians ought to be industrious. Let us consider the birds of the air: although God feeds them regularly, He does not drop the food in their nests; they have to go out to get their food. Trusting God and relying on Him for our daily needs does not exempt man from working. The process by which God prospers His children is not only by praying or giving; He also blesses them through their diligence. It is what our hands are engaged in doing that He will bless and multiply. It is also not enough to be engaged in a particular trade or venture; we ought to be diligent with it. Ecclesiastes 9:10 says, *"Whatever your hand finds to do, do it with your might..."* (NHEB.)

It is safe to say that working with diligence is a sign of godliness. *"and that you make it your ambition to lead a quiet life, and to do your own business, and to work with your own hands, even as we instructed you; [12] that you may walk properly toward those who are outside, and may have need of nothing."* (1 Thessalonians 4:11–12 NHEB.) In 2 Thessalonians 3:7–10, Apostle Paul used himself as an example to the Thessalonians on the need to be hardworking; he highlighted how he had worked tirelessly while with them to not be a burden, even though he had the right to demand support from them. *"For you know how you ought to imitate us. For we did not behave ourselves rebelliously among you, [8] neither did we eat bread from anyone's hand without paying for it, but in labor and travail worked night and day, that we might not burden any of you; [9] not because we do not have the right, but to make ourselves an example to you, that you should imitate us. ¹⁰For even when we were with you, we commanded you this: "If anyone will not work, neither let him eat.""* (NHEB.)

God knows the essence of work, as well as the effect of idleness. Work has a way of enduing us with a sense of purpose, productivity and responsibility. On the other hand, idleness not only leads to poverty but exposes us to several temptations from the enemy, just as the popular saying goes, *"An idle mind is the devil's workshop."* Those who are idle are easy targets and tools in the enemy's hands.

While remaining committed to work we must also be very cautious, for work, rather than a blessing, becomes a curse when it takes the place of God in our hearts. No matter how elaborate they are, all rewards for labour cannot give the ultimate fulfilment that a healthy relationship with God provides. The great King Solomon, who had all the riches and achievements in his days, gives us a hint to this truth. *"Then I looked at all the works that my hands had worked, and at the labor that I had labored to do; and look, all was vanity and a chasing after wind, and there was no profit under the sun."* (Ecclesiastes 2:11 NHEB.)

It is quite easy for people's hearts to be consumed by the labour of their hands to the extent that they go against the word of God and endanger their souls. Furthermore, as we go about our work, what we achieve from it should be used not only for our betterment but also for the glory of God and the benefit of fellow men. It should be noted that the problem with the rich fool in the parable given by Christ was not that he possessed abundant possessions but that he was not rich towards God (Luke 12: 3–21). His possessions possessed him. All our achievements and labour are only meaningful when dedicated to the Lord and when God resides in our hearts and influences our actions. At such an instance, whether we serve in the church as ministers or work in the secular sphere, all we do will align with God's will.

TOPIC 5: CHOICES AND CONSEQUENCES

GENESIS 2:16–17

Adam and Eve were clearly instructed to eat fruits from every tree in the garden except the tree of the knowledge of good and evil. They flouted this instruction. Their wrong choice affected them and caused a separation of the entire human race from God and subjected all creation to decay. This is a typical example of the terrible effect wrong choices can have. Many of us may wonder why God would create and put the tree of knowledge of good and evil in the garden. Maybe if the tree were not there Adam would not have sinned and the world would not have been in this state.

It is essential to note that man was not created as a robot automatically programmed to love and submit to God. He was created in the image of God, having reason and freewill; hence, it will undermine the justice of God if obedience is compelled. Man is supposed to love God and submit to Him by choice – not compulsion or without option. The presence of an option reveals the genuineness and sincerity of man's love for God as expressed in his obedience.

Although man possesses freewill, he is both free and bound; he is free to carry out any action but he is not free from the consequences of such actions. Going by this principle, it is safe to say that man is generally a product of his decisions. Choices can determine the course of our entire lives and our eternal destination; some might seem insignificant at the point when they are made, but they have the propensity to determine the shape of our lives and that of those connected to us. This is why we must be cautious about the choices we make in life because the consequences will come and may often present themselves more strongly with no opportunity to make amends.

A common and fatal error among many is the minimal importance accorded to the consequences of their actions. One of the verses in the Bible that clearly describes wrong choices and their consequences is Proverbs 20:17: *"Fraudulent food is sweet to a man, but afterwards his mouth is filled with gravel.* "(NHEB.) Although this verse speaks explicitly about gains obtained by deceit and the consequences that follow, it can be applied generally to sin and its effects; it gives an idea of the anguish or discomfort of what is pleasurable but wrong. There is general deceitfulness in the appearance of sin; it usually looks attractive, and there is that tendency for people to be so consumed by the momentary pleasures and gratifications it promises that they lose consciousness of the gravel inside the bread. Only after we have bitten the bread do we realise that the discomfort of the gravel in our mouths far outweighs the sweetness of the bread.

The fact that we are Christians and recipients of God's love and grace might not exempt us from the earthly consequences of bad choices. If David had thought about the consequences of killing Uriah and taking his wife, his feet would not have been so quick to tow the path of sin. Even though God forgave him when he repented, he was not spared from the dire consequences of his misconduct (2 Samuel 12:1–12). A man who is convicted of a crime may still have to serve a sentence even though he repents.

God does not encourage rebellion and cannot excuse rebels by approving their lifestyle against His revealed justice plan, otherwise man would continue to sin forever. God treats everybody in the same way, based on His eternal principles. He is the God of justice. He rewards the obedient and punishes the disobedient; this He does for the good of all. There might be times when divine justice might seem sluggish in catching up with the wicked or rebellious; this should not be a reason to envy them, for by the justness of God every man will reap the consequences of his actions either in this life or/and in eternity.

Seeing the importance of our choices in life we must endeavour to make the right ones. Our choices can only be right if they are made in line with the desires of God. If Adam and Eve had followed this principle, man's relationship with God would not have been broken. Thank God Jesus came in the flesh to restore our broken fellowship with God due to Adam's sin. *"For if by the trespass of the one, death reigned through the one; so much more will those who receive the abundance of grace and of the gift of righteousness reign in life through the one, Jesus Christ."* (Romans 5:17 NHEB.)

We have a responsibility now to obey God. Hence, the word of God must be the guide and final authority over all our actions. Those who reject the love of God expressed to the world through salvation in Christ Jesus will be damned for eternity.

TOPIC 6: MARRIAGE: ORIGIN AND PURPOSE

GENESIS 2:18, 21–25

One intimate, complementary and lifelong relationship God designed, where two human beings cleave as one, is the institution of marriage. As a holy institution, marriage is purely God's idea, and, like any idea of His, it is good. God instituted it in the Garden of Eden between a man and a woman – Adam and Eve – with well-defined purposes: companionship, procreation and support for one another. Marriage is an exclusive union between a man and a woman, not between the same genders or between humans and any other creature.

Seeing that the man He had created was alone in the Garden of Eden, God said, *"It is not good that the man should be alone..."* (Genesis 2:18 NHEB.) Going by this statement, man needed a companion because he would thrive better with the companion. In solving Adam's loneliness, God caused him to fall into a deep sleep, took one of his ribs and made a woman for Him. When God brought her to Adam, he remarked, *"This at last is bone of my bones, and flesh of my flesh. She will be called Woman, because this one was taken out of Man."* (Genesis 2:23 NHEB.)

The woman was created for man, and they are to be best friends in a companionship rooted in God's word. It should be a companionship that is devoid of fear and deceit. It should be a companionship where trust exists and where love prevails because, without trust and love, there will be no genuine companionship. The issue of companionship is fundamental to the success of a marital institution. However, several people have a misplaced expectation of marriage. They go into marriage for other reasons, such as financial gains, material benefits or social status, rather than for companionship. This is one of the major reasons for divorce around the globe today. Marriage cannot thrive without sincere companionship. Hence, companionship should be the primary reason for going into marriage.

Apart from companionship, the woman made for man was given a responsibility; she was created to be a source of help. God says, *"I will make him a helper suitable for him."* (Genesis 2:18 NHEB.) Before the making of the woman, God gave responsibilities to Adam. His responsibilities were to honour God and take care of the garden. The woman, as his helpmeet, was expected to partner with the man to fulfil his God-given purposes. She was not created to lead him but to support him. She was not made to be idle but to lend a supporting hand. In some societies, a woman's role has not changed and every wife is expected to be a source of help to her husband. In such circumstances children are brought up in God's way and the wife is expected to support her husband. In home management she is expected to be there for her husband and to always support the godly cause of her husband to bring glory to God.

The oneness of a man and a woman in a marriage is revealed in the scripture under consideration. By the principle of mathematics, a man plus a woman makes two individuals, but God does not just see them as two individuals; He sees them as one. *"Therefore a man will leave his father and his mother, and will join with his wife, and the two will become one flesh."* (Genesis 2:24 NHEB.) After coming together as husband and wife, they are one flesh. The "one flesh" speaks of unity. They were created to function together in harmony, complementing each other's strengths and weaknesses. Jesus reaffirms that solemn fact in Matthew 19:4–6: *"Have you not read that he*

who created them from the beginning made them male and female,
⁵ and said, 'For this reason a man will leave his father and mother,
and be joined to his wife; and the two will become one flesh?' ⁶ So
that they are no more two, but one flesh. What therefore God has
joined together, do not let man tear apart." (NHEB.) Jesus ended
with a statement that emphasises unity and discourages separation in
the marriage union.

Further, we cannot write about marriage without mentioning
procreation, which is one of the purposes of marriage. Genesis 1:28
says: *"And God blessed them. And God said to them, 'Be fruitful,*
and multiply, and fill the earth, and subdue it...'" (NHEB.)
Procreation within the marital union is how the purpose of populating
the earth should be fulfilled.

Since God is the Originator of marriage, the union of marriage can
only thrive by the Originator's wisdom. It takes God, a man and a
woman to make a good marriage. Marriage is a sacred and unique
human relationship and must thrive on the principles and purpose of
the Originator – God. We must operate within the confine of God's
purpose for the union to thrive. Marriage can only succeed with an
absolute dependence on God and reliance on His word to guide every
decision in the home.

The pages of the Bible are filled with several principles we need to
have a blissful marriage. But how can someone who does not have a
relationship with God depend on Him and His word for guidance
in marriage? Therefore, one must develop a relationship with
God – the Originator of marriage – before venturing into marriage.
"House and riches are an inheritance from fathers, but a prudent
wife is from the LORD." (Proverbs 19:14 NHEB.) A man can
inherit riches and wealth from his parents, but only God can give a
wife suitable for him.

How should the relationship between the husband and his wife be?
The relationship between Christ and the church perfectly represents

what an ideal marriage should be. Christ's love for the church is provided as a model for how a husband's love for his wife ought to be. As Christ is the Bridegroom and Head of the church, so is the man the wife's head. And as the church is subject to Christ, so is the wife subject to her husband in all things. The husband should love and cherish his wife for as long as he lives. The Bible admonishes wives to submit themselves to their husbands as unto God, and husbands to love their wives as Christ loves the church and gave Himself for it. Love and commitment are vital ingredients in marriage. This kind of love is not like the one practised by the world but such which is of God. It is the kind of love that considers first the interest of others. A man who loves his wife will not consider mistreating her; instead, he will respect and cherish her. 1 Peter 3:7 says: *"You husbands, in like manner, live with your wives according to knowledge, giving honor to the woman, as to the weaker vessel, as being also joint heirs of the grace of life; that your prayers may not be hindered."* (NHEB.) Marriage should make both parties become more like Christ by loving each other perfectly in their imperfections, just as Christ loves us perfectly in our imperfections. It is a union that does not run on autopilot but requires partners to be committed, with a desire to grow daily in love with absolute dependency on God, the Originator.

God intends to be our guide and ever-present help in times of difficulties in our marital union. We should make every necessary effort to include Him as the foundation in all we do. When the oil of our relationship is on the verge of getting finished, we can call on Him for a fresh refill, for we cannot walk effectively and in consonance with God's purpose in marriage without His help.

CHAPTER 3

TOPIC 1: TEMPTATION: ORIGIN AND STRATEGY

GENESIS 3:1–6

The inglorious fall of man brought about a whirlwind of troubles for humanity after man could not overcome the temptation in the Garden of Eden. The ultimate aim of temptation is to make a person fall into sin.

Temptation is the attraction the devil presents to lure people into disobeying God. The first act of temptation in Bible history is recorded in Genesis 3:1–6. From here, we can notice that the power of temptation is its ability to firstly attract the target's attention and convince its victim to try out the exact opposite of what God commanded or do what God said should not be done.

'Did God really say you should not eat of every tree of Eden?' That looks or sounds harmless. After all, that first statement did not come with an encouragement to disobey, but it was the first bullet thrown at Eve. The tempter got her attention. We can see that Eve was in a serious discussion with the serpent the next moment. Satan knew what God had said, but he purposely twisted it, and that got Eve's attention.

Usually, the point the tempter gets the target's attention is not where the target sins, but it is an area he should always watch out for, lest he is led to sin. If he resists the devil at this point, the devil will not get on to the next level of his tempting process. James 4:7 says, **"Be subject therefore to God. But resist the devil, and he will flee from you."** (NHEB.)

If the devil succeeds in getting the target's attention, he proceeds to the next stage of convincing the person. Concerning Eve, after his success in getting her attention, he moved to the next stage of trying to convince her. He said, *"You won't surely die..."* (Genesis 3:4 NHEB.) Often, men fall into temptations by following the lust and desires of their hearts, which makes it easier for the devil to convince them. It makes them susceptible to the schemes and ploys of the evil one in making them go against the word of God. James 1:14–15 says, *"But each one is tempted, when he is drawn away by his own lust, and enticed. ¹⁵ Then the lust, when it has conceived, bears sin; and the sin, when it is full grown, brings forth death."* (NHEB.)

Satan used different methods of persuasion with different people, but the basic strategy is the same — he appeals to the weakness of the flesh. Most of the temptations we fall into result from our inability to resist the appeals of the flesh. Sometimes, what we desire may not even be sinful, but the process of satisfying those desires might involve going against the word of God. For instance, desiring a job or business promotion is in no way sinful, but we must ensure that we do not go against God's word to satisfy these desires.

Our victory over temptation depends on how we handle the devil's attempt to convince us. Jesus handled this stage by stating and relying on the word of God. *"And the tempter came and said to him, "If you are the Son of God, command that these stones become bread." ⁴But he answered and said, "It is written, 'Man does not live by bread alone, but by every word that proceeds out of the mouth of God.'""* (Matthew 4:3–4 NHEB.)

All Christians should emulate Jesus' approach to His temptation in the wilderness. God's wisdom is expressed through His words, and only by the wisdom of God can we overcome the craftiness of the devil. The psalmist wrote, *"Your commandments make me wiser than my enemies..."* (Psalm 119:98 NHEB.) Note that Jesus did not have a scroll with Him in the wilderness; the scriptures by which

He overcame the devil were already a part of Him. We are to regularly study the word of God with emphasis on salvation and make it a part of us. *"In my heart I have hidden your word, that I might not sin against you."* (Psalm 119:11 NHEB.)

More often than not, temptations do not come in the most expected ways. Eve never encountered a petrifying image of the devil, which many assume but rather a friendly form. We must understand that temptations could manifest in any form and could come through anyone. 2 Corinthians 2:11 admonishes, *"that no advantage may be gained over us by Satan; for we are not ignorant of his schemes."* (NHEB.) Only by the Holy Spirit within us, guiding us with God's word, can we accurately discern all forms of temptation and soar above them.

Temptation does not have a timetable. Before Eve's encounter with the devil, there was no warning or announcement of the exact period the devil would approach her. Thus, we must be spiritually prepared at all times to avoid being caught unawares.

The devil does not force anyone to fall into temptation; it is the yielding of the person that makes him become a victim. The main key to living a life of continuous victory over Satan's temptations is to walk in the Spirit, which is possible when we study and obey the word of God. Paul wrote in Galatians 5:16–17, *"But I say, walk by the Spirit, and you will not carry out the desires of the flesh. [17] For the flesh lusts against the Spirit, and the Spirit against the flesh; and these are contrary to one another, that you may not do the things that you desire."* (NHEB.)

Eve's mistake was to allow the serpent to engage her in a conversation and not resist him when he created doubt about God's word. For a successful Christian journey, it is binding on us not to allow any opportunity or room for temptation while also ensuring that we are not tools used by the devil as sources of temptation to others.

TOPIC 2: RIGHT ATTITUDE TOWARDS SIN

GENESIS 3:8–13

"Adam, where are you?"

"I heard you walking in the garden, so I hid. I was afraid because I was naked."

"Who told you that you were naked? Have you eaten from the tree whose fruit I commanded you not to eat?"

"It was the woman you gave me who gave me the fruit, and I ate it."

"Woman, what have you done?"

"It was the serpent that deceived me; that's why I ate it."

This was the conversation that ensued between God, Adam and Eve after they had sinned against Him. God did not need to hear from them before knowing everything that had happened between them and the serpent because He sees all and knows all. However, He did not punish them without allowing them to speak for themselves.

Instead of accepting responsibility for his actions, Adam blamed Eve and, by extension, God. He said: ***"The woman whom you gave to be with me, she gave me of the tree, and I ate."*** (Genesis 3:12 NHEB.) This implied that the woman gave him the fruit, and that that would not have happened had God not given him the woman. When God asked Eve, rather than accept responsibility for her actions she blamed the serpent in turn.

Giving excuses, blaming others or hiding from the sins we commit amplifies our weaknesses and reflects our ignorance of the mercies of God. By doing this, we tend to wrongfully justify our actions, which prevents us from humbling ourselves before God in repentance for our sins and from pleading for God's mercy, forgiveness and help in not falling into sin again.

God is more interested in repentance than in punishing anyone. God's desire for His children, who have wandered away, is for them to return to Him in repentance. *"The sacrifices of God are a broken spirit. A broken and contrite heart, O God, you will not despise."* (Psalm 51:17 NHEB.)

King David shows us the right approach when we sin. When confronted by God through Prophet Nathan, he said, *""I have sinned against the LORD." Nathan said to David, "The LORD also has put away your sin. You will not die.""* (2 Samuel 12:13 NHEB.) His repentance led to his forgiveness and restoration. Also, Peter, the disciple of Jesus, wept bitterly when he had denied his Master thrice. He repented and went ahead to preach the gospel of the same Christ whom he had denied. God desires a humble and repentant heart. It takes meekness and humility to walk with God, for God guides the meek and teaches them His ways, but He resists the proud.

Repentance is a pivotal element in the process of salvation. To claim salvation without repentance is self-deceit. Repentance is a change of mind that leads to a change of life. It is a change of the heart reflected in a practical change of character due to the knowledge of God's word and remorse for the evil of sin. Godly sorrow is essential for repentance: *"For godly sorrow works repentance to salvation, which brings no regret. But the sorrow of the world works death."* (2 Corinthians 7:10 NHEB.)

Salvation begins with godly sorrow, a kind of sorrow that emanates from the realisation of one's sinful state. It is a profound sorrow derived from the knowledge of the evil of sin, which leads to a deep desire to be completely free from it. This desire leads to repentance (change of mind) which leads to salvation. Salvation is the answer to the prayer of one who earnestly desires righteousness. God would not grant salvation to one who has not repented from his sins, who sees nothing wrong with his sinful way of living. An attitude of repentance is essential for both Christians who fall and for the salvation of unbelievers. We should examine ourselves daily to ensure that we never get to where it becomes more difficult to turn to God in repentance.

It was futile and worthless for Adam and Eve to hide from God. God is omnipresent and omniscient. He sees and knows everything, so there is no hiding place for sin. Sinners can never hide from God's eyes and can never escape from the judgement of God. Hebrews 4:13 says, *"There is no creature that is hidden from his sight, but all things are naked and laid open before the eyes of him with whom we have to do."* (NHEB.) Adam and Eve tried to use their human sense to hide from God. The attitude of sinners or believers who fall into sin and try to hide it from God is futile; it cannot bring about any solution to sin. *"He who conceals his sins doesn't prosper, but whoever confesses and renounces them finds mercy."* (Proverbs 28:13 NHEB.)

The prevalent attitude of turning away from God and shifting blame, instead of owning up and seeking forgiveness, makes it difficult to reconcile with God. The right attitude of one who sins is to accept fault, humbly seek the face of God in repentance and endeavour to please God by living in obedience to His word. We have to remember that one day we will all stand before God to give an account of how we lived our lives while on earth.

TOPIC 3: CONSEQUENCES OF THE FALL

GENESIS 3:14–19

Disobedience to God usually comes with grievous consequences. Being the first man, Adam was a representative of humanity, and when he fell, the whole world was affected. His disobedience broke the harmony mankind had with God, corrupted his state of righteousness and brought death upon the entire human race.

The verses under consideration highlight the punishments of God as a result of Adam's disobedience. God judged them for their disobedience by imposing penalties on them. God did curse the serpent saying, *"Because you have done this, cursed are you above all livestock, and above every animal of the field. On your belly you shall go, and you shall eat dust all the days of your life."* (Genesis 3:14 NHEB.)

For the woman, God said, *"I will greatly multiply your pain in childbirth. In pain you will bring forth children. Your desire will be for your husband, and he will rule over you."* (Genesis 3:16 NHEB.) This verse clearly reveals that pain at childbirth for the woman was part of the consequence of the fall. God's statement implies that the woman was not originally created to bring forth children in pain. Furthermore, her husband is to rule over her and she is to submit herself to him.

For the man, he was now required to work extremely hard for his survival. Working became tedious because of the curse of the ground. For him to eat, he had to labour continuously throughout his life. Only through painful toiling and the sweat of his brow would he be able to eat each day. The earth would produce thorns and thistles for him.

Sin brought about the separation between God and man. Man was created in righteousness and holiness; he was perfect without any knowledge of evil, but sin corrupted this nature after the fall. Adam and Eve hid from God out of guilt and shame. They were later chased out of the garden to prevent them from eating the fruit from the tree of life and living forever. This affected the glorious communion and their relationship with God. Sin brought about both physical and spiritual death. Spiritual death is separation from God, for God is life and the source of it. Adam's divine nature was corrupted by sin; he lost his spiritual life and became dead. This sinful nature was transferred to mankind; hence every man born of a woman is born sinful by nature, guilty of Adam's sin and alienated from God. *"So then as through one trespass, all people were condemned; even so through one act of righteousness, all people were justified to life. ¹⁹For as through the one man's disobedience many were made sinners, even so through the obedience of the one, many will be made righteous."* (Romans 5:18–19 NHEB.)

The inherent evil in man is too conspicuous to be unnoticed. Today, some people promote ungodly practices such as homosexuality, pornography, and the like. The world has had terrible leaders who had no love for the people and who were only interested in oppressing and making life unbearable for their people for selfish gain. There have been numerous cases where violent men have acquired guns, gone to public places and killed fellow human beings for no just cause. A world without God is a world of chaos. All these are but a few consequences of man's separation from God.

Although God permitted us to suffer the consequences of Adam's sin, He has not left us to the ultimate and eternal consequence; this is why He made provision for our salvation in Christ. Christ came to die, to save mankind by reconciling a depraved world to the Father. In Christ, humanity will have eternal life rather than eternal damnation. *"For if by the trespass of the one, death reigned through the one; so much more will those who receive the abundance of grace and of the gift of righteousness reign in life through the one, Jesus Christ."* (Romans 5:17 NHEB.)

CHAPTER 4

TOPIC 1: ACCEPTABLE OFFERING: THE GIVER AND THE GIFT

GENESIS 4:3–7

Genesis Chapter 4 records the first instance in the scripture of man offering a sacrifice to God. Here, we see two brothers giving offerings to God – each with different items from their various vocations. We can observe how God responded differently to each person and his offerings. We can also obtain vital information on the expectations of God on whatever offerings we present to Him.

Cain was a farmer; he offered the harvests from his fields to God, while Abel, a shepherd, gave offerings from his flock as a sacrifice. God honoured Abel's offerings but dishonoured Cain's offerings. What could have been the reason for this outcome?

When we carefully study the person of God from the scriptures, we understand that He values both the giver and the gift. God first considers the person and then his offerings, as seen in Genesis 4:4–5: *"The LORD respected Abel and his offering, ⁵but he did not respect Cain and his offering…"* (NHEB.) Abel was righteous, and Jesus attested to his righteousness in Matthew 23:35: *"that on you may come all the righteous blood shed on the earth, from the blood of righteous Abel to the blood of Zechariah son of Berechiah, whom you killed between the sanctuary and the altar."* (NHEB.)

It must be understood that God examines the heart – the giver's intentions. Unlike Abel, Cain's heart was not right with God. The

4 4

Bible declared Cain's ways were evil while Abel's were righteous: *"unlike Cain, who was of the evil one, and killed his brother. Why did he kill him? Because his works were evil, and his brother's righteous."* (1 John 3:12 NHEB.) God is holy; to honour Cain's offerings would have been to contradict His nature of holiness.

Expecting God to accept an offering from an armed robber suggests that God condones robbery, which He undoubtedly does not. Regardless of what anyone gives to God, it will not be accepted if their ways and lifestyles do not conform to God's standard. Proverbs 21:27 says: *"The sacrifice of the wicked is an abomination: how much more, when he brings it with a wicked mind."* (NHEB.)

In giving to God we must ensure that we give our best to Him, with humility, cheerfulness and gratitude. We must also ensure that our hearts are right with God and our ways pleasing to Him enough to make our offerings acceptable.

Many worshippers are always eager to give offerings and render other services to God, which are good, but their hearts are far from God. *"These people honor me with their lips; but their heart is far from me. ⁹And in vain do they worship me..."* (Matthew 15:8–9 NHEB.) Let us keep our hearts pure and upright because the state of our hearts determines God's acceptance of our offerings and acts of service.

About the quality of their offerings, Hebrews 11:4 states: *"By faith, Abel offered to God a better sacrifice than Cain, through which he was attested as righteous, God testifying with respect to his gifts..."* (NHEB.) The phrase: "a better sacrifice" strongly points to the different qualities of their offerings – Abel's was superior and Cain's inferior.

The most important offering to God is presenting our bodies as living sacrifices in holy living and continual fellowship with God. This should be done before presenting material sacrifices. Presenting our bodies as living sacrifices means having no will of our own and letting

Christ live through us. Paul, in Romans 12:1, admonishes: *"Therefore I urge you, brothers, by the mercies of God, to present your bodies a living sacrifice, holy, acceptable to God, which is your spiritual service."* (NHEB.)

TOPIC 2: DOMINION OVER SIN: CAIN'S EXAMPLE

GENESIS 4:6–7

What would be your reaction if someone called to inform you that an assassin is crouching by your street on a mission to eliminate you? Your first reaction would probably be to stay indoors, call the police and wait in safety. Until the threat has been successfully neutralised you are unlikely to rest. Even after that, you would take precautionary measures to guard yourself against a similar threat in the future. However, even though men are more cautious about physical harm, they are sometimes less cautious concerning a more dangerous foe: sin.

Cain had the privilege of having God personally warn him about sin. Unfortunately, sin still had its way in his life even with the warning, because he did not heed the warning.

The verses in context, Genesis 4:6–7, show sin being figuratively presented as crouching at the door. Cain was envious of his brother, Abel, on seeing that God had accepted his brother's offering and rejected his. He got angry and purposed in his heart to kill his brother. Shortly before, God had warned him sternly, telling him that sin lay in wait at his door and desired to have him and to rule over him, and that he must master it. In other words, he was to ensure that sin did not gain dominance over his life. Cain was to be careful not to enslave himself or commit himself to sin. Sin was already lurking, but he was to shut the door of his heart against it. He was to resist it and subdue it. However, Cain could not dominate sin; instead, he allowed it to grow and gain control over him, which resulted in him killing his brother. *"The LORD said to Cain, "Why are you angry? Why has the expression of your face fallen? [7]If you do well, will it not be lifted up? If you do not do well, sin crouches at the door. Its desire is for you, but you are to rule over it.""* (NHEB.)

Although the warning in Genesis 4:7 was directed at Cain, it is still God's warning to every believer today. As long as we live, Satan – the tempter – will be at the door of our hearts, ready to come in and derail us from the path of righteousness if we give in to his enticements. No wonder the Bible says we should not be ignorant of the devices of the devil.

Temptation itself is not a sin; falling into temptation or being a source of temptation is. Sin is the major problem God has with man; it is what separates man from God. No man can serve God acceptably while living in sin. Sin has an entangling nature; it seeks to rule and dominate every man.

God's warning to Cain was that he must master and subdue sin. There is no neutral ground in our battle against sin; one must rule over the other. The one who lives in sin is a slave to sin. Jesus spoke about this in John 8:34: *"Truly I tell you, everyone who commits sin is the slave of sin."* (NHEB.) No one can serve two masters. For there to be a union with Christ, there must be a divorce with sin. Those who have failed to renounce sin cannot please God. The word of God declares that sin shall have no dominion over God's children. God would not request what is impossible; He has made provisions for every task He demands of us.

Dominion over sin requires making efforts on our part. This includes faith in the finished work of Christ regarding our salvation, praying, relying on the Holy Spirit and continually studying and obeying the word of God. Jesus said, *"You will know the truth, and the truth will make you free."* (John 8:32 NHEB.) Knowing the truth implies believing and obeying the word of God. God's power of saving men is the gospel of Christ. We must make conscious efforts to resist sin. It takes determination on the part of the person not to yield. Job was determined against sin when he declared, *"I made a covenant with my eyes, how then should I look lustfully at a young woman?"* (Job 31:1 NHEB.)

The cravings of the sinful nature – the flesh – are against the will of God. The flesh is an enemy of God; it makes it difficult for a man to serve God. Christ came to die to end the dominion of the flesh over mankind. Just as Adam represented mankind in Eden, Christ represented mankind on the cross. When He died, all who believe in Him died as well; when He resurrected, all who believe in Him were resurrected to new lives free from sin. *"We were buried therefore with him through baptism to death, that just like Christ was raised from the dead through the glory of the Father, so we also might walk in newness of life. ⁵For if we have become united with him in the likeness of his death, we will also be part of his resurrection"* (Romans 6:4–5 NHEB). Christ's death frees us from the consequences of Adam's sin and allows us to be right with God. Therefore, anyone who receives Christ would not perish on account of Adam's sin but will be accountable to God for what he did as a person.

Christ bore our sins in His body; He was crucified on the cross of Calvary so we can live our lives above the dictates of the flesh. Romans 6:7-8 says: *"For he who has died has been freed from sin. ⁸But if we died with Christ, we believe that we will also live with him."* (NHEB.)

Christians are often defeated and subdued by sin when they fail to notice the 'little foxes' in their lives and to deal with them. Instead, they nurse and pamper them with such words as "It does not matter; we are saved by grace," when they are called to be watchful. They allow these sins to grow gradually and steadily till they are overwhelmed and subdued by them. Songs of Solomon 2:15 says: *"Catch for us the foxes, the little foxes that spoil the vineyards; for our vineyards are in blossom."* (NHEB.)

Sin is powerless in Christ Jesus; this does not mean the absence of temptations, but by faith in the finished work of Jesus Christ, we know that we are no longer captives to sin. Since sin is by choice and not by compulsion we should decide firmly to serve God.

TOPIC 3: MURDER

GENESIS 4:8

Murder is the crime of deliberately killing a person. The fact that the first case of murder mentioned in the Bible occurred within the first family of the human race is a manifestation of the inherent evil in mankind after the fall. One might have thought that the members of this little family could exist in harmony with each other, but this was not the case.

Cain and Abel brought offerings to God. As a result of the righteousness of Abel, Abel offered a more excellent offering than Cain. *"By faith, Abel offered to God a better sacrifice than Cain, through which he was attested as righteous, God testifying with respect to his gifts; and though he died he still speaks through it."* (Hebrews 11:4 NHEB.)

The Lord accepted Abel and his offering but rejected Cain and his offering. As a result, Cain became angry and slew his brother for no just cause. The anger and hatred in his heart subsequently led to murder. God warned Cain against the anger in his heart because of its effects if it was not controlled, but he failed to heed. The murder was only a physical manifestation of the state of his heart. Cain had murdered Abel in his heart before he carried out the act. The moment love was replaced with hatred for Abel in the heart of Cain, Abel was murdered.

Every life is precious to God. How then will He not look with great displeasure upon men who murder or seek to murder others? Murder is forbidden in the sight of God. Man was created in God's image and to attack someone made in His likeness is to transgress against the One who created him.

The act of murder is one of the most grievous offences to commit against a fellow man. It is essential to note that murder does not begin with the act. This is what Jesus Christ emphasised in Matthew 5:21–22 when He said: *"You have heard that it was said to the ancient ones, 'Do not murder;' and 'Whoever murders will be liable to judgment.' 22But I tell you, that everyone who is angry with his brother without a cause will be liable to judgment; and whoever will say to his brother, 'Raqa,' will be in danger of the council; and whoever will say, 'You fool,' will be in danger of the fire of hell."* (NHEB.) Jesus Christ does not merely address the act but the source from which the act emanates – the heart. It is not only the one who strikes another down who is guilty of murder, but also the one who harbours indignation or hatred against another. 1 John 3:15 says: *"Whoever hates his brother is a murderer, and you know that no murderer has everlasting life remaining in him."* (NHEB.)

Jesus intends to keep us as far away from the root cause of murder as possible. He warns us from even uttering insulting words to others. Before an insult is meted out from one person to another, there is already a preconceived intention to hurt the person's feelings. This is how it begins – the intention to hurt someone else. To the natural man, this is a good way to satisfy the rage resulting from an attack on one's ego, but just like every other fleshly desire, it is an easy way to offer oneself as an instrument for the devil to use.

God sees beyond what we say or do to the intentions for saying or doing them. If the intention is not borne out of love, then it is a sin against God, and the one who sins against God will be liable to the lake of fire.

A similar case in the Bible that shows the progression of anger to murder is the story of Dinah and Shechem. Dinah was raped by Shechem and her brothers were not happy about it. In their quest for vengeance Simeon and Levi were blinded to every diplomatic means of settlement, despite Shechem and his kinsmen's attempt to make right the wrong that had been done. Simeon and Levi committed a massacre because of their uncontrolled anger.

Whenever we are faced with offences from others and become indignant, let us remember and heed God's warnings to Cain, *"sin crouches at the door. Its desire is for you, but you are to rule over it."* (Genesis 4:7 NHEB.)

Anyone who harbours hatred or indignation towards his brother is a murderer. The man who hates his brother has the same spirit or impulse in his heart as did Cain and, if it is not controlled it will lead to the same outcome. The one who has eternal life is one with the Spirit of God. When there abound such things as bitterness, malice, indignation and grudges within a man's heart towards his brother, it is proof of the absence of the Holy Spirit within such a heart. The antidote to murderous thoughts is love, which manifests in forgiveness and tolerance. A heart without love would be filled with hatred, pride, envy, bitterness and so on, but love dispels all of these. Love is proof that we are of God and that we walk in the light, *"He who says he is in the light and hates his brother, is in the darkness even until now."* (1 John 2:9 NHEB.)

We must keep our hearts from all evil by renewing our hearts with the word of God every day. The message of salvation is a message of love for the entire world. Love itself is not a static feeling; it is usually expressed. We are to love, not in words but in deeds and truth. God expressed His love to us while we were yet sinners, by giving us His Son Jesus Christ to die for the salvation of our souls. We are to replicate this act by expressing love to everyone, including those who hate and treat us despitefully. By this, the world will know that we are His disciples. John 13:34–35 says, *"A new commandment I give to you, that you love one another. Just as I have loved you, you also must love one another. ³⁵By this everyone will know that you are my disciples, if you have love for one another."* (NHEB.)

CHAPTER 5

TOPIC 1: INDIVIDUALITY OF OUR RELATIONSHIP WITH GOD

GENESIS 5:1–32

Genesis Chapter 5 is a list of direct descendants of Adam up to Noah and his three sons. The passage lists individuals – their ages and how they fathered sons and daughters. As we study the scriptures, we see how God relates with people individually and in groups, such as nations, communities and families. In a world with many people, no one is lost in the crowd or unnoticed by God, and no one is a purposeless individual.

Genesis 5:24 records that Enoch walked faithfully with God all his life and as a result God took him. *"Enoch walked with God, and he was not, for God took him."* (NHEB.) Enoch's record of holiness was an individual one; it was not about God's covenant relationship with his nation or fathers, but about the fact that "Enoch walked with God".

God is interested in every detail of our lives: our eternal destination matters to Him. God wants a personal relationship with us. That was why He commanded through Christ that the gospel of salvation be preached to all people. Jesus' death was meant to restore man's relationship with the Father. Therefore, each person has been given the opportunity to obey and be saved.

Jesus taught using the parable of the good shepherd in John Chapter 10 that though He has many sheep in His flock He knows every one of them and no one will be neglected. He stated in verse 14, *"I am the good shepherd. I know my own, and my own know me."* (NHEB.) God loves us and gave His only Son to die so that we might be saved. God longs for us to have an uncompromising relationship with Him.

As we journey through this life we should trust God for our unique personal relationship, following His will for our lives. God gives each person a unique purpose in life. He said to prophet Jeremiah: *"Before I formed you in the belly, I knew you. Before you came forth out of the womb, I sanctified you. I have appointed you a prophet to the nations."* (Jeremiah 1:5 NHEB.) Since every individual is unique before God, He relates with us individually and according to His divine and unique plans for our lives. Even though things may seem not to go well with us sometimes, we should know that in that situation, God is with us and that He is working His way through us so that when the situation is over we will not have anything to glory about, but instead all glory will be ascribed to Him alone. We should be more concerned about our relationship with God, trusting Him and focusing on doing His will to fulfil His purpose in our lives.

God's relationship with us as individuals entails us being individually responsible for our own actions and conduct. *"So then each one of us will give account of himself to God."* (Romans 14:12 NHEB.) Matthew 25:14–30 records a story of three individuals entrusted with different talents by their master. Verse 15 says, *"To one he gave five talents, to another two, to another one; to each according to his own ability. Then he went on his journey."* (NHEB.) Subsequently they were called to give an account of how they utilised their talents. Just as they gave their accounts individually, so also were they judged. In the same vein, each of us will account for how we spent our lives on earth to God. For this reason, we should ensure that our relationship with God is intact by being faithful in our stewardship. 1 Corinthians 4:2 says, *"Here, moreover, it is required of stewards, that they be found faithful."* (NHEB.)

One would correctly point out instances where God related with nations and families – whether in blessing them as a group, rebuking or chastising them. A close look at those relationships would reveal that they all started with the actions of individuals. For instance, God's covenant with Israel as a nation started with an individual's walk with God – Abraham. Zachariah, John the Baptist's father, praying in Luke 1:72–73, said, *"to show mercy towards our fathers, to remember his holy covenant, ^{73}the oath which he spoke to Abraham, our father"* (NHEB). Also, God's relationship with the kings of Judah was based on an individual's relationship with God – David. When speaking of His plan to divide the nation of Israel during the reign of Rehoboam, God reserved the nation of Judah for the sake of David: *"However I will not take the whole kingdom out of his hand; but I will make him prince all the days of his life, for David my servant's sake whom I chose, who kept my commandments and my statutes"* (1 Kings 11:34 NHEB).

Today, our relationship with God is based on an individual – Jesus – who lived in obedience to God to the point of death. Romans 5:17-18 says: *"For if by the trespass of the one, death reigned through the one; so much more will those who receive the abundance of grace and of the gift of righteousness reign in life through the one, Jesus Christ. ^{18}So then as through one trespass, all people were condemned; even so through one act of righteousness, all people were justified to life."* (NHEB.) Notwithstanding what Jesus had done, our individual level of experiencing God and His anointing depends on our level of seeking and hunger for the things of God individually. Matthew 5:6 says, *"Blessed are those who hunger and thirst after righteousness, for they will be filled."* (NHEB.)

God also holds individuals accountable for their actions and inactions. It is good to belong to a denomination or a godly family; these groups help guide our norms and values. However, we will not be judged as a denomination or a family on the last day; we will be judged as individuals. Belonging to a family can influence a family member's salvation by way of parental guidance and teachings, but the salvation of the head of a family or of a parent can never translate into the salvation of individual members of that family, except when members take personal steps to accept the Author of salvation – Jesus. For example, the Jews believed that being an Israelite afforded them free entry to God's kingdom. However, John the Baptist rebuked them in Luke 3:8, saying: *"Bring forth therefore fruits worthy of repentance, and do not begin to say among yourselves, 'We have Abraham for our father;' for I tell you that God is able to raise up children to Abraham from these stones."* (NHEB.) God's special relationship with Abraham and God's dealings with Israel as a nation could tempt a natural Israelite to believe that he is entitled to salvation because he is a seed of Abraham.

God is searching for individuals ready to be committed to Him, not minding nationality, family or denomination. Although families and denominations could help us in our race, salvation is ultimately based on a personal relationship with God.

TOPIC 2: STANDING OUT: ENOCH – A CASE STUDY

GENESIS 5:21–24

In a world filled with sin and temptations, a child of God whose main focus is to please God would find himself living in contradiction to worldly standards and a worldly way of life. It is like swimming against the tide. In a world of compromise, anyone who wants to stand out in righteousness would get more buffeted with distractions than others who just wanted to flow with the world.

Although less detailed in the Bible, Enoch's life portrays how living a distinguished life in a sinful environment could be acknowledged, honoured and rewarded by God. Enoch stands out from the list of men mentioned in Genesis Chapter 5. We are informed that he walked with God; his righteousness made him stand out among the people in his generation.

Another exemplary figure of one who walked with God was Job. He was adjudged to have lived exceptionally compared to everyone on earth during his time. *"The LORD said to Satan, "Have you considered my servant, Job? For there is none like him in the earth, a blameless and an upright man, one who fears God, and turns away from evil.""* (Job 1:8 NHEB.) He lived such a blameless life among men that God boasted of him to the devil. As children of God, we should aim at having God develop a similar level of confidence in us.

Standing out in a generation that is increasingly deviating from the road of righteousness is what we should strive for. This would be possible to achieve if we sincerely desire to please God in all we do by living our lives according to God's instructions. Walking with God in this context means having a close personal relationship with God. We see that God had always desired to walk with man from the beginning of creation. That was seen in His fellowship with Adam and Eve in Eden. That fellowship was strained when man fell. We cannot attain an abiding fellowship and walk with God if sin resides in our lives. 1 John 1:6 states: *"If we say that we have fellowship with him and walk in the darkness, we lie, and do not tell the truth."* (NHEB.) Only when sin has been eliminated can we proceed into God's presence and begin walking with Him. God's way is the way of holiness. To walk with God is to comply with His ways and make His word our guide. We must have a constant desire to please Him always in this depraved world. There is no way an association with sinners will set us on the right path to walk with God or make us stand out from the crowd. 1 Corinthians 15:33 warns us: *"Do not be deceived. "Evil companionships corrupt good morals.""* (NHEB.) We should endeavour to associate and keep company with others who walk with God. And if everyone in our immediate environment is living contrary to God's word we must resolve not to be influenced by them.

Furthermore, Hebrews 11:5–6 reveals to us that, *"By faith, Enoch was taken away, so that he would not see death, 'and he was not found, because God took him away'. For before he was taken he was attested as having pleased God. ⁶Now without faith it is impossible to be well pleasing to him, for he who comes to God must believe that he exists, and that he is a rewarder of those who seek him."* (NHEB.) We cannot be distinguished from those who do not serve God unless we live by the standards of God's word. The book of Jude reveals to us that Enoch prophesied the second coming of our Lord Jesus Christ: *"About these also Enoch, the seventh from Adam, prophesied, saying, "Look, the Lord comes with ten thousands of his saints""* (Jude 1:14 NHEB). The passage further buttresses the fact that Enoch had a close relationship with God.

It is also worth noting that Enoch lived the least of years among the men mentioned in Chapter 5 of Genesis but was recorded as creating the most notable impression on God. We must resolve to make our time on earth count. It is not the length of our days that matters but the impact we create, the kind of life we live and those we lead to Christ through our lifestyle and witnessing. These are part of what will make God pleased with us and reward us with an eternal fellowship with Him. One does not need a long life to please God and fulfil a divine purpose. You need to live every day of your life, maintaining a healthy relationship with God.

If Enoch could walk with God in his time we also can do it in ours, because God is the same and He never changes. Enoch might not have imagined how his life would end when he began walking with God; he would have never thought of the glorious way in which his life would end on earth. Walking with God is the greatest adventure a man could have in life. The future of a man who makes a firm decision against all odds to follow God is unimaginable. As it is written: *"No eye has seen, and no ear has heard, and no mind has imagined the things which God has prepared for those who love him."* (1 Corinthians 2:9 NHEB.) When we decide to follow God, God could do with our lives things that have never been done before to the glory of His name.

CHAPTER 6

TOPIC 1: GRIEVING GOD

GENESIS 6:5–7

Not many people can stand seeing their parents grieve. Children with good moral upbringing even go to the extent of inconveniencing themselves to make sure that their parents are not heartbroken concerning them. One of the things that would make a good child sad is seeing their parent grieve over them because of their action. Only people whose hearts have got to the point Paul described as "seared with hot iron" would repeatedly do things that would grieve their parents without feeling any remorse.

Genesis 6:6 paints a picture of God sorrowing over the sinful state of man whom He created in His image. The Bible lets us understand that man's wickedness was extremely great and that the imagination of his heart was continually evil. The human race had descended so low into iniquity that God became grieved in His heart to the point that He resolved to wipe humanity from the face of the earth.

The expression in Genesis 6:6, "It repented the Lord, the Lord was sorry, or the Lord regretted", as expressed in various versions of the Bible, should not be interpreted in the sense of God having a change of mind about a wrong committed. It means that God was grieved. Yes, God was pained – and He still feels pain today anytime any of His children behave contrary to His word. Just as He rejoices over righteousness He is saddened about sin.

The people of Noah's days were wiped out because they grieved God, leaving only Noah and his family. Some other people in the Bible who grieved God were King Saul whose deliberate sin made God regret anointing him king. God said in 1 Samuel 15:11: *"It grieves me that I have made Saul king; for he has turned back from following me, and has not carried out my commandments..."* (NHEB.) And also, Judah's continual sin which caused God to turn against them. Isaiah lamented: *"But they rebelled, and grieved his holy Spirit: therefore he was turned to be their enemy, and he himself fought against them."* (Isaiah 63:10 NHEB.) God's turning and fighting against them eventually led to their Babylonian captivity. From the cases of Saul and Judah and from the account of Genesis Chapter 6 we can learn that the main reason God would grieve over a man to the point of turning against him is when a man commits sin and refuses to repent.

Another way we could cause God to feel regret is putting the resources God has given us to negative use. Sometimes God blesses someone with material resources that should be used in serving Him, but instead they are used in ways contrary to God's will. Also, commercialising spiritual gifts and blessings makes God regret giving such gifts and blessings. Our intellect, strength and other inborn traits are all divine endowments that can result in God regretting endowing us with such blessings if they are not carefully used to please Him.

People of Noah's days experienced God's wrath through destruction by flood. Saul experienced God's wrath through the departure of God's Spirit, which resulted in him being possessed by evil spirits and his eventual death in battle. Judah experienced it through Babylonian captivity. It is best to learn of the consequences of making God regret through other people's experiences and not experience them ourselves. 1 Corinthians 10:5–6 teaches us that several Israelites who came out of Egypt grieved God's heart and, as a result, were destroyed in the wilderness. *"However with most of them, God was not well pleased, for they were overthrown in the wilderness. ⁶Now these things were our examples, to the intent we should not lust after evil things, as they also lusted."* (NHEB.)

God has no pleasure in the death of a sinner. However, if someone lives their life, making God grieve over them by refusing to accept Jesus as their Lord and Saviour, that person will be condemned to eternal death.

It is not only people who refuse to accept Jesus Christ as Lord that grieve God. The other set of people who grieve God more are those who claim to be God's children, know His word and even preach it, yet live in disobedience to God. In Ephesians 4:30, Paul said: *"Do not grieve the Holy Spirit of God, in whom you were sealed for the day of redemption."* (NHEB.)

Just as God made a way of escape for Noah, his family and everything in the ark, God has also made a way of salvation for humanity through Jesus Christ. God might be grieved today about a person sinning, but if that person repents, believes in the Lord Jesus and forsakes their sins, God forgives. However, if that person continues in sin, eternal separation from God in hell awaits.

Our lives should be lived for God's pleasure. Nothing gives Him more pleasure than when we present our bodies as living sacrifices – handing our will completely to Him. Romans 12:1 says, *"Therefore I urge you, brothers, by the mercies of God, to present your bodies a living sacrifice, holy, acceptable to God, which is your spiritual service."* (NHEB.)

TOPIC 2: RIGHTEOUSNESS: THE ONLY ESCAPE ROUTE FROM DESTRUCTION

GENESIS 6:8–9

The entire world was in a progressive state of rebellion against the principles and desires of God. Moral decadence was at an all-time high; mankind had come to embrace evil and immorality as the norm. All of these grieved the heart of God to such an extent He regretted ever creating man. In His righteous anger, God resolved to judge the entire world by destroying every living creature on the face of the earth with a flood.

Amid all these, one man caught the attention of God. God was willing to exempt this man and his household from destruction, *"But Noah found favor in the eyes of the LORD."* (Genesis 6:8 NHEB.) One might wonder, among the entire human race at that time, what was so special about this one man? What was it about him that attracted God? Why will an Almighty God, who can do whatever He desires without being questioned, be concerned about preserving one man's life from a fate that is to befall the entire human race? The Bible offers us an accurate answer: *"Noah was a righteous man, blameless among the people of his time. Noah walked with God."* (Genesis 6:9 NHEB.) God values the righteous, even if it is one person, and will not destroy the righteous with the wicked. Genesis 18:25 says, *"Be it far from you to do things like that, to kill the righteous with the wicked, so that the righteous should be like the wicked. May that be far from you. Shouldn't the Judge of all the earth do right?"* (NHEB.)

Noah was a just man, blameless and upright among his generation. He had a relationship with his Maker. It is essential to remember that Noah's generation was not conducive for one determined to live for God. Nothing about the age in which he lived could encourage him to serve God. Noah was committed to God in a world in which righteousness was strange and considered foolishness, in a world where all others pleasantly accepted sin. Sensuality was the habitual lifestyle of those around him. He would have been tempted countless times to blend in with the crowd but was determined to stand out for God. His uncompromising lifestyle of holiness made him "a lily in the mire".

Noah's story is a warning to us all, for there is a certain judgement coming on sinners – eternal damnation in the lake of fire. Just like the ark of Noah, which carried Noah and his family to safety, Jesus is the ark that takes the righteous safely out of this world to save them from eternal damnation. Therefore, everyone who desires to be saved must come to Him, live by His word and continue in it till the end of life. Jesus Christ related His second coming to the days of Noah and the days of Sodom. Luke 17:26–29 says, *"As it happened in the days of Noah, even so will it be also in the days of the Son of Man.* *²⁷They ate, they drank, they married, they were given in marriage, until the day that Noah entered into the ship, and the flood came, and destroyed them all.* *²⁸Likewise, even as it happened in the days of Lot: they ate, they drank, they bought, they sold, they planted, they built;* *²⁹but in the day that Lot went out from Sodom, it rained fire and sulfur from the sky, and destroyed them all."* (NHEB.)

It is worthy of note that the wide margin between those preserved and those who perished did not prevent the judgement of God. Our present world is not different from the world that was destroyed before the flood or the cities of Sodom and Gomorrah. If God did not spare the world in those times, He would certainly not spare this world from judgement.

Eternal separation from God is not an option. One can make mistakes in life and correct them, but an eternity in the lake of fire is an irretrievable mistake. Life is brief compared to eternity, for eternity is endless. The eternal lake of fire was not created for man but for the devil and his angels. Nevertheless, those who choose to tow the devil's path by disobeying God will end up with him. *"Then he will say also to those on the left hand, 'Depart from me, you cursed, into the everlasting fire which is prepared for the devil and his angels'"* (Matthew 25:41 NHEB).

God's will is for mankind to be saved, but we all have a role in fulfilling this will for each of us. God has given us life freely, but the way we live is our responsibility. We must accept Jesus as our Lord and make a firm decision to submit ourselves to Him, living our lives in anticipation of His second coming. Since we do not know the exact day or time of His coming we must be prepared at all times by being consistent in living righteously so that His coming will not meet us unprepared.

It was living righteously that saved Noah from the judgement in his time. Similarly, only living rightly will save us from eternal damnation. Like Noah, we must be determined to pursue righteousness in a godless generation. Our lives should be governed not by the world's principles and ideologies but by all the instructions of Christ. We could say to ourselves that Christ might not come during our lifetime; this could be true, but we should also consider that we most likely do not know the day of our death, and nothing more can be done regarding the salvation of our souls after death. The grace of God for repentance and forgiveness ends when our life on earth ends.

Furthermore, we are to win souls to the kingdom. It would be joyous to see our loved ones in heaven, not them alone, but all those we met on our pilgrimage through life. Like Noah, a preacher of righteousness, we should also be custodians, warning everyone about the judgement to come. We must make it a responsibility to preach the gospel in words and deeds, bearing in mind that any soul not saved could be lost forever. *"For if God did not spare angels when they sinned, but cast them down to the lower parts of hell, and committed them to chains of darkness, to be reserved for judgment; ⁵and did not spare the ancient world, but preserved Noah with seven others, a proclaimer of righteousness, when he brought a flood on the world of the ungodly; ⁶and turning the cities of Sodom and Gomorrah into ashes, condemned them to destruction, having made them an example of what is going to happen to the ungodly; ⁷and delivered righteous Lot, who was very distressed by the lustful life of the wicked ⁸(for that righteous man dwelling among them, was tormented in his righteous soul from day to day with seeing and hearing lawless deeds): ⁹the Lord knows how to deliver the godly out of temptation and to keep the unrighteous under punishment for the day of judgment"* (2 Peter 2:4–9 NHEB).

TOPIC 3: GOD REVEALS HIS PLANS

GENESIS 6:5–13

God's purposes are generally hidden to all until they are revealed, and He usually reveals them to those who are closest to His heart. *"Surely the Lord GOD will do nothing, unless he reveals his secret to his servants the prophets."* (Amos 3:7 NHEB.) This truth is conspicuously revealed throughout Bible history.

When God intended to destroy the world by flood due to the gross rebellion of humanity, He did not carry out this plan until He had revealed it to His servant, Noah. When the outcry of sin against Sodom and Gomorrah reached His throne and He had purposed to destroy the cities with fire, He paid His friend Abraham a visit and shared everything with him. *"The LORD said, "Will I hide from Abraham what I do?"* (Genesis 18:17 NHEB.) God revealed the rise and fall of the four empires to Daniel, the events that will accompany the close of age to His servant John just to mention a few.

The primary purpose for which God created man is fellowship. God desires intimacy. He wants to share His plans and secrets with men, but just as it was with Abraham, God will only do so with those who are His friends, those who fear Him and do not treat His instructions with levity. *"You are my friends, if you do whatever I command you. 15No longer do I call you servants, for the servant does not know what his master is doing. But I have called you friends, for everything that I heard from my Father I have made known to you."* (John 15:14–15 NHEB.) Close friends are entirely open to each other and look out for one another's best interests. They communicate in the clearest terms and do not see any difficulty sharing their hearts' most profound secrets and burdens.

God has confidants. He confides in those whose hearts are loyal to Him. God reveals His will, desires, plans and the mysteries of His word to those who truly honour and reverence Him and who live their lives in complete obedience to His instructions.

The greatest gift in the history of the world is salvation. God did not hide this from mankind, as seen through the pages of the scriptures. The life, ministry and death of Jesus Christ were revealed to several of His servants at various times in history, long before the birth of Christ. God desires that all mankind be saved. *"For God so loved the world that he gave his only Son, so that whoever believes in him will not perish, but have everlasting life."* (John 3:16 NHEB.)

Those who believe in Christ for their salvation are saved from the power of sin and its consequence. Just as it was in the days of Noah, there is a particular judgement coming upon sinners at the close of age – eternal damnation. God has also not been quiet about this. He revealed it to saints of old such as Daniel: *"Many of those who sleep in the dust of the earth shall awake, some to everlasting life, and some to shame and everlasting contempt."* (Daniel 12:2 NHEB.) Christ also spoke of this severally in the gospels. Matthew 25:41 says, *"Then he will say also to those on the left hand, 'Depart from me, you cursed, into the everlasting fire which is prepared for the devil and his angels'"* (NHEB). Also, in Mark 9:43, He said, *"If your hand causes you to stumble, cut it off. It is better for you to enter into life maimed, rather than having your two hands to go into hell, into the unquenchable fire."* (NHEB.)

We can learn from the account of Jonah and Nineveh that many times when God reveals His plan, it is because He desires a corresponding action from us. When the people of Nineveh received the news of the judgement of God that was to befall them, their godly sorrow and repentance saved them from the judgement. In the same way, only repentance and forsaking our wicked ways of life will save us from eternal damnation. We are not to trivialise or ignore the warnings of God as did the people in Noah's days who ignored His warnings and paid dearly for it. 2 Peter 2:5 says, *"and did not spare the ancient world, but preserved Noah with seven others, a proclaimer of righteousness, when he brought a flood on the world of the ungodly"* (NHEB).

If we know God well enough, if the history of His dealings with man has taught us anything, it is that God cannot lie and that His word is infallible – none of His warnings will go unfulfilled. We must believe in Christ and submit ourselves entirely to Him, living our lives in complete obedience to His demands.

We must decide to truly follow Christ because hypocrisy will not save us from judgement. God cannot be mocked. He knows those who are genuinely His: those who do not tolerate sin in their lives, no matter how seemingly little it is; those who are actively seeking the kingdom and His righteousness; those who have renounced the world and all its glory and pleasures and who are not slaves to the appetites of their flesh. These are the kind that will be delivered from judgement at the close of the age.

TOPIC 4: BE STRONG AND COURAGEOUS: NOAH'S EXAMPLE

GENESIS 6:13–22

All the people who had good standing with God in the Bible had one thing in common – obedience to God's instructions. At a glance, obeying God's instructions might seem simple. However, that could be one of the most mentally exerting tasks. Many times, God gives instructions that might stretch our mental and emotional faculties to their limits. There are times when one might look at God's instructions and conclude that it is humanly impossible to carry them out. The case of God instructing Noah to build an ark is a good example. It takes both courage from a man and grace from God to obey Him at such moments.

People of Noah's time were evil before the Lord. God decided to carry out judgement against the entire world. He had purposed to wipe out the entire living creatures from the face of the earth by flood. However, Noah found favour and grace with God; consequently, God preserved his life and his family.

God gave him instructions to build an ark that would preserve his life, his family and pairs of various kinds of creatures on the earth. Noah was to build the ark to the exact specifications that God gave. God told Noah in the passage: *"This is how you shall make it. The length of the ship will be three hundred cubits, its breadth fifty cubits, and its height thirty cubits. ¹⁶You shall make a roof in the ship, and you shall finish it to a cubit upward. You shall set the door of the ship in its side. You shall make it with lower, second, and third levels."* (Genesis 6:15–16 NHEB.) Although the Bible does not specifically tell us how long it took Noah to construct the ark, building an ark of this magnitude to God's specification would have been extremely strenuous and time consuming.

The Bible calls Noah a proclaimer of righteousness in his time. 2 Peter 2:5 says, *"and did not spare the ancient world, but preserved Noah with seven others, a proclaimer of righteousness, when he brought a flood on the world of the ungodly"* (NHEB). This implies he had attempted to convince those in his generation to repent, but to no avail. Apart from preaching, he needed the courage to remain righteous and blameless and obey God in everything. He remained courageous even in the face of discouragement. Noah's courage was not only admirable, it was outstanding. This courage came as a result of his faith in God. Hebrews 11:7 says, *"By faith, Noah, being warned about things not yet seen, in reverence prepared a ship for the salvation of his household..."* (NHEB.) Noah's faith in God enabled him to carry out the task. It is impossible to please God without faith.

One thing that can easily kill courage is fear. It causes you to disobey God. It tells you that you will not sail through difficult times, and you cannot overcome opposition if you dare try to do the will of God. Courage enables us to be steadfast in the face of danger, resistance and challenge.

The antidote to fear in the heart of a Christian is the knowledge of God and trust in Him. Fear is conquered by faith which has its roots in the knowledge of the person of God. The more we grow in the word and have experiential knowledge of God, the more we trust God. The more trust we have in God, the more courageous we become. *"So faith comes by hearing, and hearing by the word of Christ."* (Romans 10:17 NHEB.)

Fear is not of God, *"For God did not give us a spirit of fear, but of power and love and of a sound mind."* (2 Timothy 1:7 NHEB.) We are courageous when we believe in God and focus on Him. Peter could have continued walking on water if his focus had remained on Jesus and his faith fixed on Him. Because of his faith in Jesus, he got down from the boat onto the water. He continued walking on water until his attention turned to the boisterous wind around him; then, he began to sink. *"He said, "Come." Peter stepped down from the boat, and walked on the water and went toward Jesus. ³⁰But when he saw the strong wind, he was afraid, and beginning to sink, he yelled, saying, "Lord, save me." ³¹Immediately Jesus stretched out his hand, took hold of him, and said to him, "You of little faith, why did you doubt?""* (Matthew 14:29–31 NHEB.) When we take our focus away from Jesus, we see the challenges around us, creating fear and troubles within us. Isaiah 26:3 says: *"You will keep him in peace, in peace whose thoughts are fixed on you, because he trusts in you."* (NHEB.) We can either be fearful or courageous, but we cannot be both simultaneously.

Looking at the narration of the heroes of faith, Hebrews 11:13 remarks: *"These all died in faith, not having received the promises, but having seen them and embraced them from afar, and having acknowledged that they were strangers and temporary residents on the earth."* (NHEB.) We know them as heroes today not because they had easy lives but because of their tremendous courage towards life's challenges. They could carry out God's will in their generations because of their faith in God, reflected in their courage. They made the mountains in their lives look like stepping-stones.

In our generation, courage is needed to carry out God's will. We must understand that the One who calls us has all the power to bring His will to pass. Our responsibility is to submit ourselves to His will as Noah did. The Bible says, *"Thus Noah did. According to all that God commanded him, so he did."* (Genesis 6:22 NHEB.)

TOPIC 5: ATTENTION TO DETAILS

GENESIS 6:13–22

One essential benefit of studying God's word is understanding several attributes of God that were revealed in His dealings with mankind throughout the ages. God is wisdom, and He is perfect. We can benefit from these attributes when we pay attention to the details of His instructions. He does not act sporadically; He always has plans for His actions, and He accords much value and significance to every detail, however little or inconsequential they might seem, in actualising these plans.

As the engineer of the universe, everything He did at creation was done in a methodical and orderly fashion. For instance, not until He had created a perfectly suitable environment did He create the living creatures.

His disposition towards detail was apparent in the architectural specifications provided to Noah in the building of the ark purposed to preserve Noah and his household. The ark was not to be constructed based on Noah's discretion; God gave him the blueprint for going about it and strict adherence was required.

Noah's disposition towards God's demands is worthy of emulation. His complete trust in God was revealed in his absolute adherence to every detail of the instructions God gave to him in constructing the ark. He followed every detail of God's command to the letter just as the scripture says, *"Thus Noah did. According to all that God commanded him, so he did."* (Genesis 6:22 NHEB.)

Noah seemed to have understood the high priority God placed on the details of His instructions and to have realised that any alteration – addition or omission – made by him to God's instructions regarding the construction of the ark, no matter how little, would be detrimental.

Examining the ark's construction critically, we can draw vital connections to our own lives. The Bible, to us, could be likened to an instruction manual filled with instructions from God on the best way to ensure the salvation of our souls. It contains directives that will enable us to make decisions according to godly wisdom to get the best from our lives. It contains specific instructions on the right way to worship God and godly counsel in managing all forms of human relationships – how best to relate with leaders, subordinates, spouses, parents, children, elders and even our enemies. *"All Scripture is God-breathed and profitable for teaching, for reproof, for correction, and for training in righteousness, [17] that the person of God may be complete, thoroughly equipped for every good work."* (2 Timothy 3:16–17 NHEB.)

The importance of obedience and attentiveness to detailed instructions cannot be treated with levity. No one has ever profited from neglecting the instructions of God. We must note that half or incomplete obedience is disobedience in God's sight. In 1 Samuel 15, God instructed Saul to annihilate the Amalekites, but he spared their king, the best sheep, fat calves and everything good in the land. 1 Samuel 15:8–9 says, *"He took Agag the king of the Amalekites alive, and utterly destroyed all the people with the edge of the sword. [9]But Saul and the people spared Agag, and the best of the sheep, and the cattle, and the fat ones and the lambs, and all that was good, and wouldn't utterly destroy them; but everything that was despised and rejected, that they utterly destroyed."* (NHEB.) This grieved the heart of God. If Noah had, in any way, altered the instructions handed to him by God, he would have grieved the heart of God.

There are instances of people altering God's instructions to excuse their act of disobedience or sinful lifestyle. They aim to justify their disobedience by trying to find a neutral ground between obeying and disobeying. More bothersome is when such people see those who take obedience to God seriously and, rather than consider them a source of inspiration, discriminate against them and call them names.

The highest form of honour any man can give to God is complete obedience to His instructions. This is also the only way by which we can express our love for Him. Jesus said, *"If you love me, you will keep my commandments."* (John 14:15 NHEB.) We must not only be hearers of the word but doers as well. Apostle James admonished us in James 1:22–25, *"But be doers of the word, and not only hearers, deluding your own selves. **²³For if anyone is a hearer of the word and not a doer, he is like someone looking at his natural face in a mirror; ²⁴for he sees himself, and goes away, and immediately forgets what kind of person he was. ²⁵But he who looks into the perfect Law of freedom, and continues, not being a hearer who forgets, but a doer of the work, this person will be blessed in what he does."* (NHEB.)

When we thoroughly obey the instructions of God, we become worthy examples to those of the world. Some of them might persecute us or consider us overzealous, but we are not to worry, for we are cherished in God's sight.

God's love and attention to all of His creation are expressed in His care for us. We are to replicate this love by obeying His instructions to the letter. We must be cautious about our actions, for nothing we do goes unnoticed before God.

CHAPTER 7

TOPIC 1: RIGHTEOUSNESS: GOD'S PRIORITY

GENESIS 7:1, 23

The fact that man possesses freewill does not entirely make the world a lawless place in which everyone can act in any way they desire without supervision or consequence. Since God is the Source of life, every living thing exists because He wills it to, and, as such, everyone is accountable to God for their deeds. By right, God is the Supreme Ruler and Judge over His entire creation –rewarding the righteous and punishing the wicked. *"For the LORD is righteous. He loves righteousness. The upright shall see his face."* (Psalm 11:7 NHEB.)

This truth was revealed in His acts of judgement against the people in the days of Noah. The people in those days had come to embrace sinfulness as a general way of life. They delighted in acts that were abominable in the sight of God. They were morally depraved, and all their thoughts and actions were increasingly rebellious to God's principles and desires; all of these provoked His judgement.

Another instance of God's judgement is the account of Sodom and Gomorrah. Just like the people in Noah's days, their way of life grieved the heart of God. Their ways were abominable in His sight. They had given themselves to all forms of immorality and sexual perversion; hence, God rained down fire upon the entire inhabitants of the cities. *"As it happened in the days of Noah, even so will it be also in the days of the Son of Man. ²⁷They ate, they drank, they married, they were given in marriage, until the day that Noah*

entered into the ship, and the flood came, and destroyed them all.
²⁸Likewise, even as it happened in the days of Lot: they ate, they
drank, they bought, they sold, they planted, they built; ²⁹but in the
day that Lot went out from Sodom, it rained fire and sulfur from
the sky, and destroyed them all." (Luke 17:26–29 NHEB.)

There are essential lessons worthy of note to be learnt from the incidents
in the days of Noah, and Sodom and Gomorra. Firstly, no sinner will
escape the judgement of God. Secondly, God will never punish the
righteous with sinners; He will always deliver those who are His from
the ill fate that is to befall the wicked. *"Be it far from you to do things*
like that, to kill the righteous with the wicked, so that the righteous
should be like the wicked. May that be far from you. Shouldn't the
Judge of all the earth do right?" (Genesis 18:25 NHEB.) Thirdly,
God's judgement cannot be influenced by the significant margin
between the righteous and the sinners. One might have thought that
the number of the ungodly who were to perish would have hindered
God's judgement or made Him reduce His standard by pushing some
unrighteous individuals to the margins, but this was not the case. God's
priority is righteousness and not the numerical strength of the ungodly.
We need to understand that if Christ returns today and finds just a few
righteous people among the billions of people in the world, He will save
them only. It does not matter how much He loves the world, even to the
point of dying for it.

Although God is Love, He is also a God of justice. The opinion that
God is too loving to punish the disobedient in the eternal lake of fire
is unfounded. God does not change, and His standard of judgement
is still the same. The God that judged the world in Noah's time is the
same God that will judge this world at the close of the age. That is
why we must be very cautious about how we are living our lives.
We ought to be ready at all times so that Christ's second coming does
not meet us unprepared. *"Therefore also be ready, for in an hour*
that you do not expect, the Son of Man will come." (Matthew 24:44
NHEB.) Only those living in obedience to God's word will be saved
from the impending judgement coming on this world.

It is not enough to believe that God exists; that kind of faith cannot save us. Our faith must be backed up by deeds; it should manifest itself in how we live our lives. We must firstly believe in the finished work of Christ on the cross of Calvary for the salvation of our souls and then live the rest of our lives in complete obedience to His instructions. *"You believe that God is one. You do well. The demons also believe, and shudder. [20]But do you want to know, foolish person, that faith apart from works is useless?"* (James 2:19–20 NHEB.)

The path of Christianity is usually a lonely one, but we must not be afraid to tread it. Standing for God is never the norm in any generation; it will attract persecution and antagonism from the world and sometimes from self-acclaimed Christians who are not born again. If we must walk with God, we must forsake the world; if we are to be alive in Christ, we must be dead to sin; if we intend to dwell with Him in eternity, we must be willing to submit to Him now; if He is to be our Saviour, He must be our Lord.

Let us always consider His words, *"Enter in by the narrow gate; for wide is the gate and broad is the way that leads to destruction, and many are those who enter in by it. [14]How narrow is the gate, and difficult is the way that leads to life. Few are those who find it."* (Matthew 7:13–14 NHEB.) The broad way is the path without caution or restrictions. It is the path of one given to the appetites of the flesh and the pleasures of this world. This path leads to eternal destruction. On the other hand, the narrow way is one of discipline and sacrifice. It is saddled with trials, temptations and every form of obstacle to our eternal destination. We must be determined to be among the few who would tread this path to eternity.

Furthermore, it is incumbent on teachers of the word of God to let the people know that God is not more interested in large congregations than in the kind of life each member of the congregation is living, for this is the only proof that they are children of God. *"However God's firm foundation stands, having this seal, "The Lord knows those who are his,"* and, *"Let every one who names the name of the Lord depart from unrighteousness.""* (2 Timothy 2:19 NHEB.)

TOPIC 2: OUR PART AND GOD'S PART

GENESIS 7:7–9

Imagine if the entry of all the animals into the ark was left to the human abilities of Noah. How possible would it have been for him to bring the birds of the air? Or how could he have controlled the carnivores walking among the herbivores? It is really something marvellous – this extraordinary coordination in a seemingly uncontrolled environment – and something Noah on his own would not have been capable enough to carry out. The eighth verse of this chapter tells us that all the creatures came to Noah and entered the ark just as God had told Noah in the 20th verse of the previous chapter. This was not something humanly possible; it was divine, and had the handwriting of our great God.

Nevertheless, Noah also played his part by complete obedience to the instructions given to him by God. God does not just leave us when He gives us instructions to follow; He walks with us through the whole process. Noah played his part by obeying in detail all the instructions of God regarding the construction of the ark. At the same time, God played His part in sending the animals and preserving Noah's life and the rest of the ark's inhabitants from the flood. There are two parts to our relationship with God – our part and God's part; they work in pari passu with each other.

God's part and our part are mutually inclusive; although that does not make God dependent on us, He demands that we play our role to fulfil His purpose in our lives. In walking with God, we must learn to balance fulfilling our part and believing Him to fulfil His. This will avoid the error of becoming indolently dependent on God and being complacent regarding our responsibilities or overly depending on our abilities and not seeing the need to rely on Him. The fact that we have

God on our side, and the fact that He is willing to help us when we are in need, is not an encouragement to be irresponsible. A student going to an examination, having not studied at all but with a mindset that God will miraculously help him simply because he prayed, stands a risk of failing that examination. Likewise, a lazy man who is unwilling to work but prays earnestly for food would most likely go hungry. Let us always remember that *"faith, if it has no works, is dead in itself."* (James 2:17 NHEB.) God will not do for us what we are to do for ourselves.

Just as Noah and his household's deliverance from the flood required both human and divine roles, the salvation of our souls is a combination of God's role and ours. God offered His Son to be sacrificed for the sins of the world. Our part is to willingly accept the salvation provided to us by God. We are to repent from all forms of unrighteousness and believe in Christ's finished work on the cross for the salvation of our souls.

The grace to obey God is made available to us at the point of salvation; after that, we are required to live the rest of our lives here on earth in complete submission to the commandments of God. Indeed, we are saved by our faith, but any form of faith that is not backed up with works – a lifestyle of obedience – is a dead faith. We are to work out the salvation God has already worked in us. *"So then, my beloved, even as you have always obeyed, not only in my presence, but now much more in my absence, work out your own salvation with fear and trembling. ¹³For it is God who works in you both to will and to work, for his good pleasure."* (Philippians 2:12–13 NHEB.) We are to carefully study God's instructions in the Bible and be committed to obeying all that is written regarding the salvation of our souls. We can get the best out of our relationship with God by perfectly submitting to His will.

Furthermore, in God's overall plan for the world's salvation, every believer has the responsibility to preach the gospel to the lost across all nations and trust Him to do His part. A sinner is not saved by our strength but by the power of God, and it is God who convicts souls to repentance and grants salvation to all men. *"I planted. Apollos watered. But God made it grow."* (1 Corinthians 3:6 NHEB.)

TOPIC 3: FULFILMENT OF GOD'S JUDGEMENT

GENESIS 7:21–23

The execution of God's pronouncement of judgement on the ungodly who refuse to repent and renounce their wickedness is always fulfilled at God's appointed time. No matter how long, none of God's words ever go unfulfilled. *"so shall my word be that goes forth out of my mouth: it shall not return to me void, but it shall accomplish that which I please, and it shall prosper in the thing I sent it to do."* (Isaiah 55:11 NHEB.)

In the previous chapter, God had earlier informed Noah about the impending doom that would befall the earth's inhabitants because of mankind's tremendous acts of wickedness and horrific, sinful deeds. He would destroy the earth with a flood and He instructed Noah to build an ark for his safety, the safety of his family and other living creatures. *"By faith, Noah, being warned about things not yet seen, in reverence prepared a ship for the salvation of his household, through which he condemned the world, and became heir of the righteousness which is according to faith."* (Hebrews 11:7 NHEB.) God warned Noah of a happening that had never been seen and had never occurred on the face of the earth. Nevertheless, he acted upon God's instructions by faith and was delivered from destruction. All living things that moved on the earth's surface were destroyed except Noah and the rest of the ark's occupants.

All these things were written for our learning, *"Now these things were our examples, to the intent we should not lust after evil things, as they also lusted."* (1 Corinthians 10:6 NHEB.) We ought to learn from these events about the character of God – for sin attracts God's judgement, and He hates it. Also, we are made to know of the integrity of God; when He says a thing it must be fulfilled. By the justness of God, just as it was in the days of Noah, God will judge mankind for sin, and His warnings concerning this are numerous within the scriptures. One of such is Matthew 13:41–43: *"The Son of Man will send out his angels, and they will gather out of his kingdom all things that cause stumbling, and those who do iniquity, ⁴² and will cast them into the furnace of fire. There will be weeping and the gnashing of teeth. ⁴³ Then the righteous will shine forth like the sun in the kingdom of their Father. He who has ears, let him hear."* (NHEB.) These verses describe the two separate destinies of two sets of people – the righteous and unrighteous. The former will shine forth as the sun eternally in the kingdom of God, while the latter will have their eternal abode in the furnace of fire. The reason for the separate eternal destinations of these two categories of people is their disposition to God's instructions during their lifetime. Anyone who trivialises or outrightly rejects God's instructions prepares for himself a place in the lake of fire.

We are not to live like those in the days of Noah who were busy about their daily lives, unconcerned about their sinful ways until the judgement came. *"As it happened in the days of Noah, even so will it be also in the days of the Son of Man. ²⁷ They ate, they drank, they married, they were given in marriage, until the day that Noah entered into the ship, and the flood came, and destroyed them all."* (Luke 17:26–27 NHEB.) Likewise, the fiancés of the daughters of Lot perished because they did not think it possible that their city was about to be destroyed with fire. Genesis 19:14 records this: *""Get up. Get out of this place, for the LORD will destroy the city." But he seemed to his sons in-law to be joking."* (NHEB.)

God's instructions are serious and must be treated with the utmost priority. We do not have to experience the consequences of disobedience for us to learn that we ought to have obeyed Him in the first place. Note that these warnings are out of love and for our best interest. They are not to frighten us but to get us prepared so as not to be caught on the wrong side of His judgement. We ought to accept

Christ as our Lord and Saviour and live the rest of our days in complete obedience to all His instructions. Those who live their lives as though the warnings of God are of little significance to them will have no excuse when the judgement comes. Psalm 9:17 says: *"The wicked shall be turned back to Sheol, even all the nations that forget God."* (NHEB.)

CHAPTER 8

TOPIC 1: GOD NEVER FORGETS HIS OWN

GENESIS 8:1

You might have heard some heart-wrenching stories of children being abandoned by parents and left to fend for themselves. In other cases, people may have felt abandoned by their loved ones during their trying moments. In situations like these, we say those loved ones had forgotten them. We use the expression "forgotten" not because thoughts of them never flashed through the minds of their loved ones at any time, but because the loved ones never took action to show that they cared about them in times of suffering. Ironically, some of those loved ones may not have had the ability to offer help when it was needed, but when they eventually provided the long-awaited support, we hear words such as "Ah, thank God, my loved one has remembered me."

Some people who come across Genesis 8:1, that says, **"God remembered Noah…"** (NHEB) may ask: "Did God forget Noah?" Of course not. We can rest assured that God never forgets His own. Sometimes the Bible uses the expression *remember* to refer to God taking action to deal with the situation of His loved ones after a period of apparent silence.

The deluge was God's response to man's wickedness; Noah's ark was God's medium of refuge. After months of rain, the bursting of the earth's fountain and flooding, it might seem that Noah was abandoned in the ark, forgotten by God, because there was no record of interaction between God and Noah during that period. Amid this apparent hopelessness we come across one of the most soothing lines in the Bible: *"God remembered Noah, all the animals, and all the livestock that were with him in the ship; and God made a wind to pass over the earth. The waters subsided."* (Genesis 8:1 NHEB.)

Just as it was recorded that God remembered Noah after months of rain and flood, it was also recorded that God remembered the Israelites after years of slavery. *"God heard their groaning, and God remembered his covenant with Abraham, with Isaac, and with Jacob."* (Exodus 2:24 NHEB.) By the time Moses, the instrument God would use in delivering the Israelites, was born, Israel was groaning in bondage like a woman in labour pains without any sign of respite. The recurring thoughts on many Israelites' minds would have been: "God has forgotten us." Notwithstanding, God responded to their cry, not because Israel remembered God's covenant with their patriarchs, but because God remembered His promise to their fathers. He told Moses: *"Moreover I have heard the groaning of the sons of Israel, whom the Egyptians keep in bondage, and I have remembered my covenant."* (Exodus 6:5 NHEB.) That God remembered them means it was the appointed time for His intervention. God's announcement of His intervention was followed by His action. The challenge we have as humans is that when we wait for His intervention we see that period of God's apparent inactivity and silence as a time when God has forgotten us.

In Genesis 22:18, God reiterated the promise He had made earlier to Abraham about making him a blessing to all the nations of the earth. *"And in your offspring all the nations of the earth will be blessed..."* (NHEB.) Paul, writing to the Galatians in Galatians 3:16, says that the referred "seed" is Christ. *"Now the promises were spoken to Abraham and to his offspring. He does not say, "And to offsprings," as of many, but as of one, "And to your offspring," which is Christ."* (NHEB.) However, the waiting for that promised seed, the Saviour of the world, took thousands of years. Eventually, God remembered His covenant to Abraham. At the birth of John the Baptist, the forerunner of Christ, John's father, through the inspiration of the Holy Spirit, declared that John's birth was part of God's process of performing what He promised the patriarch: *"to remember his holy covenant, [73] the oath which he spoke to Abraham, our father"* (Luke 1:72-73 NHEB). The Saviour was long in coming, or so it seemed, *"But when the fullness of the time came, God sent out his Son, born to a woman..."* (Galatians 4:4 NHEB.)

What should be our attitude during dark hours and storms of life when it seems God has forgotten us? Why is trust necessary in seasons of God's seeming silence? Often, when it seems God is silent in our lives, it does not mean He has forsaken us. His silence could be to bring to fulfilment His plans for our lives. That is why we need to trust Him and not doubt. We are oblivious of the background work being carried out, and because we do not see it plainly in black and white, we despair and feel God has forgotten us. We can count on God's faithfulness during the silence, taking great confidence from the fact that He has saved us in the past, that He has promised to preserve us in the future and that He is providing for us in the present.

As we trust Him, another attitude we should put on is obedience. Obedience to His word is vital. Even when our stormy situation is caused by disobedience, God can still turn it for our good if we repent and fully return to Him in obedience.

It is quite sad that God's children tend to forget God whenever life becomes too easy but then accuse God of forgetting them when life becomes challenging. We are to actively watch and pray that we are not broken by circumstances or go against the word of God in trying times. Instead of doubting or concluding that "God has forgotten me" let us be assured by the word of God spoken through Isaiah: *"Can a woman forget her nursing child, that she should not have compassion on the son of her womb? Yes, these may forget, yet I will not forget you."* (Isaiah 49:15 NHEB.)

God's ultimate promise to us, living in this age, is found in Jesus' statement in John 14:1-3, *"Do not let your heart be troubled.*

Believe in God. Believe also in me. [2]In my Father's house are many dwelling places. If it weren't so, I would have told you; for I go to prepare a place for you. [3]And if I go and prepare a place for you, I will come again, and will receive you to myself; that where I am, you may be there also." (NHEB.) Although we may not know when God will bring this promise to fulfilment, we should not relent in our obedience to, and trust in, Him. When trials and persecutions seem to persist and when answers to prayers seem to be delayed, we should not give room for discouragement and despondency; instead, we should be faithful and patient so that His coming does not meet us unprepared.

TOPIC 2: APPRECIATION AND GRATITUDE

GENESIS 8:20–21

When we consider the limitless height of God's mercies, the bottomless depth of His goodness and the boundless dimensions of His faithfulness, we realise how much gratitude we owe Him. It is a common courtesy to say "thanks" when someone does something in our favour. We appreciate fellow men whose acts of kindness can be underlaid with ulterior motives. God's goodness is devoid of such machinations and should be greeted with nothing less than an appreciation from a sincere heart.

After Noah and his family were spared from the colossal destruction that engulfed the world, being counted worthy of remaining alive constituted a reason for Noah to react with gratitude. He was not only grateful for himself; he was grateful for his family as well. After spending so many months in the ark Noah sent out birds to scout for land. The long wait may have created boredom and uncertainty of what would follow or prompted the question "For how much longer?" Nonetheless, when he finally saw that the waters had dried and they were on land he did not act in haste but waited until God asked him, his family and all the animals to come down. When he finally came out of the boat he was thankful that God had spared him and his family. As a demonstration of his gratitude, Noah built an altar and gave thanks to God. Noah did not take the grace of God's preservation for granted, and from God's response it is obvious that God appreciated Noah's thanksgiving. We are to appreciate God daily for His blessings. It is worth noting that Noah offered his sacrifice voluntarily. A worthy act of thanksgiving offered to God must be done willingly and not grudgingly.

The act of thanksgiving is a way of acknowledging God's faithfulness in our lives; it is a way to express our gratitude to Him consciously. It is always imperative to thank God for His blessings. Psalm 92:1 says: *"It is a good thing to give thanks to the LORD, to sing praises to your name, Most High"* (NHEB). Cultivating an attitude of thanksgiving to God is good for us because it refreshes our consciousness always – the consciousness that all we have come from God and, therefore, must be used for His glory.

The Bible records the story of ten lepers whom Jesus healed. Only one out of the ten returned to Jesus to worship and give thanks. Like the other nine lepers who never returned to give thanks, sometimes many of us forget God and what He has done for us; we only remember Him when facing problems. We pray and pray until the Lord answers us, then we say, "Thank you, God! See you next time." We must note that God wants our gratitude to Him to be genuine; only when rendered genuinely is our love and devotion acceptable to Him.

Beyond a shadow of a doubt, thanksgiving is an essential component of the Christian life and the capstone of a grateful life. While it is expected that we appreciate God whenever our needs are met, it is essential to be thankful at all times: *"Do not be anxious about anything, but in everything, by prayer and petition with thanksgiving, let your requests be made known to God. ⁷And the peace of God, which surpasses all understanding, will guard your hearts and your thoughts in Christ Jesus."* (Philippians 4:6–7 NHEB.)

Apart from giving thanks to God when we have a reason – such as recovering from an illness, we should also give thanks to God when we cannot see anything significant – such as having a normal day – and when we seem not to have reasons – the loss of a job or the loss of a loved one, for example. The Bible says, *"In everything give thanks, for this is the will of God in Christ Jesus toward you."* (1 Thessalonians 5:18 NHEB.)

Furthermore, the best expression of gratitude we can give God for all we have received from Him is our bodies as a living sacrifice. Romans 12:1 says, *"Therefore I urge you, brothers, by the mercies of God, to present your bodies a living sacrifice, holy, acceptable to God, which is your spiritual service."* (NHEB.)

As believers, let us live a life of gratitude to God and be the reason others are thankful to Him as well.

CHAPTER 9

TOPIC 1: LIFE OF THE FLESH IS IN THE BLOOD

GENESIS 9:3–5

""Foods for the belly, and the belly for foods," but God will bring to nothing both it and them..." (1 Corinthians 6:13 NHEB.)

After the flood, God gave Noah and his family instructions on what to and what not to eat. The instructions were for them to live by and be passed down to their descendants – the whole of humanity, which God would later raise out of them. God gave all plants and animals that man may desire as food, except for the blood of animals.

Remember that God's instructions to Adam and Eve, to keep them from eating from the fruit of the tree of the knowledge of good and evil, was for their good. Likewise, all God's instructions to man are for the benefit of man, not God. If we know this, we will strive to obey His every command with complete trust that He would never lead us to destruction. Noah and his family must have kept to the words of these instructions precisely, but as time went by and their offspring populated the earth, the effect of the sinful nature of man had a domino effect on man's relationship with God, causing man to continually go against the commands of God, question the importance of His commandments and, in some cases, deny His existence. If we must walk with God, we must get rid of ignorance by familiarising ourselves with His words, through which we can know His mind and be willing to uphold only those standards recommended by Him.

In light of the above mentioned, let us consider the command not to eat the blood of animals. The command can be stated as:

- Do not eat the blood of animals directly as a meal.
- Blood must be sufficiently drained from an animal before its flesh can be used for food. Meat must be properly washed with water to get rid of blood before cooking.

God gave His reason for this command through Moses to the Israelites when He said: *"Any man of the house of Israel, or of the foreigners who sojourn among you, who eats any kind of blood, I will set my face against that soul who eats blood, and will cut him off from among his people. ¹¹For the life of the flesh is in the blood; and I have given it to you on the altar to make atonement for your souls: for it is the blood that makes atonement by reason of the life. ¹²Therefore I have said to the sons of Israel, "No person among you shall eat blood, neither shall any stranger who lives as a foreigner among you eat blood." ¹³"'Whatever man there is of the sons of Israel, or of the foreigners who sojourn among you, who takes in hunting any animal or bird that may be eaten; he shall pour out its blood, and cover it with dust. ¹⁴For as to the life of all flesh, its blood is with its life: therefore I said to the sons of Israel, "You shall not eat the blood of any kind of flesh; for the life of all flesh is its blood. Whoever eats it shall be cut off."'"* (Leviticus 17:10–14 NHEB.)

We can see that the command of God to Noah concerning the eating of blood transcended through ages and was reiterated in the days of Moses. Apart from the fact that God had said that blood is sacred and had accepted it as a sacrifice for the atonement of sins, we may not adequately decipher the divine significance of the blood and why our eating it translates to sin. Nonetheless, it would be in our best interest if we stayed away from it because God said so.

The apostles under the new covenant, while accepting that the Gentiles do not need to be circumcised to be saved, also upheld the prohibition placed on eating the flesh with its blood, saying: *"But concerning the Gentiles who believe, we have written our decision that they should keep themselves from food offered to idols, from blood, from strangled things, and from sexual immorality."* (Acts 21:25 NHEB.)

The command of God concerning the eating of blood transcends eras in the Bible; it was before the law, in the law and reaffirmed after the law by the apostles, after Christ's death and resurrection.

God cares about us. He knows what we need more than we could ever know; therefore, it is in our best interest to trust Him that, when we do what He requires of us, it will be well with us.

TOPIC 2: THE SANCTITY OF HUMAN LIFE

GENESIS 9:5–6

Taking a person's life is one of the highest offences that one could commit against an individual or a society. Everyone generally perceives the cruelty of the act, and there is hardly any culture or society where murder is permitted in the constitution. It is worth mentioning that not all acts of killing are considered murder. Accidentally killing another would not be termed as murder. Murder is the act of willingly and unjustly taking the life of another.

When God established His covenant with Noah after the flood, He gave him some commandments applicable to humanity. The commandments in Genesis 9:5–6 depict the sanctity of every man's life: *"I will surely require your blood of your lives. At the hand of every animal I will require it. At the hand of man, even at the hand of every man's brother, I will require the life of man. ⁶Whoever sheds man's blood, his blood will be shed by man, for God made man in his own image."* (NHEB.) It gives us an understanding of how valuable human life is to God. God's commandment regarding the prohibition of murder transcends the three eras of His dealings with man. It was given before the law, as seen in the verses in context (Genesis 9:5–6). It was given as part of the law through Moses: ***"Do not murder."*** (Exodus 20:14 NHEB.) It can also be found within the pages of the New Testament: ***"19Now the works of the flesh are obvious, which are: sexual immorality, uncleanness, lustfulness, 21envyings, murders, drunkenness, orgies, and things like these; of which I forewarn you, even as I also forewarned you, that those who practice such things will not inherit the kingdom of God."*** (Galatians 5:19, 21 NHEB.)

God said, ***"Whoever sheds man's blood, his blood will be shed by man..."*** (Genesis 9:6 NHEB.) Note that this does not in any manner permit vengeance or retaliation. During the time of Noah, when God said, "by humans shall their blood be shed", there was no stated method for the execution of this. However, when the law was given to the Israelites, such justice was to be administered by their judicial system. By God's command to Noah, we understand that the sanctity of human life is protected by divine authority. Every life belongs to God and no man has the right to take the life of a human being; more so, no man has the right to take his own life.

The crime of murder committed against another is actually committed against God, because man was created in God's image and likeness. Therefore, anyone who commits murder disregards the image of God and dishonours God. ***"for God made man in his own image"*** (Genesis 9:6 NHEB). According to the law of Moses, anyone who willingly and unjustly takes the life of another man would be accountable to God. Such a person will be required to pay with their life. Life can only be repaid with life; therefore, when God demands a man's life from a murderer, the murderer cannot give this, so he must give his own life instead. Only the life of the murderer will atone for the life he took. Numbers 35:31 and 33 buttresses this fact, ***"31Moreover you shall take no ransom for the life of a murderer who is guilty of death; but he shall surely be put to death. 33So you shall not pollute the land in which you are: for blood, it pollutes the land; and no expiation can be made for the*** *land for the blood that is shed in it, but by the blood of him who shed it.* (NHEB.)

Jesus is the only hope for a murderer. The only reason for God forgiving a person who takes another's life is if he runs to Jesus. There is forgiveness in Jesus because He has satisfied God's divine justice by giving His own life as a ransom for the life of the murderer. The murderer must be willing to accept Jesus as his Lord – deciding to live his whole life in complete obedience to Him – to be saved from his sins. There is no sin beyond the pardon of God provided the wicked are willing to repent: *"let the wicked forsake his way, and the unrighteous man his thoughts; and let him return to the LORD, and he will have mercy on him; and to our God, for he will abundantly pardon."* (Isaiah 55:7 NHEB.)

Note that God's mercies at salvation might not necessarily exempt the murderer from the earthly consequences of capital punishment or imprisonment by the state, but God's pardon on him means that he has the hope of eternal life.

TOPIC 3: THE RAINBOW

GENESIS 9:13–16

The rainbow is one of the most awe-inspiring atmospheric phenomena that has characterised our world since God created it. It is a bow in the sky made of nothing but colours perfectly aligned as it arcs its way along the horizon. Its dazzling array of colours, ravishing radiance and irrepressible iridescence evokes a euphoric feeling. Indeed, it is a delightful sight to behold.

Beyond its physical properties, however, the rainbow is a divinely ordained symbol of God's faithfulness and mercy. After the destruction of the earth by water, God instituted it to be a flag of peace, an assurance of His resolve never to destroy the world again with water.

As a result of the great transgression that pervaded in the days of Noah, an unprecedented flood brought about the destruction of the world. Consequently, placing the rainbow in the clouds marked an epoch-making moment that signifies God's commitment to His promise, a promise that assures us that He would never again repeat the magnitude of the deluge that would destroy all flesh.

It must be noted that God said that the rainbow will remind Him of His covenant. Not a reminder such as to one who may forget, but a source of comfort to the ones He made the promise to, that they may look upon it and be assured that God has not forgotten. Although there have been many floods since then, there has never been one with the destruction of the days of Noah – an indication that God has kept His promise. Therefore, we can be assured that our God is a promise-keeping God whenever we see a rainbow in the sky.

Furthermore, the covenant God made with Noah never again to destroy the world with water was the first recorded covenant of God with man. It was a covenant but was also more of a promise because man had no part in maintaining its validity; it solely depended on God. Yet, God bound Himself with His words and put up a sign as a witness as if to say, "From generation to generation, let the inhabitants of the earth know of this promise and see if I will ever fail." The sovereignty of God is clearly revealed here, seeing that He did not require any role from man for the covenant to remain valid, yet sealed His promise with a mark and called it an "agreement". God fulfilled the covenant simply because it is His desire, and He has said so.

As a sign in the sky to show that the earth will not be destroyed by flood anymore, the rainbow does not signify that there will be no more destruction for the wicked by God. God still frowns at sin just as He did in Noah's days, and He has resounded this truth in the ears of men from generation to generation. God destroyed the nations of Sodom and Gomorrah with fire because of their immoral lifestyles; He destroyed Korah and his companions in the wilderness for their rebellion against Moses and He has announced through prophets and through His Son that there will be another destruction of those that do not obey or regard Him. 2 Peter 2:4–9 says: *"For if God did not spare angels when they sinned, but cast them down to the lower parts of hell, and committed them to chains of darkness, to be reserved for judgment; [5]and did not spare the ancient world, but preserved Noah with seven others, a proclaimer of righteousness, when he brought a flood on the world of the ungodly; [6]and turning the cities of Sodom and Gomorrah into ashes, condemned them to destruction, having made them an example of what is going to happen to the ungodly; [7]and delivered righteous Lot, who was very distressed by the lustful life of the wicked [8](for that righteous man dwelling among them, was tormented in his righteous soul from day to day with seeing and hearing lawless deeds): [9]the Lord knows how to deliver the godly out of temptation and to keep the unrighteous under punishment for the day of judgment"* (NHEB).

In the event of Christ's second coming, those who lived in obedience to the instructions of God will be rewarded with eternal life and glory, while those who lived in disobedience to God's instructions will be cast into the lake of fire together with Satan and his demons. *"He who overcomes, I will give him these things. I will be his God, and he will be my son. [8]But for the cowardly, unbelieving, abominable, murderers, sexually immoral, sorcerers, idolaters, and all liars, their part is in the lake that burns with fire and sulfur, which is the second death."* (Revelation 21:7–8 NHEB.) This shows that while we are assured through the rainbow sign that the earth is not about to be destroyed when the clouds converge in a threatening sky in preparation for rainfall, we must know that there will be a future global judgement.

Whenever we look to the sky and see the magnificent bow with all its beautiful colours we are to be reminded of the integrity and faithfulness of God in keeping His promises. By this remembrance, we should act wisely to escape the coming destruction of the ungodly and teach others to do so as well, both by preaching and by living our lives in consonance with the word of God.

TOPIC 4: EFFECTS OF DRUNKENNESS

GENESIS 9:20–21

Should one who seeks to follow God take alcoholic drinks? Does the drinking of alcohol pose any risk to a person's salvation? Does God approve of or condemn the drinking of alcohol or is He just indifferent about it? These are commonly asked questions whenever the topic of drinking alcohol is raised. The answers to these questions are essential for our guidance. (Wine in this write-up refers to alcoholic drinks.)

Noah was the first man recorded in the Bible to have been drunk. He had consumed wine in excess from his vineyard. Drunkenness plunged him into an embarrassing state – he was naked and unaware of his environment; such is its effect as recorded in the Bible. *"Wine is a mocker, and beer is a brawler. Whoever is led astray by them is not wise."* (Proverbs 20:1 NHEB.) Ham had seen Noah – his father – lying naked in his drunken state; he resorted to telling his brothers about it. Shem and Japhet honoured their father by refusing to look upon his nakedness and covered him instead. This appalling scenario resulted in Noah pronouncing a curse on Canaan – Ham's son. *"Noah awoke from his wine, and knew what his youngest son had done to him. ²⁵He said, "Canaan is cursed. He will be servant of servants to his brothers.""* (Genesis 9:24–25 NHEB.) God did not reprimand Noah for his drunkenness, most likely because there was no command against it at that time; hence, Noah must have acted out of ignorance. For us today, there is no excuse because the Bible has expressly stated that drunkards will not inherit the kingdom of God. *"Or do you not know that the unrighteous will not inherit the kingdom of God? Do not be deceived. Neither the sexually immoral, nor idolaters, nor adulterers, nor effeminate, nor men who have sexual relations with men, ¹⁰nor thieves, nor covetous, nor drunkards, nor slanderers, nor swindlers, will inherit the kingdom of God."* (1 Corinthians 6:9–10 NHEB.)

When people are drunk they lose their grip on reality, and their actions are contrary to what they may have done in a sober state.

Drinking wine in itself would not have been a sin; taking certain types of wine in the right proportions can be of medical benefit to a person. In 1 Timothy 5:23, Apostle Paul advised Timothy to *"Be no longer a drinker of water only, but use a little wine for your stomach's sake and your frequent infirmities."* (NHEB.) However, caution must be applied because excess wine has several disadvantages, such as toxifying the body, damaging the liver and being addictive. An alcohol addict was not born that way; it began with a harmless little sip, then a glass, a bottle and many more bottles. The best prevention of addiction is total abstinence. We should not use Paul's advice to Timothy as an anchor to conclude that God has no problem with us consuming wine until we get drunk. Proverbs 31:4–5 further emphasises the effect of drinking: *"It is not for kings, O Lemuel; it is not for kings to drink wine, or for princes to take strong drink, ⁵lest they drink, and forget the decree, and pervert the justice due to anyone who is afflicted."* (NHEB.)

From the above Bible verses we can see that God warns us against drunkenness for our good; it is little wonder that it is listed among the works of the flesh.

Furthermore, drunkenness can lead to poverty. *"for the drunkard and the glutton shall become poor; and drowsiness clothes them in rags"* (Proverbs 23:21 NHEB). Those addicted to alcohol spend most of their money satisfying that urge; at the same time, they become more and more physically unproductive. Drunkenness can lead to severed relationships, broken homes, depression, violent behaviours, accidents and other problems and judging from this, we can see that drunkenness does more harm than good; this is why God hates it.

God forbade those who were called to priestly service of the Levitical order from consuming alcohol; those who intended to take the Nazarite vow of dedication to Him were also to abstain entirely from wine and other fermented drinks. *"The LORD spoke to Moses, saying, ²'Speak to the sons of Israel, and tell them: When either man or woman shall make a special vow, the vow of a Nazirite, to separate himself to the LORD, ³he shall separate himself from wine and strong drink. He shall drink no vinegar of wine, or vinegar of fermented drink, neither shall he drink any juice of grapes, nor eat fresh grapes or dried. ⁴All the days of his separation he shall eat nothing that is made of the grapevine, from the seeds even to the skins.'"* (Numbers 6:1–4 NHEB.) Also, in Luke 21:34, Jesus inferred that a drunk person could not act with the consciousness of the kingdom of God: *"So be careful, or your hearts will be loaded down with carousing, drunkenness, and cares of this life, and that day will come on you suddenly."* (NHEB.)

As believers, we ought to be concerned about each other's spiritual health as we relate to one another. Mature believers should be careful not to lead the babes in faith astray. If we encourage a brother to drink by our act of drinking and that brother gets into the habit of drinking, getting himself drunk in the process, we sin against God, not because we drank wine but because we caused a brother to sin. 1 Corinthians 8:9–13 says, *"But be careful that by no means does this liberty of yours become a stumbling block to the weak. ¹⁰For if someone sees you who have knowledge sitting in an idol's temple, won't his conscience, if he is weak, be emboldened to eat things sacrificed to idols? ¹¹And through your knowledge, he who is weak perishes, the brother for whom the Christ died. ¹²Thus, sinning against the brothers, and wounding their conscience when it is weak, you sin against Christ. ¹³Therefore, if food causes my brother to stumble, I will eat no meat forevermore, that I do not cause my brother to stumble."* (NHEB.) And Romans 14:20–22 says: *"Do not overthrow God's work for food's sake. All things indeed are clean, however it is evil for anyone who creates a stumbling block by eating. ²¹It is good to not eat meat, drink wine, or do anything by which your brother stumbles, or is offended, or is made weak. ²²Do you have faith? Have it to yourself before God. Happy is he who does not judge himself in that which he approves."* (NHEB.)

Believers should be good role models for others to look up to and, since we know that the things we do can influence others, it is best to totally abstain from drinking alcohol so that weaker believers will not take our drinking as an endorsement and encouragement to drink, which may lead them to drunkenness and addiction.

TOPIC 5: RIGHT ATTITUDE TO PARENTAL MISCONDUCT

GENESIS 9:20–23

Many children grow up seeing their parents as super role models; to these children, their parents are always right, and every other person is measured by what they see of their parents. They eventually grow up realising that their super role models are humans with weaknesses after all. Imagine a child who grew up seeing his father as a perfect husband to his mother and suddenly realised that the father had been having an extra-marital affair. That child will undoubtedly be disappointed. But each child in that situation would react differently. Some children could react with disrespect, others could tell the mother, and some others could even cease any care they had for the father as a way of expressing their displeasure. The question is, how should a child rightly react to parental misconduct?

When Ham saw his father's nakedness as Noah laid drunk, instead of covering him he exposed his father's shameful deed to his brothers. Let us agree that seeing his father lying naked under the influence of alcohol must have been shocking or disappointing, but Ham's fault lies in telling others with a disrespectful motive. Children cannot be held accountable for their parents' misbehaviour; instead, it is the other way round. But children should surely be held liable for their negative reaction towards their parents' misbehaviour. Proverbs 30:17 says: *"The eye that mocks at his father, and scorns obedience to his mother: the ravens of the valley shall pick it out, the young eagles shall eat it."* (NHEB.)

While many see only the openly shameful behaviours such as drunkenness, infidelity and domestic violence as parental misconduct, there are still subtle behavious such as a reluctance to sponsor a child's education, being insensitive to a child's emotional challenges, and having extreme expectations of a child – especially if unduly comparing them with their peers in the academic sphere, looks and talents. Over time, children react to these misconducts by cultivating hatred, which could lead to open disrespect.

God expects all children to take proper care of their parents, and not mind their misconduct. Without excusing the behaviour of 'delinquent parents', we should remember that parents are humans and as such are prone to errors. To start with, exposing other people's shameful weakness is not a mark of a true believer. ***"Brothers, even if someone is caught in some fault, you who are spiritual must restore such a one in a spirit of gentleness..."*** (Galatians 6:1 NHEB.) The above Bible verse is valid in our relationship with other brethren and our parents.

It is essential to see parents as humans and not perfect beings. As humans, we are prone to errors, and parents are no exception. Also, we could notice parents displaying some childhood traits as they grow older because life is a cycle; their assimilation and comprehension rate could decline with age. Some of their misconducts could be due to the decline in their mental capacity. As the saying goes, "Once a man twice a child." We are to understand them and give them the honour they deserve as elders.

We should learn to approach our parents in love, humility and wisdom regarding their weaknesses, to help them overcome them. It is advisable to watch out for an appropriate opportunity to approach the parents in question. The stage of meeting the parent is a sensitive one; a wrong approach could be destructive. Young adults should use this method with care. They should seek the assistance of a wise person who has the fear of God whom the parent gives an audience to when they speak. Some parents would not take it lightly if a young adult advised them on their misconduct, even if they inwardly admitted that the younger person was correct.

God takes severe displeasure in children dishonouring parents and, worse still, exposing their nakedness or shameful acts to others, even family members. *"Children, obey your parents in the Lord, for this is right. [2] "Honor your father and mother," which is the first commandment with a promise: [3] "that it may be well with you, and that you may live long in the land.""* (Ephesians 6:1–3 NHEB.)

Another response we should make when we notice parents' misconduct is to pray. Prayers here should be with two primary focuses. The first focus should be on the parents – for God to touch, open their eyes to their errors, and change them. The second focus should be on ourselves – to relate well without allowing hurt and disappointment to take the better part of us. Note that some misconducts could have spiritual manipulations. What else is the best weapon against spiritual manipulation than being watchful in prayers? When Satan desired to sieve Peter like wheat, Jesus warned Peter, *"Simon, Simon, look, Satan asked to have you, that he might sift you as wheat, [32] but I prayed for you, that your faith would not fail..."* (Luke 22:31–32 NHEB.) It was Jesus' prayers that saved Peter. Our prayers could deliver our parents from misconduct – whether demonically manipulated or not.

Note that honouring one's parents does not entail supporting them in their wrong-doings, nor does it mean obeying and granting their requests which are against the word of God. Sometimes, believing children may face persecution at the hands of unbelieving parents due to their incompatible lifestyles. The instruction of God concerning such parents is: "Honour them as well." We can honour them by not speaking slanderously concerning them, making a mockery of them or exposing their shameful deeds, but always seizing every opportunity to show love to them while trusting God to do His part.

Regardless of how parents must have conducted themselves, children must show their parents the way of the Lord and prayerfully lead them to the Lord instead of abandoning them. Romans 12:21 admonishes: *"Do not be overcome by evil, but overcome evil with good."* (NHEB.)

Children should try as much as possible to avoid Ham's mistake. Love remains the most potent force within the human mind. No matter how humanly wise it is handled, criticism is counter-productive without love. Love is more effective in winning a sinner to Christ than criticism. Disrespectful corrections build walls and can harden the corrected parent's heart. Remember, honour to one's parents is a command to be obeyed irrespective of the parent's spiritual state.

TOPIC 6: RIGHT PARENTAL ATTITUDE TO PROVOCATION

GENESIS 9:24–27

To an average person, words are nothing more than mediums of expressing thoughts, but to the spiritually enlightened, words are far more than the simplest unit of language. They could be mediums of moulding or destroying destinies. People who understand the power of words are cautious with their use when provoked or when overly excited. They understand that blessings are not just expressions of approval towards a person; they are tools to build lives. Conversely, curses are more than expressions of anger or disappointment; they are instruments with which generations unborn can be marred. For that reason, curses have no place in the heart of a child of God, much less on their lips.

Noah had woken from his drunken stupor to discover that Ham had disrespected him by telling others about his nakedness. Probably embarrassed by his son's act, he cursed Ham's son. In a moment of rage, the fate of generations unborn was declared and sealed. Noah's curse was not to enemies or strangers, it was directed at one of his three sons.

What would provoke a parent to curse his child? To Noah, Ham's disrespect was unpardonable. To Jacob, Reuben's sexual relationship with his concubine was inexcusable. The incident recorded briefly in Genesis 35:22 provoked Jacob: *"It happened, while Israel lived in that land, that Reuben went and lay with Bilhah, his father's concubine…"* (NHEB.) That incident, securely preserved in Jacob's heart, eventually found expression in curses at Jacob's death bed. Jacob's curse recorded in Genesis 49:4 must have come as a shock to Reuben when he would have thought it gone and forgotten. *"Boiling over as water, you shall not excel; because you went up to your father's bed, then defiled it. He went up to my couch."* (NHEB.)

For some parents, a child's constant disobedience means questioning their authority, which could lead to negative pronouncements that can mar that child's life and even that of the child's descendants. Also, parents might be tempted to curse their children when the family's name has been dragged through the mud and when their children's actions personally hurt them. However, note that there is no reason good enough for a parent to react to a child's provocation with a curse.

Parents should be mindful of their pronouncements towards their children because words are powerful. Proverbs 18:21 says: *"Death and life are in the power of the tongue; those who love it will eat its fruit."* (NHEB.) Parents could either make their child's life worthless or worthful by their pronouncements. As wonderful as it is to discipline a child, parents might need to make it a rule to postpone discipline when angry because that could make them utter words they may regret later.

As Christians, we are commanded to bless always, not to curse, regardless of the intensity of our displeasure. It is the will of God that Christians should bless even their enemies; how much more should they bless their children who provoke them? Jesus said in Luke 6:27–28: *"But I tell you who hear: love your enemies, do good to those who hate you, ²⁸bless those who curse you, and pray for those who mistreat you."* (NHEB.) Parents' first reaction to children's disobedience should be a verbal correction and then a carefully thought-out form of discipline where necessary, but never a curse.

In dealing with grown-ups, as in the case of Ham, parents should talk with them to express their displeasure and settle all grievances to preserve the relationship. Prayer is a tool that we should combine with other tools, such as a verbal correction, to bring the desired result. Parents do not need to wait until they are provoked before they employ the tool of prayer concerning their children. We are to intercede for our children, even when all seems to be well. Job 1:4–5 tells us that Job offered burnt offerings for each of his children should they have sinned or cursed God in their hearts. *"His sons went and held a feast in the house of each one on his birthday; and they sent and called for their three sisters to eat and to drink with them. ⁵It was so, when the days of their feasting had run their course, that Job sent and sanctified them, and rose up early in the morning, and offered burnt offerings according to the number of them all. For Job said, 'It may be that my sons have sinned, and renounced God in their hearts.' Job did so continually."* (NHEB.) A lot of the issues we face in life have spiritual undertones to the physical manifestations.

Additionally, we are to live exemplary lives; we are to be what we want our children to be. Children are like chameleons in nature; they tend to imitate more of what they see than what they are told to do. Verbal corrections, corporal punishments and even some prayer points could be minimised if parents simply live the way they want their children to live.

Above all, we are to love our children unconditionally. 1 Corinthians 13:4 and 7 says, *"⁴Love is patient and is kind... ⁷bears all things, believes all things, hopes all things, endures all things."* (NHEB.) Let us remember that after all is said and done, there will always be provocative situations from our loved ones; how we react matters. We must choose to respond with love and forgiveness rather than allow those situations to provoke us to anger.

CHAPTER 10

TOPIC 1: FAMILY IDENTITY

GENESIS 10:5, 20, 31

After the flood, a family of eight stepped out of the ark. The family had Noah as the head and it was from him that the family derived its name. That initial family produced several other families, then clans, tribes and nations that populated the world.

In Genesis 10, the Bible described the expansion of the earth's population. However, the verses under consideration specifically identified the people of the then world by their clans, languages and lands. The passage describes the three nations descended from the three sons of Noah – Japhet, Ham and Shem, and how they occupied different lands in their different clans' formations. Each nation had its languages and was made up of different clans and families. Thus, families were and are still the smallest units of society.

God identified people by their earthly family descent in the Old Testament. For instance, God's acceptance of worship in Deuteronomy 23:2–3 was based on family and national identity: ***"No one of illegitimate birth shall enter into the assembly of the LORD; even to the tenth generation shall none of his enter into the assembly of the LORD. ³An Ammonite or a Moabite shall not enter into the assembly of the LORD; even to the tenth generation shall none belonging to them enter into the assembly of the LORD forever"*** (NHEB). In simple terms, a man's family descent could bar him from the congregation of the Lord. A bastard is a person of illegitimate birth. That shows how important one's biological family identity was in the Old Testament. To obey this command, every Israelite was expected to trace his genealogy up to the tenth generation. After the Babylonian captivity, any Levite unable to trace his genealogy was excluded from service in the sanctuary. Ezra 2:59 and 62 record a group of families who returned from exile: *"⁵⁹but they could not show whether their fathers' house, and their descent, were from Israel: ⁶²These sought their place among those who were registered by genealogy, but they were not found: therefore were they deemed polluted and put from the priesthood."* (NHEB.)

Two gospel writers – Matthew and Luke –dedicated parts of their writing to Jesus' genealogy. While Matthew traced from Abraham down to Jesus, Luke traced from Jesus back to Adam. All these were to convince the Jewish readers that Jesus was truly the long-awaited Messiah.

In the New Testament, God still identifies people by families – not by biological descent but by the new birth. God has His family; Satan also has his. John 1:12 and 13 talks about God's family: *"as many as received him, to them he gave the right to become God's children, to those who believe in his name, ¹³who were born not of blood, nor of the will of the flesh, nor of the will of man, but of God."* (NHEB.) On the other hand, 1 John 3:10 gives the identity of members of Satan's family. *"In this the children of God are revealed, and the children of the devil. Whoever does not do righteousness is not of God, neither is he who does not love his brother."* (NHEB.)

Both God's and Satan's families have members from different tribes and nations; the point is that they will eventually end up in different destinations. God's family will end up with Christ in eternal glory. Jesus told His disciples, *"In my Father's house are many dwelling places. If it weren't so, I would have told you; for I go to prepare a place for you. ³And if I go and prepare a place for you, I will come again, and will receive you to myself; that where I am, you may be there also. ⁴And you know the way where I am going."*

(John 14:2–4 NHEB.) On the other hand, Satan's family will end up with him in eternal torment in hell. ***"Then he will say also to those on the left hand, 'Depart from me, you cursed, into the everlasting fire which is prepared for the devil and his angels'"*** (Matthew 25:41 NHEB).

The good news is that you can cross from Satan's family into God's by accepting Jesus. Sadly, you can fall from God's family into Satan's if you continuously refuse to walk in obedience to God's word.

Today, as far as God is concerned, your biological family background does not matter – whether your father's name is recognised or not. Even if your father's name is noted for evil, once you move into God's family, God accepts you as His son and identifies you by Jesus Christ.

Some family names have opened great doors in this world to members of such families; the name of Jesus opens heavenly doors for those identified by that name. It is now over to you. In whose family are you or would you like to belong?

CHAPTER 11

TOPIC 1: MOTIVE

GENESIS 11:1–4

The monumental construction of the Tower of Babel is a limpid depiction of how the element of motive plays a pivotal role in God's disposition towards our actions.

While some actions can be considered suitable by the doer and sometimes by others, if the motive behind it contradicts God's word, such actions cannot be acceptable by God no matter how grand it seems. Proverbs 16:2 says, *"All the ways of a man are clean in his own eyes; but the LORD weighs the motives."* (NHEB.)

A motive constitutes the fundamental reason for any action, and individuals can operate from a plethora of motives. Revenge, pride, anger, greed and ambition can be among the stimuli for our actions.

Genesis 11 recounts the story of a group of people exhibiting unparalleled unity, colossal ambition, and enormous determination to assemble a gargantuan edifice, popularly known as the Tower of Babel. Although this was not necessarily a bad thing, their motive was contrary to the will of God. They craved to make a name for themselves instead of glorifying God. They attempted to compromise God's intention about expansion and filling the earth by choosing to stay in one place. *"let us make ourselves a name, lest we be scattered abroad on the surface of the whole earth."* (Genesis 11:4 NHEB.) In response to their action God confused their languages to enforce

His command for humanity to spread throughout the world. What they wanted to prevent was what happened eventually.

God is interested in our motives, as well as our actions. Not only is what we do important to God but also the reason for doing what we do. We must be mindful of how we lead our lives by thoroughly evaluating our motives. One of the greatest ways to evaluate our actions is to ask ourselves, "Who am I pleasing? God, man or self?" Often, people do good works to receive recognition and praise from others. A perfect example of wrong motives in good works is seen in Jesus' teaching in Matthew 6:1–4: *"Be careful that you do not do your righteousness before people, to be seen by them, or else you have no reward from your Father who is in heaven. ²Therefore when you do merciful deeds, do not sound a trumpet before yourself, as the hypocrites do in the synagogues and in the streets, that they may get glory from people. Truly I tell you, they have received their reward. ³But when you do merciful deeds, do not let your left hand know what your right hand does, ⁴so that your merciful deeds may be in secret, then your Father who sees in secret will reward you."* (NHEB.) Hypocrites are motivated to do good by their desire to receive glory and praise from men. Some are motivated to do good when there is an audience to applaud them. Our motive for doing good must be out of love, selflessness and sincere concern for others rather than public recognition, for our Father who sees what is done in secret will reward us openly in due season.

As one of Jesus' disciples, Judas' proclivity and greed for money meant that any way to enrich himself would be exploited using a seemingly sincere action but with a deceptive motive. On one such occasion he objected to Mary's noble gesture of washing Jesus' feet with expensive perfume. He advocated that the perfume should be sold and the proceeds given to the poor. However, this was not a display of charitable affections for the poor but a scheme to enrich himself. John 12:6 captures the motive for his objection. *"Now he said this, not because he cared for the poor, but because he was a thief, and having the money box, used to steal what was put into it."* (NHEB.)

Not only do wrong motives render our actions unacceptable before God but can also prevent our prayers being answered: *"You ask, and do not receive, because you ask with wrong motives, so that you may spend it for your pleasures."* (James 4:3 NHEB.)

What should be our ultimate motivation, then? *"But even as we have been approved by God to be entrusted with the Good News, so we speak; not as pleasing people, but God, who tests our hearts."* (1 Thessalonians 2:4 NHEB.) The primary motive for all our actions, either giving, living or preaching, should be to please God and no one else, not even ourselves. There is not a thought hidden from the knowledge of God; He examines all the intents of our hearts and will only reward those whose hearts are right towards Him. If we are more concerned about external forms of righteousness instead of internal purity, we risk provoking His judgement upon us.

We should keep our motives pure by continually surrendering our hearts to the cleansing work of the word of God and the control of the Holy Spirit. Christ set the perfect example for us; His ultimate goal in life was to please the Father: *"The Father hasn't left me alone, for I always do the things that are pleasing to him."* (John 8:29 NHEB.) Pleasing God must be the priority of our lives as well.

Since Jesus, when He returns, will *"bring to light the hidden things of darkness, and reveal the counsels of the hearts..."* (1 Corinthians 4:5 NHEB), it is imperative for us to submit all the intents of our actions to the guidance of His instructions.

TOPIC 2: THE POWER OF UNITY

GENESIS 11:1–8

As an indispensable tool for success, the importance of unity among any group of people cannot be underrated.

After the flood, as people journeyed eastward, they came together to build a city and a tower whose top was to reach the sky. They intended to make a name for themselves and not be scattered over the face of the whole earth. This was against God's will for man, revealed in His blessings to Adam in the beginning, and Noah after the flood, which was to multiply and fill the earth. Although their ambition was against the will of God, God recognised the strength of their unity.

Note some key words uttered by God: *"they are one people, and they have all one language... Now nothing will be withheld from them, which they intend to do."* (Genesis 11:6 NHEB.) These words reveal both the strength and importance of unity among people. God Almighty did not dismiss their efforts as weak; He acknowledged that humanity could accomplish what they set out to do by working together. All of them came together in unity as one people, having one language with a common vision, purpose and drive, and on the strength of this unity they were going to achieve what they set out to accomplish. None of them acted of his own will – their entire will was harmonised. Notice their words: "let us make brick", "let us build ourselves a city and a tower", "let us make ourselves a name". Everything they did, they did in complete union and harmony with each other. The seventh verse of this chapter also reveals the unity of the Trinity in making decisions: *"Come, let us go down, and there confuse their language, that they may not understand one another's speech."* (NHEB.)

In preventing the people from achieving their goal, God simply neutralised their strength, which was their unity. He confused them by giving them different languages. The difference in their languages distorted their unity, making it impossible to accomplish all they had agreed. This further supports the popular saying, "United we stand, divided we fall." It is essential to note that the people's plan did not threaten God, but that was not His intention for them.

Another Biblical incident that portrays the importance of unity is the battle between the Israelites and the Amalekites in Exodus 17:11–13: *"It happened, when Moses held up his hand, that Israel prevailed; and when he let down his hand, Amalek prevailed. ¹²But Moses'*

hands were heavy; and they took a stone, and put it under him,
and he sat on it. Aaron and Hur held up his hands, the one on the
one side, and the other on the other side. His hands were steady
until sunset. ¹³*Joshua defeated Amalek and his people with the*
edge of the sword." (NHEB.) It did not matter how mighty "a
warrior" Joshua was or how anointed Moses was; Israel would have
suffered defeat without Aaron and Hur's help. Even though God was
on their side, they all had to work together to achieve victory.

Unity is vital to the success of any group. This is why our Lord Jesus
said: *"And if a house is divided against itself, that house will not be*
able to stand." (Mark 3:25 NHEB.) Our Lord is saying here that any
group that is divided or separated within itself will fall apart. Unity is
essential for any group to thrive, be it an organisation, a family, a
congregation of believers or a nation. Unity is the strength within a
group or sect that binds them together, keeping them from falling
apart to achieve the purpose for which they assembled. People achieve
more when they work together. A disunited family will most likely fall
apart, and, likewise, a congregation of believers, no matter how
anointed they are.

In the book of Acts, one phrase appears repeatedly concerning the
early church, and that is: "in one accord". The church ought to be in
one accord, having the unity that the Holy Spirit brings, as unity is
indispensable if the church must influence the world. Jesus prayed,
"that they may all be one; even as you, Father, are in me, and I in
you, that they also may be in us; that the world may believe that
you sent me." (John 17:21 NHEB.)

God knows His cause will only be advanced if we are united. The God
we serve is a God of unity who desires that His children live in unity
and harmony built on the foundation that is in Christ Jesus. The
truth of God's word should bring oneness and not disunity among us
because disunity in the Body of Christ gives the enemy, Satan, access
to our midst. Living in unity does not mean that we will agree on
everything. There might be diverging opinions but we must agree on

our purpose in life: to work for God's glory. Our outward expression of unity will reflect our inward unity of purpose. Unity, though powerful, does not just happen; we have to work at it, focusing more on what unites us. *"Now the God of patience and of encouragement grant you to be of the same mind one with another according to Christ Jesus, ⁶that with one accord you may with one mouth glorify the God and Father of our Lord Jesus Christ."* (Romans 15:5–6 NHEB.)

TOPIC 3: UNDER HIS EYES

GENESIS 11:5

M any people are driven only by sheer ambition, their pleasures and the dictates of their consciences void of any sense of accountability to God. They are only concerned about their affairs, not what God thinks of their actions. However, they do not know that God is interested in every aspect of our existence as humans and will one day demand we give an account of our lives, of all things done in public or secret, either good or bad.

Men, after the flood, found a plain in Shinar and set out to build a tower and a city for themselves. One would naturally think it was men's project; they desired to build and make a name and settlement for themselves, but God saw what they were doing and assessed the project and the motive behind it. The result of that assessment was God scattering them, introducing a multiplicity of languages. Typically, men building a tower should not be a problem to God, but this particular project caught God's attention. The Bible says God *"came down to see the city and the tower, which the children of men built."* (Genesis 11:5 NHEB.) It is not just the tower at Babel that God observed and took action about; everything He created is always under His eyes. Hebrews 4:13 says: *"There is no creature that is hidden from his sight, but all things are naked and laid open before the eyes of him with whom we have to do."* (NHEB.) And Proverbs 15:3 records: *"The eyes of the LORD are everywhere, keeping watch on the evil and the good."* (NHEB.)

For the people at Shinar, God's eyes were on them to assess their work, which unfortunately got His disapproval. It is evident in God's truncation of the project that it was against His purpose. There is no project of man that is hidden from His sight. However, it would be wrong to say that since God intervened at Shinar and scattered them at Babel, He would always intervene in everything He disapproves of. Sometimes He watches and ignores, setting His judgement for another day or, at the latest, the last day.

God is intimately interested in the lives of all His creations and watches the obedient and the disobedient persons though not for the same reasons. God may seem not to react to the evil deeds of the wicked, except when those deeds stand in opposition to His purpose. The danger here is the folly of continuing in such ways until it is too late; those who do that face the wrath of God. Ecclesiastes 8:11 says, *"Because sentence against an evil work is not executed speedily, therefore the heart of the sons of men is fully set in them to do evil."* (NHEB.)

The Lord watches over the wicked with His long rope of forbearance, but if they continue in disobedience, His tolerance stands against them in judgement. No evil gets past His watchful eyes, whether He intervenes or not. What He does with His observation is left for His sovereignty. Let no one think that the Lord does not see and that the Most High will not consider.

There are also instances when God actively intervenes. This level is mostly for believers. When we get out of God's ways, He intervenes to discipline, lead and take other similar Fatherly actions. He watches us grow, pruning and correcting us where and when necessary, so that we can bear fruits to His glory. At this level, although God provides the grace for His children to resist evil, He does not directly or remotely force a believer to act in a particular direction. Our whole life is visible to God; He discerns our thoughts and motives. We may dress up our character to create an impression and deceive men, but even our deepest intents are laid bare under His eyes. So, if we have challenges displaying the life of Christ, we should ask for help, knowing He watches over us.

God intervenes for His children; He protects them and fights for them. As a good Father, He sees our going out and coming in; He does not leave us to eventualities, fortune or chance. A Psalm of David says: *"⁵You encircle me behind and in front, and you place your hand upon me. ⁷Where could I go from your Spirit? Or where could I flee from your presence?"* (Psalm 139:5, 7 NHEB.) God is very particular about the welfare of His children. Recall how He protected the Israelites from the Egyptians, taking them through the Red Sea. *"the LORD looked out on the Egyptian army through the pillar of fire and of cloud, and confused the Egyptian army."* (Exodus 14:24 NHEB.)

God's eyes over His children also manifest in guidance. Psalm 32:8 says, *"I will instruct you and teach you in the way which you shall go. I will counsel you with my eye on you."* (NHEB.) As His children, we can boldly say, "We are under His eyes", so there is no fear of being misdirected or misled. His leading is always for our good; through life, we are assured of His guiding arms if we put our trust in Him. It can be recalled, when Joseph's brothers conspired to kill him to truncate his dreams, that God watched, guided and protected him. As Potiphar's wife falsely accused him, which led to his imprisonment, and even as Pharaoh's butler forgot him, God watched and guided him for His purpose. God will only guide us if we live only for Him. God watches over all but is only committed to those who are committed to Him in obedience.

The ultimate level of God's influence in a man's life is when the believer hands over his will to God to have total control. God directs the believer's steps by His word, daily. Even at this level, God does not control the believer as a puppet or robot. Since the believer has surrendered to God in everything, God steps in and uses His word to direct the believer's action.

The knowledge that we are under God's eyes should give us that confidence, planted only by faith in His word. With His eyes over the wicked we are sure that God will not allow them to run out of control in their wickedness; and with His eyes over the righteous we are assured of His guidance and protection.

CHAPTER 12

TOPIC 1: THE CALL OF ABRAHAM

GENESIS 12:1–4

The beginning of the gospel of salvation to all nations of the world is summarised in Galatians 3:8. *"The Scripture, foreseeing that God would justify the Gentiles by faith, preached the Good News beforehand to Abraham, saying, "In you all the nations will be blessed.""* (NHEB.)

In Eden, that old serpent – the devil – must have been rejoicing moments after he succeeded in making man disobey God. However, his joy was short lived because God started the process of salvation for man. In the process of time, God chose a man, Abraham, through whose descents the Saviour would come. Going back to where Apostle Paul referred to in Galatians 3:8, we see God calling Abraham and giving instructions. Also, He made some promises to him that led to the ultimate salvation of man – "In you all the nations will be blessed."

Whenever God calls us we have to respond decisively in such a way that all our being, actions and possessions are invested in devotion to Him. At Abraham's initial call, God only demanded Abraham's leaving, without indicating his destination. It was like travelling blindfolded, depending only on the voice of the One who commanded the movement. It only takes a wholly dedicated man to obey God to that extent.

Let us look at the background and the person of this man, Abraham. Joshua told the Israelites towards the end of his life and ministry:

"Joshua said to all the people, "Thus says the LORD, the God of Israel, 'Your fathers lived of old time beyond the River, even Terah, the father of Abraham, and the father of Nahor: and they served other gods.'" (Joshua 24:2 NHEB.) Abraham's fathers worshipped idols, yet God picked him. God's call might not match the background of some people; the background does not matter to God. When it comes to God's call, He looks at the heart of the called. There were things God saw in Abraham. Nehemiah, talking to God concerning Abraham, said: *"and found his heart faithful before you, and made a covenant with him to give the land of the Canaanite, the Hittite, the Amorite, and the Perizzite, and the Jebusite, and the Girgashite, to give it to his descendants, and have performed your words; for you are righteous."* (Nehemiah 9:8 NHEB.) God looks at a man's heart and sees what others do not see. God is like an expert craftsman: while everyone sees a forest of woods, an expert craftsman sees good furniture coming out of the woods.

Saul of Tarsus had a disreputable past and may not have looked like a perfect instrument for evangelism. Yet, God saw him as one even while he was still persecuting the church (Acts 9:10–15).

One important lesson we can learn about Abraham's call and his response to the call was that there were not many details about his destination, yet he responded in trust and obedience. Hebrews 11:8 says: *"By faith, Abraham, when he was called, obeyed to go out to a place which he was to receive for an inheritance. He went out, not knowing where he was going."* (NHEB.) Abraham was told what he must leave behind in detail, but what lay ahead was devoid of details. God would sometimes lead us without giving us much information before we set out on our journey of obedience. Yet, we know we are heading towards fulfilling His will and purpose. Let us be like Abraham; we should not wait until all assurances and proofs are obtained before obeying God's instructions. For, without faith, it is impossible to obey God.

Abraham's covenanted descendants, the nation of Israel, did not become a great nation until hundreds of years later. The blessing of

Abraham becoming a great nation was not physically manifested in his days. The universal blessing God promised him as well – the blessing of the salvation of the entire world through his Seed – actually came into effect after the birth, death and resurrection of Jesus. Those who are beneficiaries of this blessing of salvation, who have accepted Christ as their Lord and Saviour, have become Abraham's spiritual descendants. *"Know therefore that those who are of faith, the same are children of Abraham."* (Galatians 3:7 NHEB.) When we accept Jesus as Lord, we become Abraham's spiritual children.

Abraham's call was to prepare the human lineage of the Saviour of the world. Stephen started his defence before the Sanhedrin by referring to Abraham's call as the beginning of God's salvation plan.

God, at sundry times, has called men, primarily to have a relationship and secondarily for a particular assignment in His kingdom or what is popularly known as a call to service. The call that is crucial today is the call to salvation; He is calling all to accept Christ as their Lord and personal Saviour.

God called Abraham, and He is calling us today to leave our former ways of life and take a walk with Him to a promised home in heaven that is flowing with joy and eternal life. This walk begins with becoming born again, living in obedience to His word, and serving God. This call to walk with God will not be a leisure stroll but will require self-denial and sacrifice. If we respond in obedience and trust, we will undoubtedly end up in our heavenly 'Canaan land'. Abraham's attitude to God's call was that of obedience in trust.

Amid these times of a plethora of voices, calling for our commitment to various causes, we should pray that God teaches us to listen. Let us hear Him speak in our hearts, let us get used to the sound of His voice and realise that its tone may be resounding above the sounds of the world and be the only voice we will respond to in obedience.

TOPIC 2: THE BLESSING OF ABRAHAM

GENESIS 12:2–3

"that the blessing of Abraham might come on the Gentiles through Christ Jesus; that we might receive the promise of the Spirit through faith." (Galatians 3:14 NHEB.)

Many Christians often see the blessing of Abraham as tangible things such as financial prosperity or material possessions, but to solely attribute Abraham's blessing to mere physical gains in this world would be to trivialise it. Although the blessing contains physical connotations, the crux of the Abrahamic blessing is spiritual.

When Abraham was called out of his land of nativity, God made several promises to him. God called Abraham to a strange land and made him a promise at Shechem to give the land to his descendants. *"In that day the LORD made a covenant with Abram, saying, "To your descendants I have given this land, from the river of Egypt to the great river, the river Perath: ¹⁹the Kenites, the Kenizzites, the Kadmonites""* (Genesis 15:18–19 NHEB). This was a promise fulfilled without fail: *"So the LORD gave to Israel all the land which he swore to give to their fathers. They possessed it, and lived in it."* (Joshua 21:43 NHEB.)

God assured Abraham that He would bless him; bless those who bless him, and they that curse him will be cursed. He would also make his name great and make him into a great nation. From Abraham came the 12 tribes of Israel, which became the great Hebrew nation. This nation helped in preserving the knowledge of God through several centuries. God was assuring Abraham of His presence throughout their walk together. He was going to make him great and protect him from those who desired to harm him. God would favour those who were his friends, while those who plotted against him will have God to contend with.

God said to him further, *"and in you all the families of the earth will be blessed"* (Genesis 12:3 NHEB). God was not only concerned about Abraham but the rest of the world. The promised Seed, the Messiah, by whom the whole world would receive the blessing of salvation, was to come through Abraham. God further emphasised this to him after his obedience regarding the sacrifice of his son, Isaac. *"And in your offspring all the nations of the earth will be blessed, because you have obeyed my voice."* (Genesis 22:18 NHEB.) By this, God announced the gospel in advance to him. The redemption message did not begin with the ministry of Jesus; it goes back into the Old Testament. The call of Abraham was a piece of God's ultimate plan of redeeming the world. Galatians 3:8 and 16 says, *"[8]The Scripture, foreseeing that God would justify the Gentiles by faith, preached the Good News beforehand to Abraham, saying, "In you all the nations will be blessed." [16]Now the promises were spoken to Abraham and to his offspring. He does not say, "And to offsprings," as of many, but as of one, "And to your offspring," which is Christ."* (NHEB.)

Jesus is the answer to the greatest need of the world – salvation. He is the greatest blessing given by God to mankind. *"For God so loved the world that he gave his only Son, so that whoever believes in him will not perish, but have everlasting life."* (John 3:16 NHEB.)

In Christ Jesus, God's greatest desire for humanity – the salvation from the dominion and consequences of sin – is fulfilled. This blessing of salvation is available to all humanity; it is what makes us Abraham's descendants.

The true descendants of Abraham are not physical but spiritual. They are born of the Spirit, justified by their faith in God as their father, Abraham. They are those who have acknowledged the Lordship of Christ over their lives. They have made a resolute decision to follow God wherever He leads them, as did their father, Abraham. These are the ones who will receive the blessing of eternal salvation. They will live beyond this life, reigning with Christ eternally in His kingdom.

In Chapter 8 of the gospel of John, while Jesus was rebuking the Pharisees, they said to Him, *"We are Abraham's descendants, and have never been in bondage to anyone. How can you say, 'You will be made free?'"* (John 8:33 NHEB.) Dialoguing with them further, Jesus made a remarkable statement: *"If you were Abraham's children, you would do the works of Abraham."* (John 8:39 NHEB.) By this statement to the Pharisees, Christ made the clear distinction between Abraham's physical and spiritual children. The spiritual children are those who live a life of obedience to God as Abraham did. Apostle Paul sheds more light on this in Romans 2:28–29: *"For he is not a Jew who is one outwardly, neither is that circumcision which is outward in the flesh; ²⁹ but he is a Jew who is one inwardly, and circumcision is that of the heart, by the Spirit, not in the letter; whose praise is not from people, but from God."* (NHEB.)

The blessing of Abraham is available to us through Christ. God desires to walk with each of us in our time just as He walked with our father Abraham, provided we are willing to hearken to His voice and surrender our will to Him.

God's faithfulness in fulfilling His promises made to Abraham should be a lesson to us that His promises never fail, no matter how long they may take. God is reliable, and we can rest assured of the infallibility of His word, knowing full well that none of His promises goes unfulfilled.

TOPIC 3: TRUST IN GOD'S PROTECTION

GENESIS 12:10–20

Often, people act based on human wisdom – what they perceive to be right or wrong. Hence, when trapped by an overwhelming odd, when there seems to be no way out, they resort to a quick fix that goes against the word of God. The result often makes the situation more complex or leads to other problems.

Abraham's approach in the face of a potential danger contrasts with the expected reaction from someone who had a close relationship with God. He had decided to migrate to Egypt due to famine in his current settlement. Abraham's fear for his safety due to his wife's beauty propelled him to act in a manner that suggests that he depended on his strategies for protection instead of relying on God.

Abraham's survival strategy was to lie to Pharaoh that Sarah was his sister, not his wife, as clearly stated in Genesis 12:10–13: *"There was a famine in the land. Abram went down into Egypt to live as a foreigner there, for the famine was severe in the land. [11]It happened, when he had come near to enter Egypt, that he said to Sarai his wife, "See now, I know that you are a beautiful woman to look at. [12]It will happen, when the Egyptians will see you, that they will say, 'This is his wife.' They will kill me, but they will save you alive. [13]Please say that you are my sister, that it may be well with me for your sake, and that my soul may live because of you.""* (NHEB.) Abraham's intention was to preserve his life and secure the Egyptians' favour. Sarah was indeed his half-sister, and saying so was not a lie, but conspiring to hide the information that they were married and leading Pharaoh to believe that there was no intimate relationship between them made it a lie. Later on, Pharaoh's reaction to Abraham showed his ignorance of the fact that Sarah was Abraham's wife and his displeasure that he did not tell him the truth. *"Why did you say, 'She is my sister,' so that I took her to be my wife? Now therefore, look, your wife is before you. Take, and go."* (Genesis 12:19 NHEB.)

God, who saved Abraham's wife from Pharaoh, was more than capable of protecting Abraham and providing for him if Abraham had told the Egyptians the truth. Abraham should have chosen to honour God by telling the truth and trusting God to protect him and his family from the Egyptians rather than devising his safety method. This buttresses the fact that the arm of flesh, the wisdom of man, will fail us; it is only our trust in God that will guarantee our future and protection. It is better to trust in the Lord than to put our confidence in our abilities: *"Trust in the LORD with all your heart, and do not lean on your own understanding. ⁶In all your ways acknowledge him, and he will make your paths straight."* (Proverbs 3:5–6 NHEB.)

Some may say "Heaven helps those who help themselves." They may point to an action, such as the one portrayed by Abraham in this chapter, as a reference. By doing that, they suggest that God gives some allowance for certain sinful acts that seem harmless and are useful in preserving them from danger. They may use the fact that God did not reproof Abraham for what he did to support this flawed belief. The truth is that God's expectation for His children has changed with eras. For us today, a higher expectation is placed on us because of the greater revelation of the word of God which we have received.

Let us consider the growth process of God's salvation plan for humanity.

- The days when God called Abraham, through whose lineage the Saviour will be born, could be likened to the birth of Christianity. And Christianity could be said to be a baby at that time. Babies can urinate or poop where they should not but will be tolerated. Likewise, men of old could marry their close relatives, marry many wives and have concubines without risking their relationship with God.
- As children grow, the parent guides them with rules, such as when to sleep, rise from bed, brush their teeth, wash dirty dishes. Likewise, when the nation of Israel was to be formed God gave them laws forbidding them from marrying close relatives. These included all the moral and ceremonial laws.
- When children become adults, the parents no longer insist on these rules because they were meant as a guide on the right way to live. By this time, responsible children will know how to act because they understand the purpose of the rules. Likewise, as New Testament believers, we are not under the law, but it is

expected that due to the knowledge of God we now have, we should know how to act in the right manner. If we fail to do so, we will face the consequences of our actions.

In this New Testament era the death of Christ is the focal point of all of God's dealings with man since the fall of Adam. Therefore, we now have the knowledge the people of the Old Testament era did not have, and because we have this knowledge we have no excuse to act ignorantly. *"The times of ignorance therefore God overlooked. But now he commands that all people everywhere should repent, 31because he has appointed a day in which he will judge the world in righteousness by the man whom he has ordained; of which he has given assurance to everyone by raising him from the dead."* (Acts 17:30–31 NHEB.)

From the above analogy we can see that God might have overlooked Abraham's action because 'Christianity' was still at an infant stage. Abraham's act did not make him any less a friend of God, but judging from the era in which we live and the knowledge of God which we now have, no one who acts in the same manner will be held blameless.

God expects us to rely confidently on him and not trust our understanding. Like Abraham, we may be faced with situations whereby it may seem like the only way out is to go against the word of God. A student who fears God may be faced with the option of cheating in an examination or bribing a teacher to avoid failing. A person who fears God may be caught between telling the truth about what he had done and facing the embarrassment of being exposed or lying to save himself from the embarrassment. These crossroads constitute the challenges we often encounter to affirm our allegiance to God or deny His Lordship over us.

Sometimes, our actions emanate from fear of uncertainty. We hatch out designs in our homes, offices, businesses, even in church to ensure our survival and protection, leaving God out from the formula or in our calculation. We enter into a circle of deceit or lies to preserve our name or identity. At certain times we harm other people to protect ourselves, create a chain of sin and multiply our insecurity. In some cases, these methods may offer the momentary relief we seek, but that relief, compared with the risk of losing our souls eternally in hell, is like an attempt to put out a fire from a burning house with a glass of water. The option of disobeying God might seem reasonable or logical to us but not to God.

God wants us to rely on Him completely without going against His commands for any reason, even to save our own lives. Our trust should be like that of the three Hebrew young men who said: *"If it be so, our God whom we serve is able to deliver us from the burning fiery furnace; and he will deliver us out of your hand, O king. [18]But if not, be it known to you, O king, that we will not serve your gods, nor worship the golden image which you have set up."* (Daniel 3:17–18 NHEB.) Shadrach, Meshach and Abednego believed that God could rescue them from the furnace but were also determined not to sin against God even if God chose for them to die in the furnace.

Sometimes God permits us to encounter some seemingly unfavourable situations on the path of absolute obedience. Sometimes the devil causes them to happen as he tries to cause us to turn away from God; at other times we put ourselves in those dicey situations by our carelessness. Regardless of our circumstances, if our trust in God remains unconditional, unyielding and unending, God will turn it for our good in the end.

TOPIC 4: BEAUTY: INAPPROPRIATE FACTOR IN SPOUSAL CHOICE

GENESIS 12:10–20

Given the universal expectations and practices in our society today, the emphasis and pursuit of beauty as an indispensable factor in the choice of a spouse could be as misplaced as it is misleading.

As the old saying goes, beauty lies in the eyes of the beholder. To regard something as beautiful, it must meet our definition and standard of beauty. In other words, what appeals to one person may not appeal to another.

It is without a doubt that a beautiful being is an attractive being. God has wired us with physical senses to perceive and appreciate beauty. However, for all its appeal, beauty is not the singular or principal piece that makes a person attractive. While it is not wrong to wed a beautiful spouse, misguidedly basing our choice principally on beauty could expose us to enduring some untoward marital experience.

For all it is worth, having a beautiful spouse also comes with the attendant attraction and attention of other people to such a spouse, which, if not managed prudently, could lead to jealousy, distrust and insecurity. Sarah was a paragon of beauty and of resplendent charm. Even at an advanced age, anyone who saw her found her irresistible. Because of this, Abraham, who feared for his life, decided to change Sarah's status from wife to sibling when emigrating to Egypt. Although Abraham's choice to marry Sarah may not have been predicated solely on her beauty, we can still draw lessons from his experience because of Sarah's beauty.

It is often a common question and a delicate decision for Christian bachelors and spinsters regarding physical appearance in spousal choice. Sometimes, Christian bachelors could desire godly wives but make physical beauty an additional criterion for choosing a spouse. While it is not out of place to seek beauty, it would be a spousal blunder for Christians to reject a God-fearing person because they did not meet their beauty criteria. A physically attractive person is like a beautiful house viewed from the outside without seeing the inside. While the outside may be appealing, the house's foundation may be unsteady; the interior may be poorly furnished, awkwardly constructed or distastefully decorated. The same goes for a beautiful person who could have unpleasant attitudes and ungodliness oozing from them. Proverbs 31:30 cautions: *"Charm is deceitful, and beauty is vain;*

but a woman who fears the LORD, she shall be praised." (NHEB.) Failing to consider the contents of their character and relationship with God, among other things, is nothing other than preparing a recipe for marital chaos. Considering a spouse only superficially could impair our judgement.

It must also be understood that beauty is ephemeral and mutable. For people who base their choice of a spouse on physical appearance, their reaction to any downgrade in appearance will inevitably result in a monumental disappointment. Beyond the element of beauty, Christians should endeavour to look out for godly attributes in their choice of spouse.

It is said that iron sharpens iron. Therefore, it is easier for two people who fear God to build a godly home together and help each other in the heavenly race than for a person who fears God to pair with someone who will live in constant opposition to the believer's norms and values. While it is natural to be desirous of physical beauty it should never determine our spousal choice. Instead, we should look out for the true beauty in an individual who fears the Lord.

CHAPTER 13

TOPIC 1: PROVISION FOR OTHERS' GROWTH

GENESIS 13:5

A successful life is measured not only by a person's personal achievements but, most importantly, by the impact on other people's lives, out of love. One of the secrets to growth is helping others grow.

One of life's purposes is to be useful to others by being a helping hand to them when necessary: *"But do not forget to be doing good and sharing, for with such sacrifices God is well pleased."* (Hebrews 13:16 NHEB.) A helping hand that reaches down to lift others and assist them in growing in any aspect of their lives as an act of kindness is pleasing to God.

Looking back at Abraham and Lot, Lot's father, Haran, died in Ur of the Chaldeans, and from that moment, Abraham took Lot and cared for him. The call of Abraham necessitated his departure from his country, family and father's house. He did not depart with his wife alone but also with Lot, his nephew. While Lot was with Abraham, Abraham did not truncate his ambition through maltreatments but helped him grow into a successful man – he became a prosperous shepherd. With time, it is recorded that Lot had so much wealth that the land could not support both he and Abraham dwelling together, for their possessions were so great.

The prosperity of Lot clearly shows that Abraham made provision and allowance for his personal growth. He did not confine Lot to a position where he would always depend on him for his daily needs but allowed him to grow while still living with him until the land could not sustain both of them living together anymore. Consequently, there was strife between the herdsmen of Abraham and Lot. Genesis 13:6–7 says: *"The land was not able to bear them, that they might live together: for their substance was great, so that they could not live together. ⁷There was a strife between the herdsmen of Abram's livestock and the herdsmen of Lot's livestock: and the Canaanite and the Perizzite lived in the land at that time."* (NHEB.) It will not be untrue to say that Lot's successful livestock business is traceable to Abraham's support, provision and encouragement. Yet, Lot's steady business growth did not threaten Abraham.

Abraham did not only help Lot expand his business but also influenced him to develop spiritually. In 2 Peter 2:6–8, Lot is acknowledged as the righteous man whose righteous soul was tormented by the ungodly acts of the people of Sodom and Gomorrah where he lived. *"and turning the cities of Sodom and Gomorrah into ashes, condemned them to destruction, having made them an example of what is going to happen to the ungodly; ⁷and delivered righteous Lot, who was very distressed by the lustful life of the wicked ⁸(for that righteous man dwelling among them, was tormented in his righteous soul from day to day with seeing and hearing lawless deeds)"* (NHEB). One of the best ways in which to influence others to grow should be their spiritual lives.

Abraham's relationship with Lot is worthy of emulation by all and sundry. As Christians the welfare of our relatives and that of anyone under us should be our concern. We should be concerned about the wellbeing of servants or employees working or living with us by thinking about their future and making provision for what will sustain them after they have completed their services. We should never underestimate the positive difference we can make to the lives of those around us by a simple act of kindness. Colossians 4:1 says, *"Masters, give to your servants that which is just and equal, knowing that you also have a Master in heaven."* (NHEB.)

We are to treat people in our care as we want God to treat us. In our dealings with them we should not forget that we are accountable to God. Oppressing them simply because they seem helpless at that time is against God's command. Our wards should be included in our plans as we make plans for our children's education and skill acquisition programmes. We are not to leave them worse off than we met them. We are to treat matters regarding them and their physical welfare as we would our biological children and love them with the love of Christ. In planning for our children's future we are to plan for theirs as well. We are to create an atmosphere that would help them grow and prosper. We are to treat them with fairness and equity, for God will hold us accountable for how we treat them.

Abraham serves as an example for us today. In our various capacities we should make provision for our wards to be independent and self-sufficient, helping them develop to a level that they can help others and cater for their personal needs and the needs of their dependents.

Living to make other people's lives better is a way to make one's life count. Jesus, our Lord, gave us the golden rule in dealing with others: *"Therefore whatever you desire for people to do to you, do also to them; for this is the Law and the Prophets."* (Matthew 7:12 NHEB.) Christ taught us love. Therefore, it is a paradox of Christian living when we pursue self-growth while turning a blind eye to the growth of others under us. Our resources are given by God and should be used for His glory, for we are only stewards of the resources in our possession.

TOPIC 2: FAMILY STRIFE

GENESIS 13:5–9

As a result of the fallibility of human nature, strife has become a recurring reality over time. Be it among family members, friends, neighbours or colleagues, the imperfectness of human nature comes with the tendency that someone is going to say or do something that will offend us or the other way round.

Strife could be engendered through circumstances such as personal differences, misunderstandings and so on. In the passage under consideration, family strife almost ensued between Abraham and Lot because of a misunderstanding between their servants.

As Abraham's and Lot's livestock increased in number their settlement could not accommodate them and their co-existence was threatened due to their herdsmen's strife. Understanding the ills of family strife, Abraham called Lot to resolve the conflict amicably. He said to him, *"Please, let there be no strife between me and you, and between my herdsmen and your herdsmen; for we are relatives. ⁹Isn't the whole land before you? Please separate yourself from me. If you go to the left hand, then I will go to the right. Or if you go to the right hand, then I will go to the left."* (Genesis 13:8–9 NHEB.)

Strife among family members is common, and since there are no perfect human beings there are no perfect families. There are bound to be conflicts within even the best of families; the issue is how we handle them when they arise. How Abraham handled this situation is worthy of admiration and emulation. Abraham's act reflects the summary of the entire teachings of Jesus Christ on how we should relate to one another, which is love characterised by meekness and selflessness.

It is easier to humble yourself before someone older than you; it is far easier to be meek when you are not right. There were many good and justifiable reasons for Abraham to claim right of choice for himself. For one thing, Abraham was older than Lot. Abraham could have also reminded Lot that it was not Lot who took him from Ur but he who took Lot. By rights, Abraham could have chosen his portion and appointed Lot his, but Abraham gave up his rights and was willing to abide by Lot's decision and take what was left. This is humility and selflessness on display.

Abraham esteemed his relationships with God and Lot to be of a far greater value than his personal interest. He was willing to forgo his rights and desires in pure and parental affection for his nephew rather than act in any way that could have caused strife. He would rather have peace than have material possession and family strife.

Strife is one of the most potent weapons in the enemy's hands for disunity. It has permanently separated families – separated fathers from children, wives from husbands, brothers from sisters and so on. Sometimes misunderstandings arise between siblings and their children inherit these misunderstandings. Some cousins are life enemies because of unsettled grievances between their parents. This would have been avoided if only their parents had been selfless enough to put their interests aside and considered love and unity to be of greater value.

Strife fosters bitterness which defiles a man from within. It is characterised by backbiting, malice, quarrelling, bickering, disharmony and so on. Proverbs 6:16–19 lists seven things that God detests; a heart that devises wicked plans and that sows discord (stirs up strife) between brothers are fourth and seventh on the list. *"There are six things which the LORD hates; yes, seven which are an abomination to him: [17]haughty eyes, a lying tongue, hands that shed innocent blood; [18]a heart that devises wicked schemes, feet that are swift in running to mischief, [19]a false witness who utters lies, and he who sows discord among brothers."* (NHEB.) No man given to strife can please God or enter His kingdom. We are to avoid discord at all costs.

Selfishness often leads to strife. People quarrel and fight because of their desires, and there are all manner of evil works wherever strife exists. *"For where jealousy and selfish ambition are, there is confusion and every evil deed."* (James 3:16 NHEB.)

Strife between family members, friends, or the congregation of believers must be resolved without delay to avoid escalation or protraction in the form of a grudge. Unresolved strife will always escalate with adverse effects on relationships. The aim of resolving strife is to restore unity and love.

The devil is happy when conflict and bitterness exist within the family or the church, and he is delighted when nothing is done to resolve it. He fuels the conflict and ensures that relationships grow sour and degenerate into permanent division and hatred for one another. But, when there is resolution, the devil's stay is threatened because he is uncomfortable with peace, unity and love. *"26"Be angry, but do not sin." Do not let the sun go down on your anger, 27 neither give place to the devil. 31 Let all bitterness, wrath, anger, outcry, and slander, be put away from you, with all malice. 32 And be kind to one another, tenderhearted, forgiving each other, just as God also in Christ forgave you."* (Ephesians 4:26–27, 31–32 NHEB.)

We are to love and live in peace with one another. We are to be patient, kind and tenderhearted towards each other, considering others before ourselves, bearing each other's burden, being ready to forgive when offended and being eager to seek reconciliation. In the process of reconciliation or resolution, if the need arises we ought to be willing to humbly accept loss or hurt in the spirit of love, without any form of grudge or bitterness against the other party. We must value others above ourselves, not pursuing our interests but instead the interest of others, just as Abraham did towards Lot. Philippians 2:3–4 says, *"doing nothing through rivalry or through conceit, but in humility, each counting others better than himself; 4 each of you not just looking to his own things, but each of you also to the things of others."* (NHEB.)

Although we live in a fallen world, where the tendency for conflict is inescapable, either among family members, friends or at our offices, God still demands that we live peacefully with everyone. *"If it is possible, as much as it is up to you, be at peace with all people."* (Romans 12:18 NHEB.)

TOPIC 3: CHOICES BY SIGHT

GENESIS 13:5–12

There is a common saying that "All that glitters is not gold." It implies that the attractive external appearance of something is not a reliable indication of its true nature. Sometimes, things may appear perfect at first glance but a closer look might provide us with contrary information. The reliance on physical evidence and material attractions, for example, as the principal motivation for our choices could be just as flawed as it is misleading. The consequences and effects that serve as the aftermath of choices made solely on physical senses buttress the indispensability of divine direction in our decision making. We can learn a lot from men and women in the Bible by watching their choices and the corresponding consequences; a classic example is Lot.

The proposal Abraham made to Lot was selfless and Lot took advantage of this and did not have the courtesy, reverence or honour to let his uncle choose first. On hearing Abraham's proposal Lot raised his eyes, gazed around and chose for himself what seemed to be the better option. Lot's choice of the fertile and well-watered lands was one predicated solely on physical perception. What seemed like a brilliant choice for him became a snare for him and his entire household. Not only would he require the help of Abraham in saving him from the hands of the four kings who waged war against Sodom and Gomorrah (Genesis chapter 14), but the angel of the Lord would have to rescue him from the judgement of God upon those cities as a result of sin. He also lost his wife in the process (Genesis 19:1-26). What seemed to be a promise of fertility ultimately culminated in futility.

Without a shred of doubt, anything beautiful, lucrative, attractive and prestigious often appeals to human senses. While not all attractive things are sinful, it must be understood that everything that glitters is not gold. Hence, exercising caution and seeking divine direction is paramount.

Notably, some people's decisions about where to work are sometimes based on a job's lucrativeness. Some parents go to the extreme of dictatorially choosing professions for their children from a tender age due to the attendant prestige and profitability, while for others, relocating to another country is based on physical and financial appeal. For some, the choice of spouse is principally based on the person's attractiveness. In making these choices most people never consider how their lives – especially their spiritual standing – will be affected by their choices. Worse, like Lot, they never attempt to consult God for direction. Proverbs 3:5–6 says, *"Trust in the LORD with all your heart, and do not lean on your own understanding. ⁶In all your ways acknowledge him, and he will make your paths straight."* (NHEB.)

Lot's choice of settlement based on sight led to the misfortune he later encountered. Lot saw the attractiveness of his desired dwelling place but could not see the full consequences of his choice. While it is not wrong to go for the best choices available, we should also consider that they might not always be God's will for our lives.

Many believers run into errors because they do not seek God's guidance in their decisions. Some make up their minds on what they intend to do and only inform God about it; they have no intention of following His leading. A believer who is content to seek God's guidance in his actions will never make the wrong turn, for God who sees the end from the beginning will guide him step by step into His perfect will. We do not necessarily have to experience the grave consequences of wrong decisions to fully grasp the need to depend on God's leading in our endeavours.

The hallmark of a true Christian is walking by faith and not by sight. Unlike Lot, whose decision was sight based, believers must not allow their decisions to be influenced solely by their physical senses – making decisions because it looks, feels or seems good according to human reasoning. Our actions must also not be governed by the world's dictates, attractions, wisdom or standards. Rather, our choices must be ruled by the wisdom of God found in His word. We must also be sensitive to the inner promptings and convictions of the Holy Spirit within us, always bearing in mind that *"as many as are led by the Spirit of God, these are children of God."* (Romans 8:14 NHEB.)

TOPIC 4: REAFFIRMATION OF GOD'S PROMISE

GENESIS 13:14–18

Teachers often use the tool of repetition to make a lesson sink into the minds and subconsciousness of their students. They either repeat what they earlier said or ask their students to repeat what they learnt. When lessons or instructions are adequately repeated, grey areas are cleared in the hearers' minds, and skills that previously seemed difficult become part of the person. As a Father and Instructor, God often uses this tool when giving His children instructions or promises. God does not need repetition but knows His hearers are prone to forget or get discouraged along the way. For the sake of His children, God sometimes reaffirms His promises. God's reaffirmation does not mean that the promises suddenly become more authentic; it means that God gives us reasons to continue with a stronger faith.

In Genesis 12:2–3 God had promised Abraham: *"I will make of you a great nation. And I will bless you and make your name great. And you will be a blessing. ³And I will bless those who bless you, and I will curse him who curses you, and in you all the families of the earth will be blessed."* (NHEB.)

In the verses in context, Genesis 13:14–18, we see a reaffirmation of what God had earlier said, but this time the word of God comes with more specific details. In consonance with the initial promise, the reaffirmation was like God telling Abraham, "This is the place I told you about. Lift your eyes, stretch your vision; anywhere you can see from here, I will give it to you. Get up, walk through the land; it is all yours." Now, this is more reassuring and more tangible than the initial promise. God did not change and the promise did not change, but, yes, Abraham's resolve to continue trusting God would have been stronger.

It is not every time that God reaffirms His promise in the way He did to Abraham. As such, we should learn to trust God's faithfulness in keeping His promises, no matter how long it might take. We should always look to His word – the Bible – to affirm all His promises. *"For whatever things were written before were written for our instruction, that through patience and through encouragement of the Scriptures we might have hope."* (Romans 15:4 NHEB.)

God is a promise-keeping God and will fulfil His promise whether He shows up in a vision or not. Our hope and the source of our joy is in the faithfulness of God. We may be weak or discouraged and the excitement of the promise may fade because of circumstances, but God in His love will never fail us.

God's reaffirmation to Abraham was quite timely. Lot, his nephew, who had lived with him after his father's death, had just left him because the land could not bear their flocks together. Abraham gave Lot first choice over where to take his flocks and Lot chose the well-watered plains of Jordan near Sodom and Gomorrah, leaving Abraham with a less-favourable choice. Abraham's selflessness seemed to have caught God's attention, leading to a visitation from Him. God's fresh visitation did more than reaffirm an earlier promise made; it came as a comfort. In our walk with God, He occasionally shows up as a spring of refreshment to refresh and reaffirm His commitment to His promise.

In John 14:1–4, Jesus made a comforting promise, *"Do not let your heart be troubled. Believe in God. Believe also in me. ²In my Father's house are many dwelling places. If it weren't so, I would have told you; for I go to prepare a place for you. ³And if I go and prepare a place for you, I will come again, and will receive you to myself; that where I am, you may be there also. ⁴And you know the way where I am going.*" (NHEB.) These words are trustworthy enough on their merits. However, God had to reaffirm the promise of Jesus' return through angels as Jesus was ascending into heaven. *"You men of Galilee, why do you stand looking into the sky? This Jesus, who was received up from you into the sky will come back in the same way as you saw him going into the sky."* (Acts 1:11 NHEB.)

God is reaffirming His word every day through the scriptures. The more of the word of God you study, the more comfort and hope you get. As believers, let us not wait until we have a vision, a trance or other forms of theophany for us to know that God will keep His promise of saving us from this world of sin and giving us an abode in His eternal kingdom. As long as we walk according to His word, we should believe what the scriptures say about our soul's salvation and our eternal dwelling with Him, which are reaffirming enough.

CHAPTER 14

TOPIC 1: TRUE CONCERN

GENESIS 14:8–17

One of the hallmarks of children of God is the heartfelt demonstration of true concern for the plights and wellbeing of others, backed by timely and effective actions.

While Abraham was dwelling by the oaks of Mamre at Hebron he got the news that there was war in the region where Lot – his nephew, resided; the enemies conquered Sodom and Gomorrah and took some captives and possessions, including Lot and his household. On receiving this information Abraham acted swiftly, pursued the enemies for Lot's sake and recovered all the captives and plunders taken from Sodom and Gomorrah.

Abraham's action to save Lot showed his genuine love and concern for his nephew. This incident took place after the two had gone separate ways to avoid disputes caused by strife between their servants over grazing land for their flocks. Abraham first expressed his selflessness when he offered Lot the opportunity to pick where he would like to settle, while he went in the opposite direction. Coming to Lot's rescue here means that he held no grudge against him. This is truly a gesture worthy of emulation.

Many people express love as much as it is convenient for them. The extent to which they can love or express concern for others is the degree to which they are comfortable or safe. If helping others would risk their lives or tamper with their safety, that point would be their limit. But that was not the case with Abraham. Abraham started a campaign against King Chedorlaomer in a bid to rescue his nephew, Lot. Let us remember that this was a battle and could either have a negative or positive outcome. He could have died in the process, but his true concern for his nephew would not allow the possibility of a negative outcome in the battle to influence his decision. This was a selfless act in that he risked his life for his nephew, considering Lot's wellbeing before his. This kind of concern is rooted in a heart that loves God.

Christians are to be truly concerned for one another. We are to be willing to subjugate our desires and interests for the wellbeing of others. *"In love of the brothers be tenderly affectionate one to another; outdo one another in showing honor"* (Romans 12:10 NHEB). This kind of concern is sacrificial; it endures hardship, suffering and pain for the benefit of others and the pleasure of God. This kind of concern takes risks where others are shrinking; it is a kind of concern that reflects the love God has for us. It is sincere and fervent. One with such concern is sincerely bothered about others' welfare and is willing and eager to come to their aid.

God desires that we be one another's keepers and show true concern for those in need. Jesus emphasised the need to show concern for each other when He stated it as the basis of separating the goats from the sheep on the day of judgement. *"Then he will say also to those on the left hand, 'Depart from me, you cursed, into the everlasting fire which is prepared for the devil and his angels; ⁴²for I was hungry, and you did not give me food to eat; I was thirsty, and you gave me no drink; ⁴³I was a stranger, and you did not take me in; naked, and you did not clothe me; sick, and in prison, and you did not visit me.' ⁴⁴"Then they will also answer, saying, 'Lord, when did we see you hungry, or thirsty, or a stranger, or naked, or sick, or in prison, and did not help you?' ⁴⁵"Then he will answer them, saying, 'Truly I tell you, inasmuch as you did not do it to one of the least of these, you did not do it to me.'"* (Matthew 25:41–45 NHEB.)

Showing concern for people is a direct service to Christ and a command by Him. It is an expression of love and may require sacrifice in some cases to assist a person in times of need. In this chapter, Abraham's act of love was for his nephew, but we are to replicate this gesture, not just to those related to us, but to all who come our way – even our enemies. *"For if you love those who love you, what reward do you have? Do not even the tax collectors do the same? ⁴⁷And if you only greet your brothers, what more do you do than others? Do not even the Gentiles do the same? ⁴⁸You therefore are to be perfect, as your heavenly Father is perfect."* (Matthew 5:46–48 NHEB.) God has not called us to an impossible task, for He was first concerned about us and He did not want us to perish, so He sent His Son Jesus Christ to die for us so that we may gain eternal life. Now, He has called us to spread the good news, show love, and be concerned about the physical and spiritual wellbeing of all so that we can, by all means, lead as many as possible to salvation, even our enemies. *"But I tell you, love your enemies, and pray for those who persecute you"* (Matthew 5:44 NHEB).

By Christ's standard, everyone deserves to be loved, irrespective of their race, social status, religion, political affiliation, tribe or language. As Christians, showing true concern from pure hearts for others is a distinguishing characteristic that must always be seen in us wherever we go. We should radiate the love of Christ for all, which is the proof that He truly lives in us: *"Bear one another's burdens, and so you will fulfill the law of Christ."* (Galatians 6:2 NHEB.)

TOPIC 2: GOOD NEIGHBOURLINESS

GENESIS 14:13, 24

What would make a stranger able to mobilise his host community's leaders to a war that had nothing to do with the community? What would make leaders of a community march against four kings to rescue a man they probably had not met or known, just because a stranger who lives among them had asked for their help? Call it relationship or alliance, one thing is sure: how Abraham lived among the Amorites made Mamre and his brothers risk their lives for him.

Abraham, an alien living among the Amorites, had just received reports that his nephew, Lot, was taken captive in a war that King Chedorlaomer waged against Sodom, Gomorrah and other surrounding cities. Abraham quickly mobilised Mamre and his brothers. The Amorites' response was notable, considering that they might not have even known Lot in the first place. Abraham was not a blood relative; neither was he their king. As a stranger in the land, he would only have been able to mobilise these Amorites because of the good neighbourliness between them and the great respect his hosts had for him. The passage makes it clear that Mamre and his brothers were Abraham's allies: *"Mamre, the Amorite, brother of Eshcol, and brother of Aner; and these were allies of Abram."* (Genesis 14:13 NHEB.) Whether it was respect or alliance, this level of relationship would only have been cultivated by Abraham's way of life. The Bible admonishes us on how to live honourably with everyone, even those who do not share our faith: *"Beloved, I urge you as foreigners and temporary residents, to abstain from fleshly lusts, which war against the soul; [12]having good behavior among the nations, so in that of which they speak against you as evildoers, they may by your good works, which they see, glorify God in the day of visitation."* (1 Peter 2:11–12 NHEB.)

A neighbour is a person living next to or close to you. Jesus, using the story of the Samaritan who helped a Jewish robbery victim, in His illustration of who our neighbours are, however, extended the scope of the definition of neighbours to mean everyone we come across. Good neighbourliness means having a friendly disposition towards everyone we come across; it is the expression of love towards others. No one can exist as an island without a need for anyone else. The command *"whatever you desire for people to do to you, do also to them…"*

(Matthew 7:12 NHEB) could be rendered as: "be the good neighbour you would have loved others to be towards you".

A greater part of God's commands is concentrated on our relationship with others and good neighbours would not go against any of those commands. They would not steal, would not bear false witness, would not covet or lead a neighbour into any sin against God. Another hallmark of good neighbourliness is respect. We should respect other people's norms and beliefs without going against the word of God. When we have reasons to disagree with someone we should do that politely, without making the other person feel aggrieved.

Not every blood relation would elicit the kind of support Abraham elicited from his hosts, but Abraham did that as a stranger in the land. Abraham's good neighbourliness was seen in the Hittites' address to him when he wanted to buy a piece of land to bury Sarah – his wife: *"Hear us, my lord. You are a prince of God among us. Bury your dead in the best of our tombs. None of us will withhold from you his tomb to prevent you from burying your dead."* (Genesis 23:6 NHEB.) Careless and thoughtless actions do not achieve this level of relationship; it does not just come about by passively going about one's business in the community without caring about what happens to people in the neighbourhood. It involves feeling others' pains and genuinely attempting to do something about them, and avoiding causing pain to others. It means being the epitome of love manifesting in forgiveness when hurt. Paul admonished us, saying, *"bearing with one another, and forgiving each other, if anyone has a complaint against another; even as the Lord forgave you, so you also do."* (Colossians 3:13 NHEB.) It also involves sharing whatever possession we have with people in need. *"In all things I gave you an example, that so laboring you ought to help the weak, and to remember the words of the Lord Jesus, that he himself said, 'It is more blessed to give than to receive.'"* (Acts 20:35 NHEB.)

Good neighbours are treasures of inestimable value but are hard to come by. The easiest way to harvest good neighbourliness is to sow good neighbourliness. Even among people considered difficult, we can sow little seeds of good neighbourliness and watch them grow as our lives affect the neighbourhood. If we first display the love of Christ towards others we will discover that Christ's life gets replicated in others, and in time, the entire neighbourhood is positively impacted for Christ. These are the hallmarks of good neighbourliness.

Good neighbourliness earned Abraham support from the Amorites when he needed allies in battle. When we express good neighbourliness we should not always expect to be physically rewarded in like manner. On the contrary, we might receive the opposite of the good treatment we mete out. 1 Samuel 25 records David's experience in being paid back evil for the good he did to Nabal. David had been like a shield for Nabal's herdsmen and flocks while they were in the wilderness. When David heard that Nabal was shearing his sheep he sent men to Nabal requesting whatever Nabal could give to him and his men for their upkeep. Instead, he got insults. *"And David's young men came and spoke to Nabal according to all those words, in the name of David. But he became arrogant. ¹⁰Nabal answered David's servants, and said, "Who is David? Who is the son of Jesse? There are many servants who break away from their masters these days. ¹¹Shall I then take my bread, and my wine, and my meat that I have slaughtered for the shearers of my sheep, and give it to men who I do not know where they come from?""* (1 Samuel 25:9–11 NHEB.)

You may feed the poor and be accused of showing off; beneficiaries of your good deeds may even turn against you. In moments like this, remember the teachings of our Lord Jesus: *"You have heard that it was said, 'Love your neighbor, and hate your enemy.' ⁴⁴ But I tell you, love your enemies, and pray for those who persecute you, ⁴⁵that you may be children of your Father who is in heaven. For he makes his sun to rise on the evil and the good, and sends rain on the just and the unjust."* (Matthew 5:43–45 NHEB.)

TOPIC 3: TITHING

GENESIS 14:16–20

Tithing is one of the most contentious subjects in the Christian community. The argument against tithing or the continuity of tithing among believers often conveniently focuses on the act's dispensational practice instead of its general purpose. Giving our materials for the work of God is most importantly an expression of honour and gratitude to the One who possesses all things. Abraham's gesture of tithing sets a precedent that was instituted after the Israelites departed from Egypt.

The first recorded instance in the Bible where tithing was carried out was in Genesis 14:20. *"and blessed be God Most High, who has delivered your enemies into your hand. Abram gave him a tenth of all."* (NHEB.) When God gave Abraham an incredible victory over Chedorlaomer and his cohorts while on a rescue mission for Lot, he was met by Melchizedek, a priest of the Almighty God also described as the King of Salem. While Abraham did not take the spoils of war for himself, having surrendered his claim to nine-tenths of the spoil, he gave a tenth to Melchizedek. He did this in reverence and honour to God, who had given him victory over his adversaries.

The second instance of tithing in the scriptures is in Genesis 28:20–22, where Jacob promised to give God a tenth of his possessions if God protected and provided for him on his journey and brought him back safely to his father's house. *"Jacob vowed a vow, saying, "If God will be with me, and will keep me in this way that I go, and will give me bread to eat, and clothing to put on, ²¹so that I come again to my father's house in peace, and the LORD will be my God, ²²then this stone, which I have set up for a pillar, will be God's house. Of all that you will give me I will surely give the tenth to you.""* (NHEB.) Although God did not expressly command the Patriarchs to pay tithes, the fact that He later institutionalised it as part of the law implies that He was in support of it.

Following the deliverance of the children of Israel from bondage in Egypt, God commanded tithing as part of the law given to them. According to James Strong, the Hebrew word translated as tithe in the Bible is *"mah-as-raw"*, which literally means tenth. A closer look at tithing – and its intricacies – might offer a clearer understanding of whether or not a believer in this dispensation is obligated to keep the commandment of tithing. Leviticus 27:30–33 says, ***"All the tithe of the land, whether of the seed of the land or of the fruit of the trees, is the LORD's. It is holy to the LORD. [31] If a man redeems anything of his tithe, he shall add a fifth part to it. [32] All the tithe of the herds or the flocks, whatever passes under the rod, the tenth shall be holy to the LORD. [33] He shall not search whether it is good or bad, neither shall he change it: and if he changes it at all, then both it and that for which it is changed shall be holy. It shall not be redeemed."*** (NHEB.) The entire produce of the land of the Israelites and their livestock was subject to the tithing commandment. Note that even though money existed at the time, the law specifically demanded that tithes were paid in the produce of their land and livestock; nothing else. A tenth of all the land and livestock produce were to be given to God. It was in honour and reverence to Him for the abundance of His providence. The verses above also reveal that there was a provision for tithes to be redeemed. Redemption here meant that if a person had missed a particular tithe, he was obligated to redeem it by bringing the tithe he had omitted with a fifth (20 per cent) of it in addition.

Attending to whether a Christian is obligated to pay tithe in this dispensation, the answer is no. By the life and death of Christ, He fulfilled the law on our behalf. As such, Christians are no longer under the law. An excellent illustration to drive home this truth is the incident at the church in Antioch. Certain Jewish Christians were compelling the Gentile Christians in Antioch to be circumcised by the law of Moses, as though it was necessary for their salvation. After a sharp debate with them, Paul and Barnabas were appointed to go to Jerusalem to consult the apostles and elders regarding this issue. Following much discussion in the meeting, Peter got up among them and spoke some truthful words. Some of those words are captured in the verses below. *"Now therefore why do you tempt God, that you should put a yoke on the neck of the disciples which neither our fathers nor we were able to bear? ¹¹But we believe that we are saved through the grace of the Lord Jesus, just as they are."* (Acts 15:10–11 NHEB.) The apostles and elders all agreed not to burden the Gentiles with the weight of the law, and they sent back word to them with some instructions. Thus, Christians are no longer under the law of Moses. Note that this is not a licence to live however we please. We are now under the law of Christ, which is love for God and love for one another. We are saved to walk in the liberty Christ earned for us in complete submission to His teachings. We are to acknowledge Christ as Lord and live our lives in a way that reflects His lordship over us.

Matthew 23:23 says, *"Woe to you, scribes and Pharisees, hypocrites. For you tithe mint, dill, and cumin, and have left undone the weightier matters of the Law: justice, mercy, and faith. But you ought to have done these, and not to have left the other undone."* (NHEB.) Many use this verse to support their point that Christians are still bound by the law of Moses to pay tithes to God. Let it be known that Jesus' instruction in this verse was to the Pharisees under Moses' law. Tithing was one of the righteous instructions of the law demanded by God from the Jews, but, although it was good, it did not take the place of mercy and justice. Jesus' rebuke of the Pharisees was that they should not choose lesser matters at the expense of weightier matters of the law. That said, this was not an approval of the continuation of tithing for New Testament believers. By the death of Christ, the law and its practices gave way, and a new covenant was introduced. The New Testament emphasises giving to God willingly, cheerfully and according to our ability (2 Corinthians 9:6, 7). All under the new covenant instituted by the death and resurrection of Christ are not obligated to pay tithes of any form. The payment of tithes was never emphasised in any of the books or epistles of the New Testament. What is captured is the need for willing and sacrificial giving according to one's ability to advance the work of God.

Understand that giving God a tenth of our earnings is not wrong. Also, we should not go about criticising those who, in the name of tithing, willingly and regularly lay down their resources for the upkeep of ministers and advancement of the work of God. God, who takes note of every good deed done towards Him, will reward them. What to do is enlighten them that their giving to God should not be done based on the law, but willingly, bountifully and out of love, for God loves a cheerful giver. The Bible instructs us in 2 Corinthians 9:6–8 thus: *"Remember this: he who sows sparingly will also reap sparingly. He who sows bountifully will also reap bountifully. ⁷Each person should give according as he has determined in his heart; not grudgingly, or under compulsion; for God loves a cheerful giver. ⁸And God is able to make all grace abound to you, that you, always having all sufficiency in everything, may abound to every good work."* (NHEB.) Beyond the intricacies of tithing – whether or not it is emphasised in the New Testament – we must never lose sight of the significance of the practice of tithing, which was an act of giving to God or worship. In the verses in context, Genesis 14:16–20, Abraham willingly demonstrated an act of worship and acknowledged God as the source of everything by tithing. Tithing is about giving, but we are not bound by the laws of tithing; we are obligated to give willingly as Christians. We can certainly not escape the fact that honouring and appreciating God with our resources can never be excessive nor can it be considered obsolete in His sight because such a gesture in itself is pleasing to Him. And how much do we lose – if we lose anything – by giving to God, since we own nothing?

A regular and systematic means by which we can, with our possessions, express our reverence and honour to the One who provides for us is encouraged. If we genuinely believe that all we possess in life – including our very own lives – is given to us by God, and if not for His mercies, we would have nothing, giving to God would not be too difficult. God deserves much more than the tenth of our income. Due to their love for God, whatever a person decides to give, is up to them, but know that nothing sincerely given to God out of love would ever go unnoticed, for God is a rewarder of the sower.

What and how we give to God reflects our level of love for Him. Note that love is not a static feeling; it is usually expressed. We cannot claim to love God if we find it difficult to give to Him. When Abraham was about to offer Isaac – his only son whom he loved – to God, God stopped him and said *"For now I know that you fear God, seeing you have not withheld your son, your only son, from me."* (Genesis 22:12 NHEB.) Note the words "for now, I know", which implies that at that time Abraham's love for God was proven by his willingness to withhold nothing from God, not even his dear son whom he loved.

We must understand that everything we have comes from God and that where the need arises we should be willing to use all we have for the purpose and glory of God. Christians should see themselves as custodians of the wealth God has given to them. Jesus Christ said, *"So therefore whoever of you who does not renounce all that he has, he cannot be my disciple."* (Luke 14:33 NHEB.) Those who have not surrendered their possessions, who are not rich towards God, who are so attached to their belongings and find it difficult to yield them for the advancement of His course cannot be disciples of Christ. As such, we must be willing to surrender whatever is needed of our resources for the progress of God's work.

If we consider it a great deal to part with our belongings for God, not only do we lack understanding, we do not love Him as well. We can look to the church in Macedonia as a worthy example of giving, just as Apostle Paul commended it. It gave sacrificially beyond its ability amid severe trials and poverty. *"Moreover, brothers, we make known to you the grace of God which has been given in the churches of Macedonia; ²how that in much proof of affliction the abundance of their joy and their deep poverty abounded to the riches of their liberality. ³For according to their power, I testify, yes and beyond their power, they gave of their own accord"* (2 Corinthians 8:1–3 NHEB). Believers should have this kind of attitude towards giving to God. Money is essential to the service of the kingdom. The welfare of pastors, administrative needs, building projects, catering for the needy and evangelism all emphasise the need for money in the church.

The responsibility of providing finances for the church rests on the shoulders of believers. As much as God prospers us, we should see it as our obligation to support kingdom projects.

Often, the reluctance of Christians to give to kingdom projects stems from the mismanagement of these monies by some church leaders; nevertheless, the abuse of a thing does not render it useless. Therefore, we should not be discouraged but pray for the Holy Spirit to guide us on how to give. When we give to God, it is honourable before Him, and He will never leave us without reward in due season.

TOPIC 4: CONTENTMENT

GENESIS 14:16–24

We live in a world in which the fire of discontentment is kindled in us almost everywhere we turn – TV commercials, billboard adverts, unsolicited messages on our phones; the list is endless. It is a world in which a happy person is pictured as someone with mansions, several cars and countless trips abroad. The slogan seems to be: "The bigger, the better; the more, the merrier."

In this rat race for material possessions many people are left discontented with what they already have, not because those things have suddenly lost their usefulness but because there are new ones that have been promoted higher on the social ladder. The fire of discontentment swallows up any appreciation the heart would have developed and replaces it with depression. It does not matter whether the very things they are discontented with are what many people are praying to have. Jesus taught us: *"Beware. Keep yourselves from all covetousness, for a man's life does not consist of the abundance of the things which he possesses."* (Luke 12:15 NHEB.)

It is the fear of God and contentment that would make a man turn down bounties of war. We see this virtue of contentment in Abraham when he turned down the King of Sodom's offer of spoils of war, saying that he did not want the King of Sodom to claim responsibility for his wealth. His contentment is displayed by his expressed satisfaction in wealth given by God; this constrained him from indirectly giving God's glory to a man.

Like Abraham, we are expected to be different from the rest of the world in our norms and beliefs. Godly wealth can be found in all the things that come to us through righteous and honest means; other than these, we will be giving God's glory to another or the devil in whatever we possess in this life. As good as they can sometimes be, material gains should not be our focus in any endeavour. God is calling each of us to heights where everything else in the world is less important when placed side by side with the values God expects of us. A contented Christian knows God's sovereignty and rests in it with unwavering trust that God can meet his needs. Peradventure, God in His sovereignty decides not to meet those needs; he still rests in the unwavering trust that God knows what is best for him.

Contentment is being satisfied with who you are and what you have, and having a desire to grow without feeling depressed about your current state. Human desires will always abound, but placing your satisfaction and happiness in their fulfilment will only lead to dissatisfaction and unhappiness. A wise person is satisfied with what they have, and, even while aspiring for more, does not get depressed if more is not attainable.

Solomon, the richest man who ever lived in Bible history, understood the circle of wants and discontentment. He said, *"He who loves silver shall not be satisfied with silver; nor he who loves abundance, with increase: this also is vanity."* (Ecclesiastes 5:10 NHEB.) Explicitly stated, no matter how much you acquire, the desires keep growing. If your definition of happiness is fulfilment of desires, you are treading a path of unachievable happiness and satisfaction.

A contented person might not always get what they want but will always appreciate God for what they have. When this virtue is added to our godliness it becomes of greater value than any wealth the world can offer. 1 Timothy 6:6–10 says: *"But godliness with contentment is great gain. ⁷For we brought nothing into the world, so neither can we carry anything out. ⁸But having food and clothing, we will be content with that. ⁹But those who are determined to be rich fall into a temptation and a snare and many foolish and harmful lusts, such as plunge people into ruin and destruction. ¹⁰For the love of money is a root of all kinds of evil. Some have been led astray from the faith in their greed, and have pierced themselves through with many sorrows."* (NHEB.)

We often bring the name of the Lord into disrepute by our concern for material possessions. Discontentment has trapped many Christians in a corner, where they gain materially but lose their testimonies and salvation. As a Christian, have you trodden the name of God on the ground by letting others take credit for the provisions you enjoy? God could use men to bless us materially, but when we give God's glory to those men, we lose our testimony of God's provision. Satisfaction expressed in God's provision is the right kind of attitude expected from believers.

Contentment is a pearl of great price and whoever procures it, even if it means forgoing 10,000 desires, has made a wise and happy purchase. Aspirations are good, dreams are nice, but we should pursue them in consonance with God's word. God gives us resources based on the responsibilities He has given us; when we stretch our desires beyond our resources, we end up being entrapped by many cares, leading to depression. We are not to struggle to live a Wall Street lifestyle on Main Street income.

Left on its own, the flesh will always be covetous and selfish. The only way we can curtail the cravings of this sinful nature is to constantly walk in the spirit. Galatians 5:16 says, *"But I say, walk by the Spirit, and you will not carry out the desires of the flesh."* (NHEB.)

CHAPTER 15

TOPIC 1: GOD OUR REWARD

GENESIS 15:1

We usually see the need to recompense a good deed, and usually feel the burden of compensating others for actions perceived to be highly beneficial to our interests. If this can be said of us, how much more God who is perfect in love?

In Genesis 15:1, God reaffirms His relationship with His servant Abraham. In this instance, Abraham's encounter with God is preceded by a series of events that transpired in the previous chapter. After Abraham had rescued Lot from Chedorlaomer and his allies and had given Melchizedek a tenth of the spoils, the King of Sodom approached him and demanded for his people whom Abraham had rescued. He permitted Abraham to keep the entire spoils for himself but Abraham replied to him, saying, *"I have lifted up my hand to the LORD, God Most High, possessor of heaven and earth, ²³ that I will not take a thread nor a sandal strap nor anything that is yours, lest you should say, 'I have made Abram rich.'"* (Genesis 14:22–23 NHEB.) Abraham had the right to claim his share from the plunder and to oblige the king's request by accepting the entire spoils as a form of compensation for all he had done. No matter how enticing or sumptuous the spoils might have been, if taking any of the spoils would afterwards give occasion for the king to blaspheme against God by attributing Abraham's riches to the spoils received from him rather than God, Abraham would not have any of it.

This act seemed to have caught God's attention, attracting a visitation from God and the sublime words uttered to Abraham in our verse in context. The reason for the fear in Abraham's heart when God said "Do not be afraid" is not entirely apparent. Whatever the reason, God assured him not to be afraid, for He was both his shield and his great reward. God presented Himself as a shield and a reward to Abraham. God, being his shield, meant that He was going to protect and defend him against any form of adversary. God, being his reward, meant that God was the compensation for any loss Abraham might have encountered in standing for His Name; God was his sufficiency and Abraham could rest assured that he would never lack. *"for he who comes to God must believe that he exists, and that he is a rewarder of those who seek him."* (Hebrews 11:6 NHEB.)

This account of Abraham is laced with an awe-inspiring message for every believer. On our pilgrimage through life, persecution is inevitable due to the demands of absolute consecration and obedience to God in a godless world. We could experience hurts or losses of several forms, and we could suffer the loss of opportunities, relationships, jobs, finances, material possessions and so on. Of all the rewards God could give us for the inconveniences we suffer as a result of our diligence in seeking Him, the greatest is Himself. The man who has God has everything and needs nothing more.

The greatest possession Abraham had through his life was not his wealth or numerous sheep or cattle, it was the presence of God – the presence of God with Abraham was of far more value to Him than anything he possessed. Moses understood this when he prayed to God after the children of Israel had sinned: *"If your presence doesn't go with me, do not carry us up from here. ¹⁶For how would people know that I have found favor in your sight, I and your people? Isn't it in that you go with us, so that we are separated, I and your people, from all the people who are on the surface of the earth?"* (Exodus 33:15–16 NHEB.)

The presence of God with the children of Israel was what made them defeat their enemies and what made them feared among other nations. They only suffered defeat when they lost this manifest presence due to one form of sin or the other. Also, looking at Samson's life, the secret to his tremendous strength was God's presence. Once he lost it, he became an object of ridicule in the hands of his enemies. *"He awoke out of his sleep, and said, "I will go out as at other times, and shake myself free." But he didn't know that the LORD had departed from him. ²¹ The Philistines seized him, and gouged out his eyes. And they brought him down to Gaza, and bound him with bronze shackles, and he ground at the mill in the prison."* (Judges 16:20–21 NHEB.)

The greatest reward we have for seeking the Lord is His presence with us. God desires to walk with us as He did with Abraham. Christianity is not a call to abundant possessions or a life of luxury but an entire lifetime of communion with God. We are called to spend our lives on earth walking with God, learning of Him and standing out in a godless world through obedience to His commands. We are to esteem our relationship with Him and His presence in our lives above any reward of sin. We should be careful not to trade His presence in our lives for physical gains or pleasures.

To gain eternal life and dwell in the heavenly home is more than any compensation we can imagine for overcoming all trials and persecutions. Those who overcome will finally dwell with the eternal King of kings, beholding His glory and praising Him forever. We would experience the fullness of the joy in His presence and commune with Him for eternity. This, in itself, is the greatest reward.

We are to treasure God above all else, making Him the epicentre of all the affections of our hearts. We are to love Him with all our being and esteem Him greater than anything this world has to offer.

TOPIC 2: INTERACTING WITH GOD

GENESIS 15:1–21

A certain picture frame was popular in many homes in the 1980s and on it was written the words: "Jesus is the head of this home, the unseen guest at every meal and the silent listener to every conversation." How revealing those few lines were. However, those lines could be misleading in that they could portray God as a non-interactive person.

God universally communicates with us through His word – the Bible. He does not, however, have two-way communication with everyone. While speaking to God through prayer and knowing His mind through His written word is a good and common Christian practice, being supernaturally engaged with God in an interaction represents a different dimension of communication we should aspire to attain. Interacting supernaturally with God can occur through visions, trances, dreams and hearing from Him audibly. The medium and timing of the communication is determined by Him and does not contradict His word.

Genesis 15 is an interactive session between God and Abraham. Abraham expressed the concerns of his heart, and God took His time to address those concerns. The discussion continued till evening and then night – almost as if they were two humans living in the same house. Some parts of this interaction took place in a vision.

Apart from the Bible, vision is one of the mediums through which God interacts with His children. In visions, a man receives the ability to see the invisible and hear the inaudible and sometimes interact with God or angelic beings in a dimension in which others may not be aware of his experiences. Many of the prophets of old had their divine messages in this format.

In another dimension of supernatural experience, God gives instructions in an audible voice while the hearer listens and sometimes writes instructions down or responds to specific questions. The boy Samuel in 1 Samuel Chapter 3 heard God's voice, listened attentively and relayed what he was told to Eli – less interaction took place in that instance. However, after years of walking with God, the same Samuel had several two-way discussions with God. For instance, in 1 Samuel 16:1–3, we see God telling Samuel to anoint David as king over Israel to replace the spiritually rejected Saul; Samuel expresses his fears, and God addressed those fears – a two-way interaction. *"The LORD said to Samuel, "How long will you mourn for Saul, since I have rejected him from being king over Israel? Fill your horn with oil, and go. I will send you to Jesse the Bethlehemite; for I have provided a king for myself among his sons." ²Samuel said, "How can I go? If Saul hears it, he will kill me." The LORD said, "Take a heifer with you, and say, I have come to sacrifice to the LORD. ³Call Jesse to the sacrifice, and I will show you what you shall do. You shall anoint to me him whom I name to you.""* (NHEB.)

Another example of divine interaction is the 'Moses experience'. God testified about Moses to Miriam and Aaron when they challenged Moses' leadership: *"If there is a prophet among you, I the LORD will make myself known to him in a vision. I will speak with him in a dream. ⁷My servant Moses is not so. He is faithful in all my house. ⁸With him I will speak mouth to mouth, openly, and not in riddles; and he shall see the LORD's form..."* (Numbers 12:6–8 NHEB.) Moses interacted with God on a platform more real than visions and dreams. He interacted with God to the level that he advised God against destroying the Israelites more than once, and God listened. Moses was portrayed in these instances as someone who could intervene in what God was planning to do. What a rare level of interaction.

In Genesis 18, Abraham had an angelic visitation and among the angels was the Lord. The Lord was on His way to Sodom and could not hold back mentioning His mission to Abraham: *"The LORD said, 'Will I hide from Abraham what I do?'"* (Genesis 18:17

NHEB.) In his conversation with God, Abraham attempted to change God's mind about destroying Sodom.

Children of God should aspire to experience active interactions with God. It must be understood that God has already promised us this. Prophet Joel prophesied long ago: *"And it shall come to pass afterward, that I will pour out my Spirit on all flesh; and your sons and your daughters will prophesy, and your old men will dream dreams, and your young men will see visions."* (Joel 2:28 NHEB.) On Pentecost Day, when addressing the crowd, Peter quoted Joel 2:28 to enlighten the people on what was happening. Then he said, *"For to you is the promise, and to your children, and to all who are far off, even as many as the Lord our God will call to himself."* (Acts 2:39 NHEB.) If men like us could interact with God in such ways, we should also aspire to do so.

Man was created in the image and likeness of God primarily for fellowship. God desires communion; He desires to interact and share the deepest secrets of His heart with man, but He will only do this with His friends – those who fear Him and whose hearts are right before Him. *"The friendship of the LORD is with those who fear him. He will show them his covenant."* (Psalm 25:14 NHEB.) If we are to be friends with God, we must agree with Him. We ought to love what He loves and hate what He hates. We must live our lives in complete obedience to His commandments, bearing in mind that without holiness, no man will see the Lord.

Note that the Bible remains the fundamental medium by which God speaks to His children in our times. The legitimacy of messages received through other means of communication, such as dreams, visions and trances, could be ascertained by examining such messages in light of the Bible. However, the Bible is not the only way God communicates with His children. There are times when God might desire to pass specific and timely messages to His children; God can use any other means of communication as He deems fit.

CHAPTER 16

TOPIC 1: MANAGING ELEVATION

GENESIS 16:1–9

Rising above one's current state is everyone's desire, but in rising, we need to be careful of one serious leech: Pride. Let us take a close look at Hagar in our passage. She rises from being just a maidservant to carrying a child for her master. Her mistress, Sarah, initiated this situation. Sarah's childlessness had left Abraham's divine promises to be a father of nations unfulfilled. Sarah surrendered the expectation and the hope that she would participate directly in fulfilling the divine message given to Abraham. After many years of barrenness she thought it wise to offer her maidservant to her husband for procreation. Abraham obliged, Hagar took in and then, like a snap of the finger, everything changed. Her attitude towards Sarah deteriorated, and she despised her mistress. How quickly she forgot that she had been a mere servant!

Sarah's decision to have a child through Hagar was an acceptable practice in her culture, and God did not rebuke her or Abraham for it. Sarah's actions could be seen as courageous and purposeful and born out of desperation. She would not want to be the woman who could not bear a child for her husband and who would not allow another woman to do it. After all, up to the time Sarah gave Hagar to Abraham, God had not mentioned through which woman's womb the child would come. This was Sarah's understanding at that time, and God did not say, "Sarah! What have you done?" This does not mean we should repeat the same act today; we now know better about

God and His ways. *"The times of ignorance therefore God overlooked…"* (Acts 17:30 NHEB.)

Sarah transferred her hope to Hagar; this was why she felt so disappointed when Hagar turned against her, *"It is better to take refuge in the LORD, than to put confidence in man."* (Psalm 118:8 NHEB.) Hagar's response to the pregnancy was to despise Sarah. Hagar, the slave girl from Egypt, assumed a new identity. She was now in a position of power as a mother to Abraham's child. Her pregnancy changed her from an ordinary slave to having a future with promises, purpose and meaning. Hagar's reaction to her elevation was unwise and unthoughtful. She allowed pride to cloud her judgement and treated her mistress with contempt. As Hagar showed contempt and disregard for Sarah, Sarah became upset, and her capacity to respond to Hagar with reasonable and appropriate measures was overwhelmed by indignation, causing her to deal harshly with Hagar. Hagar's poor management of her elevation left her caught up in a cycle of oppression and victimhood. Sarah's maltreatment of Hagar forced her out of the home that until then had ensured her welfare and safety, even as a slave girl. She would have gained even more if she had displayed humility to her mistress, Sarah.

Hagar's attitude while in an elevated state is typical of our societies today and cuts across every sphere of human relations such as schools, families, workplaces and churches. This attitude is characteristic of man in his natural sinful state and may come to some people subconsciously.

To some, an elevated state and pride go hand in hand. That feeling of exaltation propels them to disregard and despise those around them, not minding what role those people may have played in helping them reach the stage they are at. Hagar was quick to forget Sarah's pivotal role in elevating her in the household, but she learnt a vital but tragic lesson: *"Pride goes before destruction, and a haughty spirit before a fall."* (Proverbs 16:18 NHEB.) We should be careful not to allow pride rule us as it did Hagar.

Our elevations and successes in any sphere of life are gifts from God and should be handled with humility and respect for others, either higher or lower than us in status. They should be managed so that every person who comes into contact with us retains their human worth and dignity. Many have used their elevations and successes as a tool to oppress others, while some have used it to create a system that makes it difficult for people to thrive in comfort. Many play 'god' in people's lives and expect to be worshipped, without realising that the earth is the Lord's as is everything in it. He raises and dethrones kings.

Joseph understood that every elevation is from God and should be used according to His will and for others' good, not to downgrade others' dignity and worth or as an occasion for revenge. When Joseph revealed himself to his brothers who sold him to slavery in Genesis 45:7, he said, *"God sent me before you to preserve for you a remnant in the earth, and to save you alive by a great deliverance."* (NHEB.)

We should be mindful of how we manage our elevations and successes. God's good old principle of divine elevation is still in force. God must, in His servants, find humility and dependence. He may have to reject the person altogether if He does not detect these behaviours. James 4:6 says, *"God resists the proud, but gives grace to the humble."* (NHEB.)

TOPIC 2: ABRAHAM, SARAH AND HAGAR: RIGHT PERSPECTIVE

GENESIS 16:1–16

Many people have come to wrong conclusions about cases simply because they failed to view them from more than one perspective. From the perspective of a contemporary Christian, one might look at Sarah as one who could not wait for God's promise of a child to come to fruition. The same perspective would also conclude that Abraham, out of doubt, yielded to his wife's suggestion to bear a child through her maid, thus trying to work out God's purpose through human efforts. On the surface, that may look like a sound judgement concerning the patriarch, especially when it teaches us to trust God irrespective of the situation we go through. However, looking at the scenario from different perspectives presents a different conclusion about the action of Abraham and Sarah in the case of Hagar as a mother.

People who opine that Abraham and Sarah doubted God's word fail to mention which of God's words they specifically doubted. It should be noted that before this incident God did not tell Abraham or Sarah that the promised child would come through Sarah. Faith is trusting God's word even in the face of discomfort. If God had not explicitly said something, and the norms and values of the people gave them the go-ahead, one cannot accuse them of doubt.

Let us look at what God said in Genesis 15:4–6: *"Look, the word of the LORD came to him, saying, "This man will not be your heir [referring to Eliezer of Damascus], but he who will come forth out of your own body will be your heir." *⁵The LORD brought him outside, and said, "Look now toward the sky, and count the stars, if you are able to count them." He said to him, "So shall your descendants be." *⁶And Abram believed God, and it was credited to him as righteousness."* (Parenthesis added. NHEB.) God told Abraham that a child would come from him, which Abraham believed, and this was regarded as righteousness. Up to that point there had been no mention of Sarah as the carrier of the promised child. Thus, Abraham could not be accused of doubt. In those days, having children through maids and concubines was legitimate. However, this was not the method God had in mind. Abraham's action was guided by his norms and values. So, whether one looks at it from the perspective of a direct command from God or cultural values, it would be unfair to pass a verdict of doubt on Abraham and Sarah.

The same practice of giving out maids for childbearing was carried out by Racheal and Leah. Rachael willingly gave her maid Bilhah to Jacob, and she had two sons – Dan and Naphtali – by her. Leah also voluntarily gave her maid Zilpah to Jacob, and she had two sons – Gad and Asher– through her. These instances further buttress the claim that giving a maid to a husband to have children was not considered a sin. Nor was it a deviant act before God during that dispensation. For us today, using Abraham's and Sarah's method is a clear violation of God's instructions: *"Let marriage be held in honor among all, and let the bed be undefiled: for God will judge the sexually immoral and adulterers."* (Hebrews 13:4 NHEB.)

Another perspective that would make many change their verdict is the perspective of age. By the time Ishmael was born Abraham was 86 years old and Sarah 76. This means Sarah would have been 75 when she introduced the idea of having a child through Hagar. Naturally, Sarah, who had passed childbearing age, was not wrong to recommend Hagar to her husband. Abraham could hope to get a child but not Sarah. If God had explicitly mentioned Sarah from the beginning as the specific carrier of the promised child, Abraham would still hold on to God for the fulfilment of His promise, notwithstanding Sarah's age. A man who could believe God and move from his native land without knowing where he was going would believe God even at Sarah's age. We are to trust and obey God in the way that Abraham did in the context of his day.

It is clear from the perspectives discussed above that there is no premise for accusing Abraham and Sarah of doubt and impatience. There was never an instance of Abraham knowing what God had said and presumptuously going against it. As painful as letting Ishmael go was, the moment God told him to take Sarah's advice, he obeyed. These are the things we should emulate from Abraham. We can only benefit from the blessing God promised Abraham if we operate at that same level of obedience to and trust in God.

TOPIC 3: RESPONDING TO CHALLENGES

GENESIS 16:8–9

While the reality of being engulfed in problematic situations is not uncommon it is possible to handle them. The root cause of certain challenges we encounter in life, and our inadequate responses to them, often lies in the sinfulness of our nature. When we can see ourselves in the light of God's word and approach these challenges by His wisdom embedded in His word, we will realise that these challenges are not actually impossible to manage.

Hagar ran away from home, away from the heat of a problem her arrogance had caused. She did not want to take responsibility for the unpleasant circumstances she had created.

Having worked as Sarah's maid, Hagar's elevation to a wife's status to be a child-bearer for Abraham due to Sarah's childless predicament propelled her to exhibit loathsome attitudes towards her mistress. Although Hagar conceived after Abraham slept with her, Sarah's plan to have a son from this union backfired unbearably, for Hagar began to rebel against her mistress. She treated Sarah with contempt, lightly esteeming her due to her barrenness. This made Sarah obnoxious towards Hagar, and she maltreated Hagar until Hagar had to flee from her.

Proverbs 30:21–23 lists four things that the earth trembles under and cannot bear: *"For three things the earth tremble, and under four, it can't bear up: ²²For a servant when he is king; a fool when he is filled with food; ²³for an unloved woman when she is married; and a handmaid who is heir to her mistress."* (NHEB.) The fourth on the list is a maidservant who displaces her mistress. Sarah felt threatened by Hagar which made her unleash all her fury on her. She was determined to make their home unbearable for her so she maltreated and humiliated Hagar; this made her flee to the wilderness.

The angel of the Lord found Hagar near a spring in the wilderness and asked where she was going. She replied truthfully that she was running from her mistress. The angel of God said, *"Return to your mistress, and submit yourself under her hands."* (Genesis 16:9 NHEB.) The angel's reply may not have been what Hagar was expecting but it was the appropriate solution to her predicament. Hagar was the cause of her dilemma; she would not have been in this situation but for her earlier bad decisions; hence, running away was not the answer. The appropriate solution was to make the necessary decisions to correct her mistakes. The angel's verdict was for her to retrace her steps and not to go entirely off course. She was meant to face and manage the problem, not run from it. The solution to her troubles was a simple decision to humble herself.

In handling challenges, it is crucial to avoid denial. Denying the existence of a problem or our role in its materialisation will achieve nothing other than breathing further life into the problem. Acknowledging personal responsibility for self-inflicted situations will enable us to handle the situation. Men are essentially products of their decisions. Several people today are suffering from the bad choices they have made in their lives. They are experiencing a direct consequence of their actions, but rather than face the issues troubling them they either run away or ignore them or shift blame. For instance, losing one's temper with people and attributing provocation to one's nature is nothing but an attempt to avoid confronting the problem. Some may say they have tried to change but failed; such people should be aware that there are some problems that human efforts alone cannot remove and that seeking God's help in prayer and fasting is the right thing to do, in addition to retracing their steps or amending their ways.

Giving one's life to Christ might not necessarily exempt one from the consequences of bad decisions made in the past, if such a person is unwilling to make the required restitution. Some have marred their relationship with those who could have made this life journey easier due to pride and other negative attitudes. In addition to praying, they ought to examine their lives thoroughly to see where they have taken the wrong path and make the right decisions to fix their lives.

God will not do for a man what he is to do for himself; God will only guide and point us in the right direction – as the angel did to Hagar – but we have to retrace our steps. In such cases, we should accept responsibility for the consequences of our actions and do the needful thing to salvage them. Ignoring or running away from the problem does not mean that it will disappear; in fact, it might prolong our suffering.

CHAPTER 17

TOPIC 1: BEING PERFECT

GENESIS 17:1

After the fall of man, God started working out a plan to have a people who would live a life that conforms to His original intention. His desire is to have a people that will be an expression of His personality and glory among the inhabitants of the earth, a people that will walk and live entirely, habitually, wholeheartedly and blamelessly before Him. This desire of God began with Abraham.

God introduced Himself as the "Almighty God" to remind Abraham that the One who called him is Almighty, the All-Powerful and Supreme Ruler of all creation. This was not Abraham's first encounter with God; he had obeyed the call of God earlier in his life to leave his land of nativity; he followed and walked with God for about 24 years before this event. God at this time was calling him to a higher level of consecration with Him, for God was about to establish His covenant with him: *"I will make my covenant between me and you, and will multiply you exceedingly."* (Genesis 17:2 NHEB.)

This is noteworthy for every believer. After the event of salvation, as we grow in Him, God will demand higher and deeper levels of consecration at several intervals in our relationship. God gave Abraham two commandments – *"Walk before me"* and *"be blameless"* (Genesis 17:1 NHEB). The word "walk" literally means moving from one place to another on foot at a moderate pace (dictionary.com), but it is used in several instances figuratively in the scriptures to mean "to live". The command "be blameless" depends solely on "walk before me", for no one can live blamelessly away from God.

Picture two friends taking a walk through the park, having intimate and exciting conversations with each other. They are both enjoying their company so much that they are oblivious of the passing of time. They relish their companionship so much that they do not want the day to end, so they do not depart from each other. This is the kind of feeling one has when walking with God. "Walk before me" is a call to live our lives before His eyes, being conscious of His attention upon us. It is spending our entire lives in unbroken communion with Him to continue in eternity. It is to journey through life with God, having our hearts completely devoted to Him, fixing our attention so strongly on Him that our hearts become detached from the things of this world. It entails being in complete union and harmony with His will, for two people cannot walk together unless they agree.

According to the James Strong Bible Dictionary, the Hebrew word from which the word "perfect" is translated is *taw-meem*, which could mean "entire" or without spot or blemish, complete, undefiled or whole. Being perfect or blameless means being sincere and upright, undefiled, without fault or blemish. It is a state of righteousness before God, free from the influence and consequence of sin.

God demanded perfection from Abraham to forge a cordial and enduring relationship with him. Since God is the same forever, His demand has not changed. God's command to Abraham to walk before Him and be perfect is a command to every true (spiritual) descendant of Abraham, for this is the sole basis by which we can foster an intimate and enduring relationship with God as well. Just as God is a perfect Being by nature, His requirement for us, His creation, is also to be perfect. Jesus corroborates this expectation in Matthew 5:48: *"You therefore are to be perfect, as your heavenly Father is perfect."* (NHEB.)

While it would be understandable to be overwhelmed by the instruction's seeming impossibility from a human perspective, it is unequivocally practicable when we see things from God's view. Matthew 19:26 makes us understand that *"With humans this is impossible, but with God all things are possible."* (NHEB.) This includes living blamelessly and it indicates that perfection cannot be attained with our human strength unless we rely on God to enable us to live perfectly.

We must be careful not to be caught in the trap of complacency due to being overwhelmed by the practicability of perfection. We must not let ourselves get easily blown away by the wind of sin by deluding ourselves with the excuse that it is impossible to live blamelessly. The Bible contains some characters that were attested to have walked perfectly before God. Noah was a man who walked perfectly in his time and was spared from destruction along with his family. Similarly, Job was considered blameless by God, so much so that He permitted the devil to tempt him to prove His claim. Even through trial, Job remained steadfast.

The life of Jesus on earth also points us to the possibility of perfection. Having undergone similar temptations that confront us, Jesus' absolute obedience to God's word and submission to His will represents the perfect model we are to emulate in our walk with God. As children tend to imitate their parents, we ought to imitate our Lord in all things.

We are not to be discouraged at the demands of God. We are to look not at ourselves but at the Almighty God who is making this demand, for He who makes this demand is faithful. God would not demand from us what we cannot give or what He has not made provision for. Both forgiveness from sin and the power to live above it are available in Christ Jesus: *"⁶knowing this, that our old self was crucified with him, that the body of sin might be done away with, so that we would no longer be in bondage to sin. ⁷For he who has died has been freed from sin. ¹⁰For the death that he died, he died to sin one time; but the life that he lives, he lives to God. ¹¹In the same way, consider yourselves dead to sin, but alive to God in Christ Jesus."* (Romans 6:6–7, 10–11 NHEB.)

It is imperative to understand that walking blamelessly before God is a progressive and continuous process. It is a process that begins at salvation, and which after that involves conscious and consistent efforts to live in obedience to God's word. It does not matter what your past life might be; when you decide to follow Christ and be truly determined to be perfect, God wipes your slate clean, makes you a new creature and you can begin your journey to perfection. Abraham's continuous acts of obedience to God demonstrated a willingness to live by God's standard of perfect living. Likewise, our obedience to God's words, which remains the standard for Christian living, sets us on the path of perfection. When we take the bold step of faith towards Him in repentance, are determined and willing to please Him, live our lives in constant fellowship with Him (walking before Him), make all efforts to obey all His commands, and turn to Him for help when it seems difficult, we will grow by His grace into perfection: spiritual maturity and without blemish.

TOPIC 2: BLESSINGS AND CONDITIONS

GENESIS 17:1–2

In everyday life and our dealings with concerns there are actions and corresponding reactions. For instance, a student is not issued a certificate until he has fulfilled all the conditions for the award of that certificate. Our blessings are also premised on a condition, and we cannot receive from God when we choose to ignore and disobey Him.

When God called Abraham in Genesis Chapter 12:1–3 He declared certain promises to him. One of the promises He made to Abraham was that he would be a blessing, and that through him all nations of the earth would be blessed. ***"Now the LORD said to Abram, "Go out from your country, and from your relatives, and from your father's house, to the land that I will show you. ²And I will make of you a great nation. And I will bless you and make your name great. And you will be a blessing. ³And I will bless those who bless you, and I will curse him who curses you, and in you all the families of*** *the earth will be blessed."'"* (NHEB.) These promises form the basis for what later became the Abrahamic covenant God made with him, and God explained the terms in detail in this chapter. It was an everlasting covenant between God and Abraham and his descendants – sealed by circumcision. *"This is my covenant, which you shall keep, between me and you and your descendants after you. Every male among you shall be circumcised."* (Genesis 17:10 NHEB.) God was to multiply Abraham exceedingly, making him a father of many nations and a blessing to all generations. God made Abraham the father of Israel, and Jesus Christ – the Seed of promise – came through this nation. Through Christ, the blessing of salvation is made available to all men. As a result, all true descendants of Abraham are those who are saved by faith in Christ's sacrifice on the cross. Their circumcision is not that of the foreskin but of the heart by the Spirit: *"For he is not a Jew who is one outwardly, neither is that circumcision which is outward in the flesh; [29] but he is a Jew who is one inwardly, and circumcision is that of the heart, by the Spirit, not in the letter; whose praise is not from people, but from God."* (Romans 2:28–29 NHEB.)

This covenant God made with Abraham was conditional; it depended on the instruction given to him in the first verse. God said to Abraham, *"walk before me, and be blameless."* (Genesis 17:1 NHEB.) He said further, *"I will make my covenant between me and you, and will multiply you exceedingly."* (Genesis 17:2 NHEB.) Abraham's role in fulfilling God's promise was his faith, revealed in his obedience to God.

God's promises to His children can never fail. The problem is usually with us and not God. Usually we fail to believe in the promises of God for us and we do not trust God enough to bring His promises to fulfilment. Faith and obedience are what the Lord requires from us, which are the conditions we must meet for our blessings to be actualised.

Everyone desires the blessings of God in their lives. While it is not wrong to desire God's blessings, there are, however, conditions we must meet to access these blessings. We can only walk with God when we agree with His will. Amos 3:3 says: *"Do two walk together, unless they have agreed?"* (NHEB.)

The condition God gave Joshua in Joshua 1:8 to make his ways prosperous was to study the book of the law, meditate on it and do according to what is written in it. *"This book of the law shall not depart out of your mouth, but you shall meditate on it day and night, that you may observe to do according to all that is written in it: for then you shall make your way prosperous, and then you shall have good success."* (NHEB.) The conditions by which we can receive God's blessings are not different from the one given to Joshua. We are to acquaint ourselves with His desires in His word and ensure living our lives by His principles. God wants us to trust and obey Him; this has been and will always be the anchor point in our relationship with Him. When we study His word we learn to trust Him more. Only when we walk with Him in absolute submission can we get the best of our relationship with Him.

It is crucial to note at this point that our obedience to God should not be solely motivated by the blessings we intend to receive from Him. We should not seek God solely because we want Him to meet our needs. Our loyalty to God should be selfless and unconditional. We are to love God and submit to Him for who He is, for God is worthy of all our worship. When we relate with God with this understanding, our loyalty to Him will be unwavering, whether our desires are met by Him, delayed or even declined. We will aptly accept His will as best for our lives in any circumstance.

God's greatest blessing offered to mankind is salvation from sin – this blessing is also conditional. To be saved, we must repent from our sins, believe in the finished work of Christ and accept Him as Lord over our lives – this is just the beginning of the journey. The ultimate salvation is eternal dwelling with God which can only be attained by living a life consecrated to God in obedience to His will. *"So then, my beloved, even as you have always obeyed, not only in my presence, but now much more in my absence, work out your own salvation with fear and trembling."* (Philippians 2:12 NHEB.)

To attain the ultimate salvation, just like God demanded from Abraham, we must walk faithfully before Him, and we must be perfect. God requires we live blamelessly in a godless world. Jesus also addressed this issue in Matthew 5:48: *"You therefore are to be perfect, as your heavenly Father is perfect."* (NHEB.) We must overcome this world – all its trials and temptations for *"he who endures to the end, the same will be saved."* (Mark 13:13 NHEB.) We are to make righteousness the priority of our lives' pursuit. We are to journey through life as pilgrims, always bearing in mind that our home is not of this world, setting all our affections on things above. We are to decide firmly to live for God, no matter the cost.

TOPIC 3: IMPORTANCE OF NAMES

GENESIS 17:4–5, 15–16

As one of the cardinal features of some notable biblical characters, the issuance or modification of names was divinely orchestrated to significantly convey an air of purpose. These names were highly significant or symbolic.

When God established His covenant with Abram, God changed his name to Abraham, for God was about to fulfil His promise to make him a father of many nations by giving him a son. "Abram" means "high father" but "Abraham" means "father of many or multitude" (Campbell, 1996). God's intention for giving or changing names is not only for the names to be a form of identification but also to reflect His purpose in the individual's life and generally communicate His will. The name Abraham was a reflection of God's purpose for his life. While Abraham's physical descendants eventually became numerous, the spiritual descendants are countless, since all who belong to Jesus Christ, regardless of race or nationality, are accounted as Abraham's.

Galatians 3:29 says: *"If you are Christ's, then you are Abraham's offspring and heirs according to promise."* (NHEB.)

Another instance of God naming people is seen in the naming of Hosea's three children, as recorded in Hosea 1:3–9: *"So he went and took Gomer the daughter of Diblaim; and she conceived, and bore him a son. ⁴The LORD said to him, "Call his name Jezreel; for yet a little while, and I will avenge the blood of Jezreel on the house of Jehu, and will cause the kingdom of the house of Israel to cease. ⁵It will happen in that day that I will break the bow of Israel in the valley of Jezreel." ⁶She conceived again, and bore a daughter. Then he said to him, "Call her name Lo-Ruhamah; for I will no longer have mercy on the house of Israel, that I should in any way pardon them. ⁷But I will have mercy on the house of Judah, and will save them by the LORD their God, and will not save them by bow, or by sword, or by battle, or by chariots, or by horses, or by horsemen."⁸Now when she had weaned Lo-Ruhamah, she conceived, and bore a son. ⁹He said, "Call his name Lo-Ammi; for you are not my people, and I will not be yours."* (NHEB.) These names were messages to the Israelites concerning His will for them. Before Jesus was born, the angel of the Lord appeared to Joseph in a dream and informed him of the name God desires His Son to be called. The name "Jesus" was a reflection of God's will and purpose for the entire world through His Son. Matthew 1:21 says, *"And she will bring forth a son, and you are to name him Jesus, for he will save his people from their sins."* Later on in Jesus' ministry, when he met Simon, He named him "Cephas," or "Peter", meaning "rock." (Matthew 16:18, John 1:42). This reflected Peter's leadership role in the early church.

If God is particular about names, it will be wise for us not to treat the issue of naming our children with levity. Worthy of note is that a good name does not automatically translate to a promising future or good testimonies in life. For instance, the name Rehoboam means: "he enlarges the people" (Campbell, 1996), but the people of Israel rebelled under him; though not as a result of his making, the kingdom of Israel was divided under his leadership as God had foretold. The name

"Judas" means "Praise" (Campbell, 1996), but the life of Judas Iscariot was far from reflecting the praise of God. Nevertheless, we should always give our children names that reflect the future we hope for them.

We are to be guided appropriately. Our aim for naming should not just be to tag or label individuals to distinguish them from another. Hence, we should be cautious about the kind of names we give our children. It will be wise to prayerfully give them good names that reflect a godly heritage, pray ceaselessly for them and raise them in fear of the Lord.

Beyond our nominal identity in this world, we should look forward to and aspire to obtain a uniquely eternal name as citizens of a different world that would endure forever. Those who have accepted Jesus and followed Him faithfully in this world can rest assured that they will receive a new name in eternity. Revelation 2:17 says: *"To him who overcomes, to him I will give of the hidden manna, and I will give him a white stone, and on the stone a new name written, which no one knows but he who receives it."* (NHEB.)

Since, as believers, we are no longer citizens of this world, we must do everything in our capacity to ensure we are partakers of God's eternal kingdom, a kingdom in which our true and everlasting names will be written.

TOPIC 4: TRUE CIRCUMCISION

GENESIS 17:9–14, 23–27

At 99, Abraham was already approaching the fulfilment of God's promise of an heir, although he was not aware that the promised child was about a year away until God told him. On God's part, certain things needed to be in place before the promised child's birth. Besides his name change, God had to prepare Abraham and his household for the next phase of his relationship with Him through the covenant of circumcision.

God commanded Abraham to circumcise himself and every male member of his household of eight days old or more. This was to be a covenant between Abraham, his descendants and God. God said in Genesis 17:9–13, *"As for you, you will keep my covenant, you and your descendants after you throughout their generations. [10] This is my covenant, which you shall keep, between me and you and your descendants after you. Every male among you shall be circumcised. [11] You shall be circumcised in the flesh of your foreskin. It will be a token of the covenant between me and you. [12] He who is eight days old will be circumcised among you, every male throughout your generations, he who is born in the house, or bought with money from any foreigner who is not of your descendants. [13] He who is born in your house, and he who is bought with your money, must be circumcised. My covenant will be in your flesh for an everlasting covenant."* (NHEB.) Observance of this covenant was to prove obedience to God. Abraham asked no questions about the reasons and rationale behind the cutting off of the foreskin of males in the family; he just obeyed, and it became a seal of righteousness according to Romans 4:11. *"He received the sign of circumcision, a seal of the righteousness of the faith which he had while he was in uncircumcision..."* (NHEB.) The physical circumcision was not what made Abraham righteous: earlier, he was accounted righteous by his faith in God while uncircumcised. The obedience of circumcision was evidence of that righteousness, and the circumcision was the seal of the covenant.

From Abraham's relationship with God it is evident that what makes a man righteous with God is his faith – revealed in his obedience to God. When services are rendered to God without obedience and faith, those services do not amount to anything. Services rendered in the name of God become meaningful only when they are generated from hearts that trust and obey God.

Over the years, the term circumcision became synonymous with the law and being a Jew. The Jews were generally referred to as the circumcised while the Gentiles were generally considered uncircumcised.

It should be noted that the covenant of circumcision and its ceremonial observance were all pointers to the true circumcision of the heart, which was to come in Christ. Paul wrote: *"For he is not a Jew who is one outwardly, neither is that circumcision which is outward in the flesh;* ²⁹*but he is a Jew who is one inwardly, and circumcision is that of the heart, by the Spirit, not in the letter; whose praise is not from people, but from God."* (Romans 2:28–29 NHEB.) True circumcision is the circumcision of the heart – renewal of the heart. It is not physical but spiritual. It is the cutting off of the sinful nature – refusing to empower the flesh by refusing to walk by its dictates. It is more than cutting off the foreskin in observance of the written laws; it is the cutting off of that part of human life that is in the habit of going against God's commands. Apostle Paul was simply saying, "circumcise your hearts" when he wrote in Galatians 5:16, *"But I say, walk by the Spirit, and you will not carry out the desires of the flesh."* (NHEB.)

Long before Paul wrote about the significance of circumcision in Romans 2:28–29, Moses had already admonished the Israelites concerning circumcision of the heart. Deuteronomy 30:6 says, *"The LORD your God will circumcise your heart, and the heart of your descendants, to love the LORD your God with all your heart, and with all your soul, that you may live."* (NHEB.) It is the heart circumcision that will enable regenerated persons to love God with all their hearts and obey His word. Deuteronomy 10:16 says, *"Circumcise therefore the foreskin of your heart, and be no more stiff-necked."* (NHEB.)

Circumcision – the token of God's covenant with Abraham and his descendants, distinguished the Israelites from other nations. It also served as a shadow of the heart circumcision of every believer in this dispensation.

True circumcised persons are those who walk in the footstep of our Lord Jesus Christ. A circumcised heart is a contrite one. It is a heart that trembles at the word of God – a humble one with a broken will.

It is the heart of one who has willingly given over his will to God. The will of such a person is to please the Lord constantly. Such a heart is mouldable and teachable, always led by the Spirit of God.

Just as physical circumcision involves cutting away and putting off a part of the body, true circumcision involves putting away the indwelling sinful nature – the metaphorical old man – with its carnal wisdom, craftiness and subtlety. No human being can circumcise his heart through his effort alone. It comes through the grace of God when we willingly obey God and ask Him for help. God's help is made available through the finished work of Christ. Often, following God in contrast to our carnal desires can be inconvenient since it will go against the interest of the flesh.

Circumcision marked one out as a Jew at that time, but that could only be great if that person lived by God's law. Some of the Jews came to a point where their confidence was based on physical circumcision. Instead of craving to obey God more, they placed more value on the command of circumcision. Likewise, many Christians have come to the point where they place more importance on the name "Christians" than on obedience to God. Someone who calls himself a Christian but whose heart is not circumcised, thus having a habit of disobeying God, is worse than the person who is not carrying that name. It is the mark of God on our hearts, not that of a knife on our skins, that makes us spiritual descendants of Abraham.

In Joshua 5:2–4, the Bible records God's instruction to Joshua to circumcise the Israelites born in the wilderness. *"At that time, the LORD said to Joshua, "Make flint knives, and sit and circumcised the sons of Israel." ³So Joshua made himself flint knives, and circumcised the sons of Israel at the Hill of the Foreskins. ⁴And this is the reason Joshua circumcised the sons of Israel"* (NHEB). This incident happened at Gilgal just before they got into the Promised Land. God demanded that each of the Israelites not circumcised should be circumcised immediately. Failure to do so would attract the wrath of God. Likewise, to enter our heavenly Promised Land, we have to cut off the old man – that sinful aspect of our lives – by refusing to obey its dictates.

Praying for God's help and His will to be done in our lives helps us align our will with that of Christ. Our prayers should be accompanied by a determination to be like Christ in character. Our hearts have to desire righteousness to the point that nothing else matters in life other than to please God. It is this desire that Jesus spoke about when He said, *"Blessed are those who hunger and thirst after righteousness, for they will be filled."* (Matthew 5:6 NHEB.) It is at this point that we can honestly say, like Paul, *"For we are the circumcision, who worship God in the Spirit..."* (Philippians 3:3 NHEB.)

CHAPTER 18

TOPIC 1: FEAR OF CONSEQUENCES

GENESIS 18:9–15

To Sarah, nothing could be more amusing than overhearing her husband's respectable guests declare that she, an 89-year-old woman, would put to birth for the first time in her life within the next 12 months. From the tent door, her chuckle was within her – so she thought. Now, the men had become aware and had queried her husband to know the reason for her laughter. But how would she bring herself to admit that she was laughing at what her husband's guests were saying? On first instinct, she lied.

One of the principal reasons people lie is fear of the consequences of accepting their actions. The Bible did not mince words about what pushed Sarah to lie: *"Then Sarah denied, saying, "I did not laugh," for she was afraid..."* (Genesis 18:15 NHEB.) Sarah was afraid. When she realised that the visitors had found her out, her first reaction was to lie.

Fear can cause a person to act out of character when he perceives danger or threat. Our reactions to fear could either be positive or negative; for instance, the fear of hunger as a survival mechanism would make a man go out and work to provide for himself and his family; that is a good reaction. But sometimes we allow fear to enslave us, leading us to steal and lie, all in a bid to overcome hunger; that is when fear has become a tool in the hand of the enemy.

Abraham's and Sarah's survival instincts drove them down to Egypt during a famine. However, that natural survival instinct soon became a motivation for covering up their marital relationship. The fear of being killed led to lies. Fear paralyses and reduces our level of confidence. This reduced level of boldness sometimes makes us lie. If fear is taken out of the way and courage is enhanced, we will eliminate a great chunk of our lying. Take Peter's fear and the resultant lies, for instance: *"Now Peter was sitting outside in the courtyard, and a servant girl came to him, saying, "You were also with Jesus, the Galilean." [70]But he denied it before them all, saying, "I do not know what you are talking about." [71]And when he had gone out onto the porch, another girl saw him, and said to those who were there, "This man also was with Jesus the Nazorean." [72]Again he denied it with an oath, "I do not know the man." [73]After a little while those who stood by came and said to Peter, "Surely you are also one of them, for your accent makes you known." [74]Then he began to curse and to swear, "I do not know the man." Immediately the rooster crowed. [75]Peter remembered the word which Jesus had said, "Before the rooster crows, you will deny me three times." He went out and wept bitterly."* (Matthew 26:69–75 NHEB.) The fear of the consequences of being identified as Jesus' disciple made Peter do what he did. But when boldness came to Peter through the baptism of the Holy Spirit, fear was completely eliminated and he was able to stand up for Jesus even before the Sanhedrin.

When we display more regard for people's opinions about us than what God says we allow ourselves to be caught in the trap of disobedience. When we are scared of what they might think of us we stand the risk of disregarding God by not standing for the truth. Fear of losing our reputation can stop us from accepting our wrongs and repenting where necessary. When we do not accept responsibility or embrace repentance from our wrongdoing, we erroneously make our reputation a higher priority than the salvation of our souls.

The fear of God is the solution to the fear of man. While the fear of man leads to lies and other sins, the fear of God leads to wisdom: *"To man he said, 'Look, the fear of the Lord, that is wisdom. To depart from evil is understanding.'"* (Job 28:28 NHEB.) When we fear God, we will not lie, and we will not allow the fear of man to force us to go against the word of God. The psalmist seemed to have overcome the fear of man; that is why he wrote: *"The LORD is my helper; I will not fear. What can man do to me?"* (Psalm 118:6 NHEB.)

We should fear only God. Jesus told His disciples, *"do not be afraid of those who kill the body, but are not able to kill the soul. Rather, fear him who is able to destroy both soul and body in hell."* (Matthew 10:28 NHEB.) Out of fear, a man may tell a lie and escape physical death but forget he is in danger of eternal death.

Isaiah 8:13 says, *"The LORD of hosts is who you must regard as holy. He is the one you must fear. He is the one you must dread."* (NHEB.) The fear of man is the enemy of the fear of the Lord; it pushes us to pander to man's approval rather than yield to God's directives.

When we are pushed to lie to please others we should rather displease others than God. For Christians today, the word of God should dictate our way of life, and we should only follow those practices that align with the word of God.

There will always be consequences for our actions. If we decide to stand for God and the truth, the result could be persecution from the world while having a growing friendship with God. On the other hand, if we decide to fear man, regard personalities and opinions about us in contravention of God's word, the result could be having a friendly relationship with the world and enjoying its attendant material and social benefits, yet separating from God. In the end, the decision is ours to make: either stand with God or go with the world, but it is best to stand with God.

TOPIC 2: IS ANYTHING TOO DIFFICULT FOR THE LORD?

GENESIS 18:10–14

In this chapter, God appeared to Abraham in the similitude of man to talk with him. Part of the discussion was God's reaffirmation of His promise to him – to give him a son through Sarah. God had already spoken about this in the previous chapter to Abraham, but here, while God was speaking, Sarah overheard the discussion from the tent's entrance. She considered her age and Abraham's – for Sarah was about 89 years old at this time, and Abraham was about 99 years old – and she laughed within herself. This prompted God's reply: *"Is anything too difficult for the LORD?..."* (Genesis 18:14 NHEB.)

"Is anything too difficult for the Lord?" is actually a rhetorical question about God's ability to bring what is considered an impossibility into reality. The question is vital for every person who struggles with unbelief or the inability to trust God in difficult times. Nothing is impossible for God and nothing is difficult for Him. Some of us might think that it is easier for God to cure a headache than for Him to raise the dead, but God will both heal the headache and raise the dead effortlessly.

Sometimes we see life situations like children looking at a half-finished building and do not have the slightest idea of what it will look like when completed. We see masses of stones, bricks, timbers, mortar and dirt, all in apparent confusion. We may not see the possibility of having a beautiful building in that same place, but the architect, who designed the building sees order beyond the rubbles and quietly looks forward with joy to the day the whole building will be finished; when all that seems like confusion will be removed to present a beautiful edifice.

Sarah looked at her age and her husband's, but the Lord understood the whole situation as the architect who designed the building had. Sarah saw confusion and impossibility, but God, the master designer, saw order and possibility. He announced to Sarah that she would have a son at the same time the following year, for nothing is too difficult for Him.

There are several situations people considered impossible, which God made possible, to their amazement. We must understand that there is no such thing as impossibility with God. Who would have thought that a virgin could conceive and give birth without being with a man? Who would have thought that the corpse of Lazarus could come back to life again? Also, remember Daniel in the lion's den, Shedrach, Meshach and Abednego in the fiery furnace, Elizabeth, who gave birth to John the Baptist in her old age; the list is endless. From the Old Testament to the New, the impossible made possible by God is limitless. God never changes! So why should we doubt Him or let the predicaments of life cause us sorrow?

It is worth noting that God can make the impossible possible in our lives when we have a relationship with Him; this also implies that we must avoid sin at all costs. Isaiah 59:1–2 says, *"Look, the LORD's hand is not shortened, that it can't save; neither his ear heavy, that it can't hear: ²but your iniquities have separated between you and your God, and your sins have hidden his face from you, so that he will not hear."* (NHEB.) Regardless of the trying situations that confront us, God can fully express His ability to solve any problem and do the impossible in our lives. Even if those challenges are not solved, it is not because God cannot do it; it could be His will for us to pass through those challenges or it is not yet the set time for our deliverance. As such, we should look up to Him for the strength to remain strong and faithful in the storm.

Faith honours God; He is pleased when we believe Him. Moreover, as we look up to God we must also learn to submit to His sovereign will. We ought to always remember the words of the three young men, Shadrach, Meshach and Abednego when they came face to face with King Nebuchadnezzar: *"If it be so, our God whom we serve is able to deliver us from the burning fiery furnace; and he will deliver us out of your hand, O king. ¹⁸But if not, be it known to you, O king, that we will not serve your gods, nor worship the golden image which you have set up."* (Daniel 3:17–18 NHEB.) Right there, that very statement "But if not" is trust expressed at its peak! That is totally submitting the outcome of our situation to the will of God. This is the epitome of faith. While we believe in the all-powerfulness of God it will be wise not to relegate His sovereignty over our affairs. There are times when God's will might not be in line with ours; nevertheless, we ought to trust and accept His will as best for our lives. God may deliver us from some trying situations, and He may require us to go through others for reasons best known to Him. Whatever the case may be, we are to remain steadfast in the faith, fully convinced that *"all things work together for good for those who love God, to those who are called according to his purpose."* (Romans 8:28 NHEB.)

TOPIC 3: GOD'S CONFIDANT

GENESIS 18:17–18

Precious stones cannot just be picked up on the streets; accessing them needs capital-intensive exploration and mining for days, months and sometimes years. Likewise, much more hard work is required to access the deep things of God, which are even more precious than the finest gold. Typically, in human relationships, we tend to reveal or withhold certain information from people depending on the degree of our friendship with them. It will take a fool to divulge a bedroom secret to some neighbourhood drunk or gossip. God, who is wiser than the wisest of all beings, does not reveal His secrets to just anyone. He has confidants to whom He divulges His secrets. Getting to that level of relationship takes more diligence than digging for the finest gold.

A confidant is a person close to you, who you can confide in and trust with the most profound matters of your heart, a trusted companion with whom you can interact and share your deepest thoughts and who will not mishandle them. The fact that God, who is immortal, omnipotent and omniscient should have a mortal and frail man as a confidant is genuinely remarkable. God did not mince words when He called Abraham His friend: *"But you, Israel, my servant, Jacob whom I have chosen, the offspring of Abraham my friend"* (Isaiah 41:8 NHEB).

In Genesis 18:17 we see God desirous to divulge His plan to Abraham without Abraham's request, because of their cordial relationship. God said, *"Will I hide from Abraham what I do?"* (NHEB.)

Another confidant God had in the Bible was Moses. In the wilderness, the Israelites rebelled against God in their unbelief. God was willing to destroy all of them and make another nation out of Moses, but Moses advised God, giving Him reasons why He should not kill the people. God listened to Moses and took another decision. God once said about Moses: *"If there is a prophet among you, I the LORD will make myself known to him in a vision. I will speak with him in a dream. ⁷My servant Moses is not so. He is faithful in all my house. ⁸With him I will speak mouth to mouth, openly, and not in riddles; and he shall see the LORD's form..."* (Numbers 12:6–8 NHEB.)

Also, while God and the heavenly hosts discussed how King Ahab would be sent to his death, God's decision to let Micaiah in on the means through which Ahab would be killed reveals Micaiah as God's confidant (1 Kings 22:10-28).

At certain times when Jesus taught the crowd He would teach them in parables, but when He was alone with His disciples He would expound the meaning of the parables to them. As a result, the disciples had a deeper understanding of His teachings. His disciples noticed this and asked Him why He did what He did. He replied to them, saying, *"To you it is given to know the mysteries of the kingdom of heaven, but it is not given to them."* (Matthew 13:11 NHEB.) This buttresses the fact that the secrets of God are not for everyone. God does not reveal the deep things of His heart to just anybody. In another instance, Jesus said to them, *"No longer do I call you servants, for the servant does not know what his master is doing. But I have called you friends, for everything that I heard from my Father I have made known to you."* (John 15:15 NHEB.)

Every relationship has a starting point. The first step to becoming a confidant of God is accepting the Lord Jesus Christ as Lord and submitting to His Lordship completely. The next phase is to pursue a life of intimacy with God and make pleasing Him our utmost priority. Relationships are based on trust, and trust is built over time. The fact that God saw a confidant in Abraham meant that Abraham had earned God's trust over the years. God's statement in Genesis 18:19 buttresses this truth: *"For I have known him, to the end that he may command his children and his household after him, that they may keep the way of the LORD, to do righteousness and justice; to the end that the LORD may bring on Abraham that which he has spoken of him."* (NHEB.) For God to confide in us, we must prove ourselves trustworthy. One of the crucial elements of trust is consistency. To earn God's trust we ought to be consistent in our obedience to His commandments. Our obedience must be absolute and in every situation. Just as Abraham was obedient to God and steadfast in the faith, despite God's delay in giving him the child of promise, our loyalty to God should not waver even in challenging circumstances. Our consistency in obedience to Him makes us dependable, which in turn makes us confidants in His sight.

Psalm 25:14 says: *"The friendship of the LORD is with those who fear him. He will show them his covenant."* (NHEB.) In every generation, God seeks men He can trust with His plans or secrets. When God finds a man that genuinely fears Him and walks faithfully in His ways, He could make such a man His confidant. All God's confidants in the Bible, such as Abraham, Moses and others were humans, men of like passions. They were not different from any other person on the face of the earth. What they all had in common was the fear of God and an intimate relationship with Him. When we draw close to God, He will also draw close to us. God desires intimacy: He wants to have friends He confides in, for He does not do anything without revealing it to His servants and prophets. Amos 3:7 says, *"Surely the Lord GOD will do nothing, unless he reveals his secret to his servants the prophets."* (NHEB.) He would not do anything regarding the church or nations without disclosing it to His confidants. God shares His secrets with those who appreciate and tremble at His word. When we seek God diligently and sincerely through His word He will grant us access to the deeper meanings of scriptures. He will unravel the mysteries of His word to us as He did to the disciples. When we draw closer to Him, investing more time and consecration in our relationship with Him, He will not hold back from confiding in us. We are not to relent in our pursuit of a level of intimacy with God where nothing is hidden between us, where God would speak to us as clearly as He did with the likes of Abraham and Moses.

TOPIC 4: JUST JUDGE

GENESIS 18:23–32

Have you ever been in a courtroom and felt the judge's decision was unfair? Why did you think it was unfair? Was it because he let the offender go scot-free? Or was it because he punished an innocent person?

A judge's verdict could be influenced by a plethora of factors such as bribery, falsified information, the inconsistency of human nature, or it could just be the judge having a bad day. With all these factors that bring about wrong judgements in human courtrooms let us rest assured that it is just and fair in the heavenly courtroom of justice. Every man will get what he deserves.

God is the Judge of the whole earth. He is the Judge because He created all men so all men are accountable to Him. As the Judge of the entire world, God administers justice to all men based on their actions. He judges the righteous according to their righteousness and the wicked according to their wickedness.

God had just informed Abraham about the impending destruction of Sodom and Gomorrah. Abraham was troubled in his heart, and he imagined how everyone, both the righteous and the unrighteous, would be destroyed. This would not have been fair; hence, he said to God, *"Be it far from you to do things like that, to kill the righteous with the wicked, so that the righteous should be like the wicked. May that be far from you. Shouldn't the Judge of all the earth do right?"* (Genesis 18:25 NHEB.) In the subsequent verses, God clearly states the standard of judgement, saying that He will not destroy the righteous with the wicked. This standard remains the same through all dispensations.

In the time of Noah, sin and moral depravity were prevalent. The human race's wickedness was severe, and men's thoughts were evil continually; this made God regret that He had made man. As a result God decided to wipe out humanity from the face of the earth with a flood. Notwithstanding the high perversion and depravity prevalent in those days, Noah remained faithful to God and blameless. The fact that Noah was the only one God found righteous on all the earth did not make God destroy him with the wicked; God carefully preserved him and his household. Supposing God was to judge the entire world we live in today and out of the billions of people on the earth finds only one man righteous. God would preserve such a fellow.

In another instance, God was angry with the Israelites and resolved to judge them for their sins. They were to be taken captive for 70 years. God's verdict for all of Judah was for them to submit themselves to King Nebuchadnezzar, who would take them all to Babylon. Those who would not submit themselves to the righteous judgement of God were to be punished by the plague, famine and the sword. Although the righteous – like Daniel, Shedrach, Meshach and Abednego – were taken captive, they excelled in Babylon. In this case, God blessed the righteous in captivity, which was supposed to be a punishment. God always distinguishes between the righteous and the wicked in His judgement; He never condemns the righteous with the wicked.

Another fact about the justice of God is that it is not without mercy. God said to Abraham that He would not destroy Sodom and Gomorrah if He found as little as ten righteous persons in the city. God's mercy is available to the sinner who repents from his sinful ways. In the beginning, God told Adam and Eve not to eat from the tree of the knowledge of good and evil, but they disobeyed God. At that very moment, justice demanded action. For God to overlook or excuse their disobedience would not be just. That would mean going against the very laws He established for the universe to abide by. However, He made a covering for the sinful man in His mercies and assured Him of restoration. Several millennia later, God sent His own Son, Jesus, into the world to reconcile us to Himself. By the sacrifice of Jesus, an acceptable exchange was made to redeem mankind – a life for a life. *"Because Christ also suffered for sins once, the righteous for the unrighteous, that he might bring you to God..."* (1 Peter 3:18 NHEB.)

If we want to be saved, all that is required of us is to accept Christ as Lord and Saviour. Then live the life of Christ as revealed in the scriptures. God still calls out to us through His servants and His word but what do we do? Many still disobey. God cannot merely overlook our rebellion against Him or else He would not be just. Although Christ's sacrifice was for the redemption of man, by the justice of God, everyone who refuses to accept Him will be condemned.

There are times when people have accused God of injustice. When Job was overwhelmed by his predicaments, being ignorant of what was really happening, he said: *"he destroys the blameless and the wicked. 23 If the scourge kills suddenly, he will mock at the trial of the innocent. 24 The earth is given into the hand of the wicked. He covers the faces of its judges. If not he, then who is it?"* (Job 9:22–24 NHEB.) The answer lies in knowing and understanding God's ways and His ultimate plan for those who love Him. When God revealed Himself to Job, Job repented of the words he had spoken earlier, saying *"Therefore I abhor myself, and repent in dust and ashes."* (Job 42:6 NHEB.) Some of God's children find it hard to understand certain things they encounter in life. For instance, a righteous man's death is not God's judgement upon that man because he is not condemned to eternal damnation. In fact, the death of a righteous man is precious in the sight of God. *"Precious in the sight of the LORD is the death of his faithful ones."* (Psalm 116:15 NHEB.) God is not as concerned about the number of days we live here on earth as He is about fulfilling our purpose and where we will spend eternity. Also, the righteousness of a man is not measured by how long he lives or how prosperous he is. Jesus Christ explained to us that our priority should be to seek God's kingdom, even if it means giving up every other thing, including possessions, loved ones and even our lives. By this, we know that God's justice is not called into question when we are faced with unfavourable circumstances – even death.

CHAPTER 19

TOPIC 1: HOSPITALITY

GENESIS 19:1–3

As far back as we may go in the history of God's people, one of the virtues of righteous people is hospitality. Hospitality entails the willingness to welcome people and assist in their needs. It is the friendly and benevolent reception or treatment of guests and strangers. This could include offering shelter, food or money to people in need. The act of hospitality is not restricted to guests' reception in our homes alone; it can be done wherever we find ourselves.

Hospitality is a virtue of the righteous; the only reason why such virtue was found in Sodom is that Lot, a righteous man, lived in Sodom. Humans have a natural tendency to be selfish. Therefore, it is natural for many to tow the path of least resistance and neglect hospitality. When we yield to our self-centred natural tendency, the result will be a life so full of self that there will be no room for hospitality, but God commands us to be kind and hospitable to others. In Leviticus 19:34, God commanded the Israelites, saying: *"The stranger who lives as a foreigner with you shall be to you as the native-born among you, and you are to love him as yourself; for you lived as foreigners in the land of Egypt. I am the LORD your God."* (NHEB.) Apostle Paul admonished Christians to practice hospitality: *"contributing to the needs of the saints; given to hospitality."* (Romans 12:13 NHEB.) This is a sign of true and sincere love that Christians should possess. More important than the act of hospitality is the motive for doing it. The motive for being hospitable to someone must be predicated purely on love, not with an expectation to be rewarded or lauded by others. Some people find it easier to care for those they are familiar with, those they love and who love them in return, but the standard of God is for us to care for everyone. Hospitality should have nothing to do with nationality or race; wherever and whenever we find people in need, we ought to show hospitality. We are to be friendly and accommodating to our loved ones and strangers alike.

Lot displayed hospitality in its true sense when he entertained two men who happened to be angels of God. On sighting them from afar, Lot swiftly extended an invitation to them to be his guests. He offered them shelter and also persuaded them to honour his invitation after their initial refusal. Abraham showed similar hospitality towards three men, two of whom happened to be the same set of guests Lot received. *"The LORD appeared to him by the oaks of Mamre, as he sat in the tent door in the heat of the day. ²He lifted up his eyes and looked, and saw that three men stood opposite him. When he saw them, he ran to meet them from the tent door, and bowed himself to the earth, ³and said, "My lord, if now I have found favor in your sight, please do not go away from your servant. ⁴Now let a little water be fetched, wash your feet, and rest yourselves under the tree. ⁵I will get a morsel of bread so you can refresh your heart. After that you may go your way, now that you have come to your servant." They said, "Very well, do as you have said." ⁶Abraham hurried into the tent to Sarah, and said, "Quickly make ready three measures of fine meal, knead it, and make cakes." ⁷Abraham ran to the herd, and fetched a tender and good calf, and gave it to the servant. He hurried to dress it. ⁸He took butter, milk, and the calf which he had dressed, and set it before them. He stood by them under the tree, and they ate."* (Genesis 18:1–8 NHEB.) Both men willingly and joyfully received their visitors. They did not wait for the angels to request before obliging. We should not wait to be asked for help before offering, especially when the recipient's need is obvious and within our ability to help. Our acts of hospitality should be without grumbling. *"Be hospitable to one another without grumbling."* (1 Peter 4:9 NHEB.)

Like Lot, Manoah, the father of Samson, exhibited a hospitable gesture towards an angel of the Lord. He and his wife received an angel, thinking he was a man of God. *"The angel of the LORD said to Manoah, "Though you detain me, I won't eat of your bread. And if you prepare a burnt offering, you must offer it to the LORD." For Manoah did not know that he was the angel of the LORD."* (Judges 13:16 NHEB.) His gesture to offer refreshment to the supposed man of God demonstrates the kind, hospitable and benevolent attitude that can lead us to entertain angels unknowingly. This is confirmed in Hebrews 13:2: *"Do not forget to show hospitality to strangers, for in doing so, some have entertained angels without knowing it."* (NHEB.) We should not hunt for angels to entertain, but we should make hospitality our character.

Also, the Shunammite woman and her husband demonstrated hospitality towards Prophet Elisha when they offered him food and accommodation every time he passed through Shunem. God rewarded their good deeds by using Prophet Elisha to meet their need for a child. 2 Kings 4:12–17 says, *"He said to Gehazi his servant, "Call this Shunammite." When he had called her, she stood before him. [13]He said to him, "Say now to her, 'Look, you have cared for us with all this care. What is to be done for you? Would you like to be spoken for to the king, or to the captain of the army?'" She answered, "I dwell among my own people." [14]He said, "What then is to be done for her?" Gehazi answered, "Most certainly she has no son, and her husband is old." [15]He said, "Call her." When he had called her, she stood in the door. [16]He said, "At this season, when the time comes around, you will embrace a son." She said, "No, my lord, you man of God, do not lie to your handmaid." [17]The woman conceived, and bore a son at that season, when the time came around, as Elisha had said to her."* (NHEB.) Sometimes we are unaware of whom God has put before us to help change our situation; we do not know that all we need is to show a little kindness to that person.

Although hospitality can open doors that can change our lives, it should never be done with an expectation of reward. It should be done because we are Christians and because the love of Christ is our drive. It should not be done like the hypocrites who practise righteousness for the acknowledgement of others but should be done because God commands it, and with the knowledge that we are laying for ourselves treasures in heaven. When we are hospitable to those who cannot repay us, God becomes our rewarder. *"When you make a dinner or a supper, do not call your friends, nor your brothers, nor your kinsmen, nor rich neighbors, or perhaps they might also return the favor, and pay you back. ¹³ But when you make a feast, ask the poor, the maimed, the lame, or the blind; ¹⁴ and you will be blessed, because they do not have the resources to repay you. For you will be repaid in the resurrection of the righteous."* (Luke 14:12–14 NHEB.)

Often people neglect to show hospitality because of the cost they stand to incur in the process. They usually offer the excuse that their resources are insufficient to take care of their families, let alone strangers. Some others view hospitality as an inconvenience that disrupts their schedule and comfort. However, as believers, it is essential to understand that whatever we have in this world does not belong to us but to God. We are merely stewards of whatever God bequeaths to us and should, therefore, use it as God desires. Hospitality does not just reflect our love towards men but also towards God. *"The King will answer them, 'Truly I tell you, inasmuch as you did it to one of the least of these my brothers, you did it to me.'"* (Matthew 25:40 NHEB.)

Hospitality can be an excellent tool for evangelism. It is essential for us as believers in our bid to win souls for Christ, to cultivate the habit of hospitality regardless of the resources at our disposal. Although not everyone can offer help at the same level, everyone has something to offer. Hospitality serves as an avenue to demonstrate a Christ-like attitude. It becomes easier for people to accept Christ when they see Him living through us. The salvation of lost souls should serve as enough motivation for us to be hospitable. By serving others, we serve Christ, and by that, we promote the spread of

God's truth and love. The message of the love of Christ will be easily understood by the recipient who enjoyed hospitality from us. Not only is hospitality admirable but it also makes the world a better and more conducive place.

Since hospitality deals with strangers, we should be wise and careful not to be victims of evil men who may disguise themselves as strangers to attack innocent victims. The significant increase in crime rates around the world today, compared with those of Abraham and Lot's time, calls for caution in our hospitality. A careless person with a good heart who falls into the trap of evil marauders may never again be able to show hospitality. But the presence of evil must not prevail over good; we must be wise and strategic in showing hospitality to strangers. For example, taking a stranger in need of a place to spend a night to a shelter home or paying for a hotel room might be safer than taking them to your home. We should be wise as serpents and harmless as doves.

TOPIC 2: LIFE'S PRIORITIES

GENESIS 19:1–38

To know someone's priority in life you need to look at the choices they make. When we set a goal as the top priority, our choices are geared towards achieving it. Although we might foresee the consequences of choices we make, the outcome of most of our decisions might be humanly unpredictable, even if we apply the best analytical minds. For this reason, we need the help of the One who can see the future and knows the consequences of all our choices; this is even more the case when we know that some consequences are irreversible and of eternal dimension. Even with much prayer, if we do not align our priorities with God's will we will find ourselves making decisions that could attract eternal negative consequences.

Lot had been living with his uncle, Abraham, since Abraham moved from Haran into Canaan. It is not surprising that he had grown to be a wealthy man, even while living with Abraham. A time came that, due to the growth of their individual businesses, uncle and nephew had to separate for the sake of peace. Abraham gave Lot the privilege of choosing where he would relocate to. As most people would do today, before taking such a decision Lot took a look at the Jordan Valley and saw that it had almost everything that would make for a successful business – good pastures and proximity to the city. He chose to move there. Genesis 13:12 says, *"Lot lived in the cities of the plain, and moved his tent as far as Sodom."* (NHEB.) Good pastures meant limiting the stress of migration or looking for pastures now and again.

Oblivious to the destruction that would come on Sodom, his choice revealed what he held as a priority – business success. What you place as a priority will undoubtedly influence your choices. Take a look at a Christian who decides to work in or run a nightclub and it is not difficult to know where their priority lies. No matter the words of their confession, their priority is certainly not heaven. Many people might not know the future and eternal consequences of their choices until God reveals it to them through His word or other mediums. The best course of action is to make God part of your decision-making process; let Him be your guide and helper in setting your priorities then let Him help you with the choices you make to attain that priority.

Lot's choice landed him in a situation in which he lost everything he had. He escaped destruction only by God's mercies and ended up in a cave where he was involved in incestuous acts with his daughters. Those consequences could not have been predicted by any human.

Apostle Peter described Lot in Sodom as a righteous man who was daily tormented in his soul by the lifestyle of the Sodomites: *"for that righteous man dwelling among them, was tormented in his righteous soul from day to day with seeing and hearing lawless deeds"* (2 Peter 2:8 NHEB). This begs the question, what would make a righteous man, who is not spiritually comfortable in a place, continue living or working there? The priority of making money and being successful has caused many Christians to lose their spirituality simply because they would not want to leave a sinful relationship or career for the sake of what they stand to lose. Jesus said in Matthew 16:26, *"For what will it profit a person, if he gains the whole world, and forfeits his life? Or what will a person give in exchange for his life?"* (NHEB.)

A child of God, who has the kingdom of God as his top priority, should be mindful of his involvements wherever he finds himself and not waste his time in fighting emotions and temptations in a place or relationship that is daily tormenting his spirit and challenging his values, even if that place has significant economic benefits.

Let us be mindful of the instruction of God: *"Therefore, "'Go out from their midst, and be separate,' says the Lord, 'and touch no unclean thing,' and I will receive you."* (2 Corinthians 6:17 NHEB.) We find it hard to leave the world's practice when our priority is aligned with the world. Someone with material gains as the priority will find it difficult to leave a social club that encourages sin but provides business connections. However, the moment the priority is to please God, making the choice of leaving becomes a straightforward decision with God's help.

If the environment we live in or the friends we keep are ungodly, affecting our relationship with God, we should relocate or forgo such friendship for the salvation of our souls. 2 Corinthians 6:14 says, *"Do not be unequally yoked with unbelievers, for what fellowship have righteousness and iniquity? Or what fellowship has light with darkness?"* (NHEB.)

We need to define our priorities as believers if we want to spend eternity in heaven. It is essential to ask: is the kind of career we are in, our place of residence and the relationships we keep pleasing to God? Do we find ourselves in situations in which we are constantly tempted to disobey God? We will be doing ourselves a world of good if we sacrifice such endeavours rather than our soul's salvation. We must be careful not to let pecuniary rewards overshadow the salvation of our souls. Salvation does not come by mere wishes; it comes by setting it as our top priority and making the choice of accepting Jesus as Lord and Saviour. This must be followed by daily decisions to live in obedience to the word of God. Salvation could make us lose friends, money, power and even all the good things of this life; however, those losses are nothing compared to the loss of eternal life we would experience if we lose our salvation.

TOPIC 3: HOMOSEXUALITY

GENESIS 19:4–5

God destroyed the cities of Sodom and Gomorrah because of the sin of their people. The first mention of this sin was in Genesis Chapter 13, which says: *"Now the men of Sodom were exceedingly wicked and sinners against the LORD."* (Genesis 13:13 NHEB.) From that passage we learn that their sin was grievous, and in Genesis Chapter 19:4–5 we see a manifestation of their evil character when they tried to seize Lot's guests to have sex with them, thereby confirming the extent of their lawlessness and depravity. *"But before they lay down, the men of the city, the men of Sodom, surrounded the house, both young and old, all the people from every quarter. ⁵They called to Lot, and said to him, "Where are the men who came in to you this night? Bring them out to us, that we may have sex with them.""* (NHEB.) The act of men having sexual intercourse with men was the norm in their society.

Homosexuality is the term used to describe the sexual preference of people who are sexually attracted to people of the same sex; a man who gets sexually involved with a man or a woman who gets sexually involved with a woman is a homosexual. Homosexuality is a deviation from the natural order of the application of sex, which should be between a man and a woman. It was an abomination before God in the days of Sodom and Gomorrah; also, it attracted a death sentence in the laws given to the Israelites by God: *"If a man has sexual relations with a male, as with a woman, both of them have committed an abomination: they shall surely be put to death; their blood shall be upon them."* (Leviticus 20:13 NHEB.) Homosexuality has always been a sin, both in the Old and the New Testament. 1 Corinthians 6:9 says: *"Or do you not know that the unrighteous will not inherit the kingdom of God? Do not be deceived. Neither the sexually immoral, nor idolaters, nor adulterers, nor effeminate, nor men who have sexual relations with men"* (NHEB). God kicks against homosexuality today just as He did then; His stance about homosexuality has not changed with time, culture, modernisation, human will or sentiments.

From creation, God's intention for sex has been for sex to be between a man and a woman within the confines of marriage. *"He answered, and said, "Have you not read that he who created them from the beginning made them male and female, [5] and said, 'For this reason a man will leave his father and mother, and be joined to his wife; and the two will become one flesh?'"* (Matthew 19:4–5 NHEB.)

The inherent sinful nature in man, which came to be due to Adam's sin, engendered many behavioural depravities such as homosexuality. Hence, homosexuality represents a downright disobedience, deviation and perversion of God's original order of sexual attraction and relation among humans.

The urge for sex is not sinful but it was not meant to be directed at members of the same sex as the Bible states in Romans 1:27, *"Likewise also the men, giving up natural relations with women, burned in their lust toward one another, men doing what is inappropriate with men, and receiving in themselves the due penalty of their error."* (NHEB.)

Sex is useful and desirable but must be applied following the guidelines stated in the Bible, which is given by the One who created us. There is only one way to please our Maker and that is to obey His commands.

Our obedience cannot be complete if it is not in totality. We must not choose what is convenient to obey while making excuses for what we still want to hold on to. The standards of God cannot be compromised by the standards of the sinful flesh to create a comfortable atmosphere for men to serve God. Therefore, we must strive to overcome the flesh and yield to the instructions of God, then He will help us to overcome the cravings of the flesh: *"16But I say, walk by the Spirit, and you will not carry out the desires of the flesh. 17For the flesh lusts against the Spirit, and the Spirit against the flesh; and these are contrary to one another, that you may not do the things that you desire. 19Now the works of the flesh are obvious, which are: sexual immorality, uncleanness, lustfulness, 20idolatry, sorcery, hatred, strife, jealousies, outbursts of anger, rivalries, divisions, heresies, 21envyings, murders, drunkenness, orgies, and things like these; of which I forewarn you, even as I also forewarned you, that those who practice such things will not inherit the kingdom of God."* (Galatians 5:16–17, 19–21 NHEB.)

Homosexuality has gained increased acceptance globally as those who practise and advocate it increase in number by the day. However, Christians must be careful not to be caught in this web of rebellion, as the number of people practising a thing does not necessarily make that thing right; the measure of rightness for a Christian is the word of God. The world's system sometimes permits things that are against the word of God. The world we live in is like a slippery ground for those who genuinely love God and long to please Him, and we must tread with care lest we fall and lose our salvation. Christians who endorse the practice of homosexuality have slipped into falsehood and are propagating the standards of the world as if they are accepted by God. Of such types, Jesus said: *"And in vain do they worship me, teaching instructions that are the commandments of humans."* (Matthew 15:9 NHEB.)

Like every other sin, the sin of homosexuality is a weakness to some but is inexcusable because we are not without an option for our choices in life. A person cannot overcome his shortcomings by making excuses for them or living in denial, but by identifying them and aggressively going against the tide of his desires without relenting, while trusting God to help him overcome them. Such a person will overcome because God never abandons those who diligently seek Him.

TOPIC 4: RELATIVITY OF GOODNESS

GENESIS 19:3–8

Goodness in the world is largely relative; for instance, what seems good or appropriate for one person, might not be suitable for another. The world in which we live is a morally complex one. Evil constantly lurks around us. In dealing with the complexity of evil, sometimes we avoid it, at times we tolerate it, other times we might be faced with choosing the lesser of two immoral actions – applying the lesser-evil principle. This principle holds that when an individual is confronted with two immoral acts, choosing the less sinister option is the ideal. People who act by this principle believe that good can be achieved by doing something less evil. The danger of this principle is accepting that some evil is greater than others and then thinking that one is somehow justified by carrying out a lesser evil. Such was the case of Lot and his two innocent daughters.

The depth of corruption in Sodom is plainly revealed in this instance. People had come to embrace sexual perversion as a way of life. In their depravity, the city's men approached Lot and demanded that he hand over his guests so that they would have carnal knowledge of them. To pacify them, Lot offered them his virgin daughters instead. A similar act is recorded in Judges 19:22–25, in which a man had to offer his daughter to a gang of vile men to be raped instead of allowing them to rape his guest. *"As they were enjoying themselves, look, the men of the city, some wicked men of the city surrounded the house, beating at the door. And they spoke to the master of the house, the old man, saying, "Bring out the man who came into your house, that we may have sex with him."* [23] *The man, the master of the house, went out to them, and said to them, "No, my brothers, please do not act so wickedly; since this man has come into my house. Do not do this disgraceful thing. ²⁴Look, here is my virgin daughter and his concubine. I will bring them out now. Ravish them and do with them what seems good to you; but do not do any such a disgraceful thing to this man." ²⁵But the men wouldn't listen to him: so the man laid hold of his concubine, and brought her out to them. And they raped her and abused her all night until the morning, and when the day began to dawn they let her go."* (NHEB.) From the perspective of Lot and the old man in Judges 19, offering to hand their daughters to men to be raped was the lesser evil than allowing their guests to be raped. To them, that was the right thing to do. Christians have a lot to learn from these incidents.

Judging from the knowledge of God available to us in this dispensation, although ensuring the safety of his guest was a noble act which is highly commendable, the act of doing so at the expense of his daughters should not be emulated because, with God, the end does not justify the means. No evil action is lesser or justified in the eyes of God, and any seemingly good act carried out by a wrong means is unacceptable. For instance, a man who steals from his employer is not justified because he intends to send the proceeds to orphans in an orphanage.

The most accurate guide or indicator of the rightness of an act, especially in relating with others, is the word of God. We are not to act in a certain way simply because it is logical or culturally approved. Our paramount evaluator of what is good or bad is the principles of God. This is why our conscience ought to be influenced by the in-depth knowledge of God's word so that it could be a proper moral compass within us.

The word of God enables us to know the desired course of action that God intends us to take in every given situation. God's instruction on how we are to relate with others is given in Matthew 7:12: ***"Therefore whatever you desire for people to do to you, do also to them; for*** *this is the Law and the Prophets.*" (NHEB.) This commandment is the basis of our actions towards others under any circumstance. How we treat others should not be influenced by how they treat us. Cultural or traditional values should not negatively influence our treatment of others. We are to treat others in the way we would want to be treated if we were in their place, and whatever we hate or detest we are never to do to others.

Christ said in John 13:34: *"A new commandment I give to you, that you love one another. Just as I have loved you, you also must love one another.*" (NHEB.) We are to love one another as Christ has loved us. This means that we are to love one another to be willing to suffer in their place. Rather than put others in harm's way, we should be willing to suffer whatever it takes to do good, even if it means laying down our lives in the process. This is the kind of love Christ demands from us.

It is of the essence to note that Christ does not demand from us what He has not already done. Christ did not spare Himself but considered our salvation much more than the pains and agony of the atonement sacrifice. This is why He commands us to love one another, just as He expressed His love to us.

TOPIC 5: NEGLIGENCE TO CAUTION

GENESIS 19:12–14

As the divine clock wound down to God's judgement upon the nation of Judah – the Babylonian captivity, the Lord sent a young Levite – Jeremiah, with His word of warning. For years he preached. God's verdict was for them to hand over themselves to Nebuchadnezzar. Those who go out to Nebuchadnezzar would live; those who resist would die by the sword. While the wickedness of the people of Nineveh had gone up before the Lord, He sent His servant Jonah with a message: *"Now the word of the LORD came to Jonah the son of Amittai, saying, ²"Arise, go to Nineveh, that great city,*

202

and proclaim against it, for their wickedness has come up before me."" (Jonah 1:1–2 NHEB.)

God is always in the habit of sending messengers. While it is in His nature to punish sin, He often holds back judgement until He has given a warning. The death of a sinner is not His desire, but multitudes have perished nonetheless.

Before the destruction of Sodom and Gomorrah, Lot's sons-in-law were offered the opportunity to be spared from the cities' impending destruction. Lot approached them, warning them of God's destruction coming upon those cities, but the warning sounded like a joke to these young men. They would later share the same fate with the rest of the cities' inhabitants due to their failure to show caution. They had forfeited their opportunity of salvation from damnation because they refused to believe Lot's message.

Let us not be hasty in judging these men but rather learn from their experience. As a result of our existence in and constant interaction with our physical world, we tend to become so engrossed with this realm that we become passive to spiritual things because we try to understand the things of the spirit with our physical experience. Taking the sons-in-law who were pledged to marry Lot's daughters as a case study, they may have thought Lot was joking because they tried to compare what he said to their physical experience – what they perceived to be possible or what they have witnessed during their lifetime on earth. They had never seen God destroy cities before; hence, what Lot said sounded like a big joke. The tragedy is that, even though what Lot said sounded like a joke, they still perished.

Regarding spiritual things, faith comes before understanding. *"By faith, we understand that the ages were prepared by the word of God..."* (Hebrews 11:3 NHEB.) Note the words "By faith, we understand." If we wait to understand before we believe, we might never believe and never understand altogether. But if we are willing to believe, we will understand. If these men had chosen to believe what

Lot said to them, even though what he said did not make any sense to them at that time, when they would have reached Zoar everything would have been clearer to them. When the gospel is preached to us, everything will gradually become clearer with the Holy Spirit's help if we choose to believe. *"For indeed we have had good news preached to us, even as they also did, but the word they heard did not profit them, because they were not united by faith with those who heard. ³For we who have believed do enter into that rest..."* (Hebrews 4:2–3 NHEB.) At the end of our lives we will be glad we believed. Let us not forget that faith entails trusting God for the unseen; it is no longer faith if we trust God for what we see.

Just as Lot warned the young men concerning the impending doom coming upon the cities of Sodom and Gomorrah, God is still sending messengers to warn the world through the gospel. The gospel of Christ, the message of salvation, is not only a message of the love of a Father for a sinful world, but is also a message of warning of God's impending judgement. Judgement is coming on this world and God has not been silent about it. The Bible is filled with several warnings from the prophets of old, our Lord Jesus Christ and the New Testament's epistles. Despite several warnings of His coming judgement the disposition of many to the gospel is quite unfortunate. *"For the message about the cross is foolishness to those who are perishing, but to us who are being saved it is the power of God."* (1 Corinthians 1:18 NHEB.)

Some do not outrightly reject the gospel but are indifferent or passive towards it. Note that being passive about the gospel is no different from rejecting it. Whether a man rejects the gospel with antagonism or he rejects it passively he remains on the path of damnation if he refuses to believe in it and act upon his faith. One can easily recognise those heading for destruction by how they treat God's instructions in the Bible regarding the salvation of their souls. It would have taken believing and acting on Lot's message for his sons-in-law to be saved. Likewise, our faith must be backed up by a lifestyle of absolute obedience to God. For the young men, they were to come out of the city; for us today, we are to come out from the world by keeping ourselves undefiled by the world.

What is God commanding us to do that is not for our good? The cost of negligence is greater than whatever reason we would give ourselves for not paying heed to the gospel of Christ. Let us do our utmost not to despise the salvation that has been made available for us. *"²⁶For if we sin willfully after we have received the knowledge of the truth, there remains no more sacrifice for sins, ²⁷but a certain fearful expectation of judgment, and a fierceness of fire which will devour the adversaries. ²⁹How much worse punishment, do you think, will he be judged worthy of, who has trodden under foot the Son of God, and has counted the blood of the covenant with which he was sanctified an unholy thing, and has insulted the Spirit of grace?"* (Hebrews 10:26, 27, 29 NHEB.)

TOPIC 6: LOOKING BACK

GENESIS 19:17, 26

Towards the end of his life and ministry, Apostle Paul used athletics to illustrate our walk with God when writing to his spiritual son. He said: *"if anyone competes in athletics, he is not crowned unless he has competed by the rules."* (2 Timothy 2:5 NHEB.) Paul pointed out the requirement for being crowned at the end of our journey to heaven: complete obedience to God's instructions.

The story of Lot's wife is sad and should teach every child of God the need to run the Christian race according to instructions and keep his eye on making heaven. The angels who led Lot's family out of Sodom were very clear and specific in their instruction: *"Do not look behind you..."* (Genesis 19:17 NHEB.) As clear as it was, this instruction is what Lot's wife flouted, and she paid with her life.

For Lot and his family, escape from destruction was not a done-and-dusted deal. Their final deliverance was promised but it would be preposterous for them to assume that it was guaranteed irrespective of how they treated the angels' instruction. Likewise, as long as we are still on this heavenly journey, no one's final salvation is guaranteed as signed and sealed until the end of life; the life we live is very important if we are to finish the race successfully. Lessons from Lot's wife's experience are essential; Jesus admonished us, saying, *"Remember Lot's wife."* (Luke 17:32 NHEB.) Parents usually use the word "remember" to emphasise things they want their children to take seriously.

What should we remember about Lot's wife? Lot's wife had looked back with a desire for the life she left behind in Sodom. We should remember that, although Lot's wife escaped the fire and brimstone at Sodom, her looking back, probably desiring the life she left behind, made her miss the final deliverance. Repentance is not final; we need to remain focused until we leave this life in death or Christ's second coming. Hebrews 12:1–2 says: *"Therefore let us also, seeing we are surrounded by so great a cloud of witnesses, lay aside every weight and the sin which so easily entangles us, and let us run with patience the race that is set before us, ²looking to Jesus, the author and finisher of our faith…"* (NHEB.)

The lure of a past life, the attachment to all its pleasures and the attendant memories could prove to be a colossal impediment to a believer's progressive walk with God. "Looking back", in a broader Christian perspective, entails a craving and a decision to return to an old sinful way of life to satisfy carnal indulgences. The greatest tragedy of running the Christian race lies in not running to the end, sacrificing so much during one's lifetime only to have the same fate as those who made no commitment whatsoever to God.

Looking back is not only when we go back to sin; it can also be when we get distracted by things that might be good but are not needful for the kingdom at that moment. *"Another also said, "I want to follow you, Lord, but first allow me to bid farewell to those who are at my house." ⁶²But Jesus said to him, "No one, having put his hand to the plow, and looking back, is fit for the kingdom of God.""* (Luke 9:61–62 NHEB.) Jesus was not against saying "goodbye" to relations. The intended disciple asked to be allowed time to attain what we sometimes call "making the home front comfortable". People have often missed fulfilling God's assignment because they want everything to be perfect at the "home front" before facing kingdom work. For the purpose of that particular assignment, "home front" becomes a distraction and could cost us the kingdom. We could be wonderful children of our parents and members of our communities yet miss heaven because we fulfil our responsibilities to others at the expense of our salvation. These things are capable of making us look back and, like Lot's wife, miss our goal and make a shipwreck of our faith.

As long as we are still in this world, we should, at no point in our Christian race, say we have arrived and can afford to relax or look back. There is always the possibility of falling. Apostle Paul told us in Philippians 3:7–10 how he counted everything as loss for the sake of gaining Christ and knowing the power of his resurrection. *"However, what things were gain to me, these have I counted loss for Christ. ⁸More than that, I count all things to be loss for the excellency of the knowledge of Christ Jesus, my Lord, for whom I suffered the loss of all things, and count them nothing but refuse, that I may gain Christ ⁹and be found in him, not having a righteousness of my own, that which is of the law, but that which is through faith in Christ, the righteousness which is from God by faith; ¹⁰that I may know him, and the power of his resurrection, and the fellowship of his sufferings, becoming conformed to his death"* (NHEB). Then he went ahead to tell us the reason he let go of everything the way he did: *"if by any means I may attain to the resurrection from the dead."* (Philippians 3:11 NHEB.) Paul meant that, even at his level, he could miss the resurrection of the saints if he was not careful. It was not yet a done-and-dusted conclusion. That was why he continued in subsequent verses: *"Brothers, I do not regard myself as having taken hold of it, but one thing I do. Forgetting the things which are behind, and reaching forward to*

*the things which are ahead, ¹⁴I press on toward the goal for the
prize of the high calling of God in Christ Jesus."* (Philippians
3:13–14 NHEB.) It was when Paul knew that his time for departure
was near that he wrote in his second letter to Timothy, with utmost
certainty: *"For I am already being offered, and the time of my
departure has come. ⁷I have fought the good fight. I have finished
the course. I have kept the faith. ⁸From now on, there is stored up
for me the crown of righteousness, which the Lord, the righteous
judge, will give to me on that day; and not to me only, but also to
all those who have loved his appearing."* (2 Timothy 4:6–8 NHEB.)
Until the end, he never relaxed nor looked back.

In our heavenly race we have Jesus as our trainer. He trains us through
His word and helps us through the Holy Spirit. Whenever we
experience difficulty or feel like looking back we should cry out to
Him for help. He is ever willing to help. Heaven is not for those Peter
described as "pigs" and "dogs", those who go back to the mud they
were taken from or those who go back to their vomit. Heaven is for
overcomers, those who remain focused on heaven as their goal.

TOPIC 7: INCEST

GENESIS 19:30–38

Incest is a sexual relationship between members of the same family
or individuals closely related by blood, such as a parent and a
child, brother and sister, cousins, uncle and niece, nephew and aunt
(Oxford Learners Dictionary, 2022). It was one of God's prohibitions
to the Israelites: they were not to marry or have sexual relationships
with close family members. Incest is an act abominable before God
and a deviation from the acceptable nature of relationships between
people of the same kinship.

Following Sodom and Gomorrah's destruction, Lot's choice to settle
in a secluded mountain along with his daughters rather than his initial
decision to dwell in Zoar set up the stage for the repulsive incident of

incest that ensued after that. Having found themselves isolated in a cave with their father, Lot's daughters' despair and anxiety that their family line would be extinct drove them to a desperate decision to engage their father in a sexual affair to procreate through him. The first daughter said to the younger, *"there is not a man in the earth to come in to us after the manner of all the earth."* (Genesis 19:31 NHEB.) From her statement it can be inferred that the rationale behind her action was that she meant there was no man around where they dwelt for procreation except their father.

Whatever her reasons may be, it does not justify the act; they would have consulted their father, who would have advised them better. Although God had not expressly spoken against incest at this time, and it was an action done to preserve their family lineage, the very fact that they had to get their father drunk before they carried out the act with him shows how unnatural and ungodly the action was. They knew that their father would never have consented to it if they had approached him. This suggests that they might have suppressed their consciences in carrying out the act. Not only is their action reproachable, but it is also inexcusable and should not be emulated. Resulting from this incestuous act, the first daughter gave birth to a son – Moab – and the second daughter also gave birth to a son – Ben-Ammi.

Although marriages between close relatives were permitted at some point in man's history, sexual relations between parents and children have never been allowed in any dispensation. There was a culture that existed in the times of the patriarchs regarding marriage from a person's family. Abraham was married to his half-sister, Sarah. When it was time for his son Isaac to be married, he did not want him to marry one of the Canaanite women in the land in which they dwelt. He instead sent for a wife, Rebekah, from among his relatives, for his son. Later on, God explicitly prohibited marital union between close relatives in the law. Leviticus Chapter 18:6 depicts God's commandments against sexual relations between close relatives. *"None of you shall approach anyone who are his close relatives, to uncover their nakedness: I am the LORD."* (NHEB.)

Any sexual relationship with a close relative is a sin against God and should not be practised. Considering God's displeasure with incestuous behaviours, perpetrators must seek repentance for the salvation of their souls. In the same vein, they must maintain a constant connection and communion with God by cultivating a relationship with Him. Galatians 5:16 says: *"But I say, walk by the Spirit, and you will not carry out the desires of the flesh."* (NHEB.) They must be sure to live in fear of God by acquainting and adhering to His word.

CHAPTER 20

TOPIC 1: TRUST IN GOD'S PROTECTION

GENESIS 20:1–3

The exclusivity of divine protection revolves around an assurance of safety contingent on the cordiality of our relationship with God.

God's love for us can be likened to parental love for their children. The parent is obliged to protect their children. In the same manner, God extends His protection towards those that are His – that is, those who are devoted to serving and pleasing Him.

This chapter records the second scenario in which Abraham and Sarah lied about their relationship. The first case was when, while on their way to Egypt, Abraham requested that Sarah say they were siblings rather than married, to prevent any harm coming to him (Genesis 12:10–20). Now in this chapter the same deceitful method is put into play.

A lie is anything done to deceive. Some lies are in action – non-verbal – while the majority are spoken. Many lies come instantly – they are either compulsive or habitual. At other times, people sit down, take time to plan, and sometimes test run a lie before administering it to their target. Abraham and Sarah's lying to Abimelech was a well-thought-out plan – a conspiracy. Although Sarah was originally Abraham's half-sister, when they got married they were no longer recognised as siblings but as a couple, so introducing her as his sister was a lie.

People try to excuse these incidents by saying that Abraham told a half-truth and that Sarah was his half-sister. But the truth of the matter is that Abraham lied; if he had been sincere he would have explained in both cases that Sarah was his half-sister whom he had later married. God did not rebuke him for these incidents. The Bible does not mention why.

God would still have protected Abraham from Abimelech even if he had not lied. Christians should not emulate Abraham's fear and subsequent lie. One might say that God never mentioned it – whether in correction or judgement, but the fact that God never mentioned it does not mean He approved of it. For us, in the New Testament, we know it is wrong. Revelation 21:8 says, *"But for the cowardly, unbelieving, abominable, murderers, sexually immoral, sorcerers, idolaters, and all liars, their part is in the lake that burns with fire and sulfur, which is the second death."* (NHEB.)

However, one thing is consistent in both instances: God still protects His children as a hen would her chicks. Although the situation Abraham found himself in was of his making God still stood by him by rectifying the issue. God appeared in a dream to Abimelech, warning him of what would befall him if he did not return Sarah to Abraham.

King Jehoshaphat faced a challenge that threatened the safety of his kingdom and needed protection. The vast army from Moab, Ammon and their allies, were coming to war against him. He sought the Lord's protection and the battle was won without bows and arrows because he trusted in the Lord. 2 Chronicles 20:22–24 says, *"When they began to sing and to praise, the LORD set ambushers against the children of Ammon, Moab, and Mount Seir, who had come against Judah; and they were struck. ²³For the children of Ammon and Moab stood up against the inhabitants of Mount Seir, utterly to kill and destroy them: and when they had made an end of the inhabitants of Seir, everyone helped to destroy another. ²⁴When Judah came to the place overlooking the wilderness, they looked at the multitude; and look, they were dead bodies fallen to the earth, and there were none who escaped."* (NHEB.) It is better to trust in the Lord than to put confidence in human strategies for protection.

Daniel was another person in the Bible greatly beloved by God and who also enjoyed divine protection. The officials in Babylon had attempted to kill Daniel. They ganged up and proposed to the king that anyone who prays to any other god or human being apart from the king within 30 days should be thrown into the lion's den. The king obliged their request, not being aware of the intent behind it. By dishonouring the king's decree, Daniel honoured God; he prayed to God as usual. He was thrown into the den of lions as a result. God rescued him by sending His angel to shut the mouths of the lions. *"Then the king arose very early in the morning, and went in haste to the den of lions. ²⁰When he came near to the den to Daniel, he cried with a lamentable voice. The king spoke and said to Daniel, "Daniel, servant of the living God. Is your God, whom you serve continually, able to deliver you from the lions?" ²¹Then said Daniel to the king, "O king, live forever. ²²My God has sent his angel, and has shut the lions' mouths, and they have not hurt me; because before him innocence was found in me; and also before you, O king, have I done no wrong.""* (Daniel 6:19–22 NHEB.)

God's commitment to the wellbeing of His own is also revealed in the life of Job. Although God allowed Satan to put him through several trials, God still set a limit. There are times when God, rather than deliver us, allows us to go through certain trials to work out His purpose in our lives. We should trust that His will is best for our lives in such instances. We are to trust Him even if He requires us to lay down our lives in the process.

Let us be assured of God's protection, for *"He who dwells in the secret place of the Most High will rest in the shadow of Shaddai."* (Psalm 91:1 NHEB.) All we have to do is love Him and dwell in His shelter. The assurance as expressed in that Psalm should build our trust in the ability of God to protect us, and we should be willing to accept whatever is the outcome of our situation, knowing full well that the worst thing that can happen to us is not physical death. Paul said this about physical death: *"to die is gain."* (Philippians 1:21 NHEB.) The gain here is eternal life for Christians. 2 Corinthians 4:17 says: *"For this momentary light affliction is working for us a far more exceeding and everlasting weight of glory"* (NHEB).

We are God's treasures and He protects His treasures jealously. It is true that God jealously guards His own; however, there are times He might choose not to deliver us from danger physically as He did for Daniel. For John the Baptist, God decided to allow him to be put to death after fulfilling his purpose on earth. Death could even be considered a tool of God's protection in that God could be using death to take His children out of this sinful world for their salvation. Isaiah 57:1 says, *"The righteous perishes, and no man lays it to heart; and merciful men are taken away, none considering that the righteous is taken away from the evil."* (NHEB.) Also, Psalm 116:15 says, *"Precious in the sight of the LORD is the death of his faithful ones."* (NHEB.)

(For more on Abraham and Sarah's lie, see Chapter 12, Topic 3, Trust in God's Protection)

TOPIC 2: BEING A SOURCE OF TEMPTATION

GENESIS 20:1–6

Temptation is an inevitable part of life. It seeks to influence our choices and appeals to man's sinful nature, which is prone to deviating from doing right. Everybody has been faced with the temptation of doing the wrong thing. Sometimes it arises from within us; at other times it is instigated by others. Temptation tends to lead people astray. Therefore, we must guard against it and avoid being a source of temptation to others.

In this passage, we find Abraham putting Abimelech in a position of sinning. Abraham lied to Abimelech regarding his relationship with

Sarah, because of Sarah's beauty and his fear for his life, just as he had lied to Pharaoh. Acting on this information, Abimelech ignorantly took Sarah as his wife and would have incurred God's wrath if God had not prevented him from doing so. Although Abraham did not directly suggest that Abimelech should take his wife, his decision to conceal the truth from him misled Abimelech, putting the life of the king of Gerar at risk. Abimelech was unhappy with what Abraham had done so he reprimanded Abraham, saying: *"What have you done to us? How have I sinned against you, that you have brought on me and on my kingdom a great sin? You have done deeds to me that ought not to be done." *[10]*Abimelech said to Abraham, "What did you see, that you have done this thing?"* (Genesis 20:9–10 NHEB.) How right Abimelech was. Abraham had acted selfishly in an attempt to save his life, which was the opposite of the attitude that should be expected from someone who fears God. It is ironic when God's children put themselves in positions in which they are corrected by unbelievers on matters of godly living.

God's children should be light to the world but, just like Abraham, many have become a source of temptation to others, leading others into sin directly or indirectly. We can directly influence people to sin by deliberately suggesting to them or encouraging them to do things against God's word. Job's wife was one character in the Bible who directly suggested to her husband to sin against God because of the calamity that befell their family, *"Then his wife said to him, "Do you still maintain your integrity? Renounce God, and die.""* (Job 2:9 NHEB.) While Job was trying to be upright in the face of a tumultuous experience, his wife was trying to destroy his remaining faith. Instead of encouraging her husband she was inciting him to sin. Similarly, Jeroboam was responsible for causing the whole nation of Israel to sin, so much so that in the chronicles of the kings – 1 and 2 Kings – he was frequently referenced for his part in making Israel sin.

It is also possible to lead people to sin indirectly. While we may not offer or suggest wrong acts to people, some of our actions may actually lead people to sin. Even when our actions are not sinful in themselves, if they hurt others' consciences or cause them to sin, we must refrain from those actions. For instance, if a mature believer encourages a younger believer to drink by drinking, and that younger believer gets into the habit of drinking, getting drunk in the process, the mature believer has become the source of temptation that indirectly lured the younger believer to sin against God. *"Do not overthrow God's work for food's sake. All things indeed are clean, however it is evil for anyone who creates a stumbling block by eating. ²¹It is good to not eat meat, drink wine, or do anything by which your brother stumbles, or is offended, or is made weak."* (Romans 14:20–21 NHEB.)

No action is worth carrying out, no matter how enticing or beneficial, if it can mislead others or cause them to stumble. This may include our choices of clothing, business, food and the company we keep. If our careless, seductive dressings, conduct in our homes and offices, or the way we talk lures others to sin we are guilty of being a source of temptation. *"Therefore, if food causes my brother to stumble, I will eat no meat forevermore, that I do not cause my brother to stumble."* (1 Corinthians 8:13 NHEB.) Though the person that yields to temptation will not be declared innocent, the one who leads another astray will be held responsible for the part he played, *"It is impossible that no occasions of stumbling should come, but woe to him through whom they come. ²It would be better for him if a millstone were hung around his neck, and he were thrown into the sea, rather than that he should cause one of these little ones to stumble."* (Luke 17:1–2 NHEB.)

Our freedom to do what we feel is good for us or our safety is inseparably tied to our Christian responsibility; this is godly living. When those around us see us failing to uphold Christian values, they may not feel motivated to emulate Christ-like attitudes. No Christian should be the reason why someone whom Christ died for perished. Therefore, we must live in the consciousness that people observe us as believers, and, as such, we must be cautious of how we live our lives. If we sincerely love others as we should, our freedom of choice should be less important. We are called to spur people to righteousness, not lead them to sin.

TOPIC 3: TAKING GOD'S WORD SERIOUSLY

GENESIS 20:3–16

Having been misled by Abraham about Sarah's identity, Abimelech found himself treading on dangerous territory after taking Sarah as his wife. As a result of his innocence God visited Abimelech in a dream and warned him to return Sarah to her husband or forfeit his life if he refused. Abimelech's prompt reaction in obeying God's instruction serves as a lesson for us on taking God's word seriously. When Abimelech awoke from his sleep he wasted no time in sending for Abraham, *"Abimelech rose early in the morning, and called all his servants..."* (Genesis 20:8 NHEB.) He was not happy that Abraham had told him a lie concerning his relationship with Sarah, but that did not stop him from giving him lots of gifts. When we examine Abimelech's displeasure at Abraham and his benevolence towards him afterwards we can tell that his generosity resulted from his fear for God because of the revelation he had had.

Taking God's word seriously entails approaching it reverently, treating it respectfully and obeying it completely. God still speaks to men today through dreams on specific matters, just as He spoke to Abimelech. But for the guidance we will need to navigate our way through the journey of life He has given us the Bible. Over the years, He has inspired men to compile His instructions written down over centuries into one book – the Bible. Ignorance is not excusable, as failure to adhere to God's directives will result in wasted potentials and abuse of God's original intent for mankind.

Just as most products come with an owner's manual on how they must be used, God – our Creator – has given us the Bible as our manual on how best to lead our lives. The Bible is a manual that contains both divine revelations and human experiences, which serve as a template and guide for how we should live. It should be studied with the sole aim of attaining salvation. It is the word of God, inspired by God Himself. 2 Timothy 3:16–17 says: *"All Scripture is God-breathed and profitable for teaching, for reproof, for correction, and for training in righteousness, ¹⁷that the person of God may be complete, thoroughly equipped for every good work."* (NHEB.)

Through the Bible, God reveals Himself, His will and our purpose to us. Some believers tend to treat the Bible with little regard and take its content lightly. They tend to regard messages they receive through such means as visions, trances and prophecies more highly than the Bible, forgetting that it is the same God who gives revelations or shows visions that also speaks through the Bible. While God talks to us through other means, the Bible remains the fundamental means by which God talks to us.

The first step to taking the Bible seriously is by studying it with the sole purpose of our soul's salvation in mind. It should be understood that we cannot live our lives to please God if we do not know God's word – the Bible. God admonishes us about this in Joshua 1:8: *"This book of the law shall not depart out of your mouth, but you shall meditate on it day and night, that you may observe to do according to all that is written in it: for then you shall make your way prosperous, and then you shall have good success."* (NHEB.) Reading the Bible is essential for obtaining the truth about the mind of God. While messages from men of God and revelations are crucial, their truthfulness should be verified from the Bible. *"Now these were more noble than those in Thessalonica, in that they received the word with all readiness of the mind, examining the Scriptures daily to see whether these things were so."* (Acts 17:11 NHEB.)

Furthermore, when we take the Bible seriously, we will live according to its instructions. Psalm 119:11 says: *"In my heart I have hidden your word, that I might not sin against you."* (NHEB.) Our reverence for the Bible prompts us to obey the commands embedded in it. The way God warned Abimelech not to sin against Him in a dream is the same way in which He warns us through the Bible to prevent us from sinning. In the same vein, God is pleased with those who take the message of repentance and salvation in the Bible seriously by mourning whenever they stumble. Isaiah 66:2 says: *""For all these things has my hand made, and so all these things came to be," says the LORD: "but to this man will I look, to him who is humble and of a contrite spirit, and who trembles at my word.""* (NHEB.)

Taking God's word seriously also entails a prompt response to His word, just as Abimelech responded swiftly to God's directive. However, there is a tendency to be hesitant when it comes to obeying the Bible's instructions. The sense of urgency is often missing due to unbelief or/and the priority placed on other revelations such as dreams, visions, trances and prophecies. King Josiah's response to coming across God's word during his reign is worthy of emulation. After listening to the message from the scroll concerning God's law and realising that they had not been keeping those laws, instantly he tore his clothes and sought God for mercy. *"Shaphan the scribe told the king, saying, "Hilkiah the priest has delivered a scroll to me." Shaphan read it before the king. ¹¹It happened, when the king had heard the words of the scroll of the law, that he tore his clothes. ¹²The king commanded Hilkiah the priest, and Ahikam the son of Shaphan, and Achbor the son of Micaiah, and Shaphan the scribe, and Asaiah the king's servant, saying, ¹³"Go inquire of the LORD for me, and for the people, and for all Judah, concerning the words of this scroll that is found; for great is the wrath of the LORD that is kindled against us, because our fathers have not listened to the words of this scroll, to do according to all that which is written concerning us.""* (2 Kings 22:10–13 NHEB.) This attitude saved him from witnessing the destruction that came on Judah. It is sacrosanct to accord the Bible with the regard it deserves.

The worth of the content of the Bible will always remain invaluable and must be treated as such. We must also ensure we take all God's words recorded in the Bible seriously, not some of them or those that suit us. This should be done with an emphasis on salvation. In our treatment of the word of God, it will be eternal damnation for us if we disregard and reject it and eternal salvation if we treasure and obey it.

CHAPTER 21

TOPIC 1: FULFILMENT OF GOD'S PROMISE

GENESIS 21:1–7

When a promise is made to someone they become expectant, and disappointed when the promise is not fulfilled. The failure to fulfil promises could be due to man's fallible nature, among other factors, even if reneging on the promise was not intended. This is not the same with God.

One of God's attributes that distinguish Him from man is His unflinching commitment to the fulfilment of His promises. No factor can hinder God from fulfilling what He has promised, but He can withhold or withdraw His promise from the recipient if he rebels against Him. God's personality is characterised by integrity. We are assured that God is faithful to His word and trustworthy, as stated in Numbers 23:19: *"God is not a man, that he should lie, nor the son of man, that he should repent. Has he said, and will he not do it? Or has he spoken, and will he not make it good?"* (NHEB.)

From Abraham's story, God demonstrated His faithfulness in keeping His promises, though the fulfilment of the promise took long. This miraculous work of God also highlights that even the righteous are not exempted from life's trials.

God promised to make Abraham a great nation, though Sarah – Abraham's wife – was barren and advanced in age. To man, the promise was impossible to fulfil considering the physiological state of Sarah's reproductive system due to her advancement in age.

Notwithstanding, God fulfilled His promise without fail; Sarah conceived and bore a son for Abraham at 90 years old.

God brings joy and laughter out of seemingly hopeless situations. Abraham and Sarah's life is laced with several lessons for us. The birth of Isaac is a vivid demonstration of God's power over nature. The promises of God are not dependent on our natural condition and circumstances because God can walk over those seemingly difficult and humanly inexplicable situations. Not only is nothing impossible for God, but nothing is difficult for Him either and no situation is hopeless with Him. There is no situation God cannot fix; neither is it ever too late for Him to act. God is more powerful than we can ever imagine and He reveals His infinite superiority over the challenges of life in situations such as this.

In fulfilling His promises time is never a barrier because God exists out of time and season; He does not change with time. Asides from the promise of Isaac's birth God promised Abraham that all nations of the earth would be blessed through him. This promise was fulfilled in Christ, hundreds of years after Abraham had died. Through the sacrifice of Jesus on the cross all nations of the earth can receive the blessing of salvation. No matter how long it takes, none of God's promises ever go unfulfilled. *"He has remembered his covenant forever, the word which he commanded to a thousand generations"* (Psalm 105:8 NHEB).

Worthy of note also is the fact that the fulfilment of God's promise is according to His timing. Human nature is associated with impatience; we typically want everything done quickly and resort to taking matters into our own hands to help God fulfil His promises if it seems that what we expect is not forthcoming. We ought to learn to trust Him with all our being. God sometimes allows us to undergo the process of waiting for the fulfilment of His promise to help us develop virtues, such as perseverance and trust in Him. At other times He may let us pass through certain circumstances to bring about His sovereign will. God fulfils His promises to the very details of His word.

One thing that thwarts God's promises for our lives is sin. That was the case with Eli and his sons. God once promised that the priesthood would not leave Eli's house forever, but God withdrew that promise because of sin. *"Therefore the LORD, the God of Israel, says, 'I said indeed that your house, and the house of your father, should walk before me forever.' But now the LORD says, 'Be it far from me; for those who honor me I will honor, and those who despise me shall be lightly esteemed.'"* (1 Samuel 2:30 NHEB.) God cannot lie; neither would He decide to deceive anyone. God watches over His word to fulfil it. *"Look, the LORD's hand is not shortened, that it can't save; neither his ear heavy, that it can't hear: ²but your iniquities have separated between you and your God, and your sins have hidden his face from you, so that he will not hear."* (Isaiah 59:1–2 NHEB.) Not only is God faithful, but He also honours His word.

Our hope and the source of our joy are in God's faithfulness in keeping and making good His promises. We may be weak and discouraged and the excitement of the promise may fade because of circumstances, but never should we give up on God.

Sometimes we may feel that God's promises are not coming to fulfilment. At such points in life we must remain steadfast in faith and be faithful to God without wavering while we keep trusting His will and accepting that whatever happens is best for us at all times. And more importantly, we should remain steadfast in faith because we have the greatest promise ever that we must set our eyes upon, a promise that is unshakeable, a promise so beautiful and endearing – the promise of eternal life in paradise with God and all the saints. This is the greatest promise ever. This is the promise our very being must register with, in faith. *"This is the promise which he promised us, the everlasting life."* (1 John 2:25 NHEB.) This promise is the reason why no situation should ever make us go against the word of God. Because God's promises always come to fulfilment.

Let us believe God's promise concerning our eternal salvation and, at the same time, strive to live our lives in such a way that His eternal purpose for us is not thwarted.

TOPIC 2: HOPELESS SITUATION

GENESIS 21:14–19

Challenges in life are not strange; they are natural. Although they come in various forms, and people give them different names, one thing is sure: no one goes through life without a taste of them.

Have you ever desperately needed help but neither seen help coming nor the possibility of having any in the future? Have you ever given up on life, or tried looking into the future and seen darkness and hopelessness? At such moments, you may cry out or feel despair, not because you expected anyone to hear and help out but because that was the only expression your heart could utter. If you have experienced any of these you can identify with Hagar's ordeal in the desert of Beersheba when Abraham sent her away from his family.

On the day Isaac was weaned Abraham held a celebration and during the celebration Sarah saw Ishmael mocking Isaac. She demanded that Ishmael and his mother be immediately thrown out of the house. After initially showing reluctance but being instructed by God to heed Sarah's demand, Abraham sent Ishmael and Hagar away. Given bread and a bottle of water, Hagar and Ishmael departed and wandered in the wilderness of Beersheba. Soon, the provisions were exhausted, and death from thirst stared them in the face. Hagar, when she could no longer bear the child's anguish, had to leave him under a shrub and walk a reasonable distance away so she would not see the child die. Few situations would be considered more hopeless than this.

God is known for intervening in hopeless situations. He intervened in Hagar's case. First, God spoke to Hagar. In a helpless situation, hearing the voice of God brings succour. For a child of God, even when the solution does not come immediately, just hearing God speak to your spirit as you read the Bible or listen to messages has a way of refreshing your resolve to trust Him more. Jeremiah 15:16 says: *"Your words were found, and I ate them; and your words were to me a joy and the rejoicing of my heart: for I am called by your name, LORD, God of hosts.* " (NHEB.) In hopeless situations, what we should desire most is to hear God speak to our hearts. Let us know that nothing gives hope in a hopeless situation as much as the word of God.

Another thing God did for Hagar in her hopelessness was to open her eyes to the solution to her problem. It could be that the well Hagar saw was there all along or that God brought it into being as He spoke. In any case, God opened her eyes to a solution. In hopeless situations, God can open our eyes to an already existing solution or create a solution that was not there before. There had been testimonies of people who had been in hopeless situations financially, and God intervened in their cases by showing them a particular product to sell, investments to make or even specific skills to learn.

Hopelessness is when you find yourself in a situation in which there is no expectation for a positive outcome; it is finding yourself at your rope's end. Many things can bring us to the point of hopelessness, situations in which we lose confidence in the future. However, this is when we ought to trust God the more. It is more common to trust God when things move according to plan and expectations, but true faith means trusting God even when you go through the valley of the shadow of death. The fact that we do not see God does not mean that He is not aware of all we are going through. The fact that Hagar felt alone did not mean that she was alone. If God could show up for Hagar, an Egyptian slave whose connection with God would have been her relationship with Sarah and Abraham, know that God is fully aware and has plans concerning your case. *"He who implanted the ear, won't he hear? He who formed the eye, won't he see?"* (Psalm 94:9 NHEB.)

No matter how hopeless a situation might look, it is always within God's power to change it. Peradventure, He does not intervene at that moment as expected; we must maintain our peace and remain undaunted in our faith in Him. We must not act outside God's word in our attempt to find solutions. In those hopeless moments, console

yourself with these words: ***"Can a woman forget her nursing child,
that she should not have compassion on the son of her womb? Yes,
these may forget, yet I will not forget you."*** (Isaiah 49:15 NHEB.)
These are very comforting words, directly from the mouth of God.
We are never to compromise our faith because we are looking for a
way out of seemingly hopeless situations; instead, we should put our
faith in God. Let the story of Hagar strengthen our faith, for God
came to her aid right there in the wilderness.

There are times when God delivers us as He delivered Hagar, and
there are times God instead gives us the grace to go through the trial.
Paul narrated how he went through what he described as a thorn in
his flesh – a messenger of Satan sent to torment him. For reasons best
known to God, God refused Paul's request for deliverance. Paul said,
***"Concerning this thing, I begged the Lord three times that it might
depart from me. [9] He has said to me, "My grace is sufficient for you,
for power is made perfect in weakness." Most gladly therefore I
will rather glory in my weaknesses, that the power of Christ may
rest on me. [10] Therefore I take pleasure in weaknesses, in injuries,
in necessities, in persecutions, in distresses, for Christ's sake.
For when I am weak, then am I strong."*** (2 Corinthians 12:8–10
NHEB.) Sometimes, we may have to go through life in that situation;
if that is the case, we must remain faithful to Him. God might have
permitted that situation to strengthen or test our faith in Him, or in
other instances, God might use it to show forth His glory. Making an
uncompromising resolution to remain faithful to God and allowing
His will to be fulfilled in any hopeless situation is a perfect way to
keep our hope alive in the face of despair.

TOPIC 3: DIVINE GUIDANCE

GENESIS 21:15–19

Imagine being in a dark, unfamiliar room; moving around would
not be so easy, would it? Or how about being lost in a forest without
a map or a compass? It is quite a scary thought having to figure out

your path, not knowing exactly where you will end up. Now, put a light in that unfamiliar, dark room and provide a compass to the one who is lost in the forest; things change immediately, right? This illustrates the need for guidance. Divine guidance is likened to the light that shows the way or the compass that directs our path.

In the Bible passage, after being told to leave her master's house with her son, Hagar found herself wandering in the desert with just a water jar whose content was spent, her teenage son and her shattered dream of being the mother of Abraham's heir. She did what a depressed mother would probably have done in such a hopeless situation: she kept the child away from her but not far from her watch, for she could not bear to see him die.

One of a mother's most heart-breaking moments is seeing her child cry for help and being unable to help. Hagar's situation was such that only God could help her. She was desperate and cried out in anguish. God heard her cry and opened her eyes to see a well of water not far from them. At that point, hope was restored; she filled the jar with water and gave the boy a drink as well.

It is not clear whether the well was there or not before she arrived there, but what is revealed here is the superiority of divine direction above human senses and understanding. There are instances when solutions to our situations are not too far away, but it takes divine leading to realise it.

The God who heard the cry of Hagar can do more for His children through Jesus Christ. Every believer needs divine guidance in their relationship with God for their sojourn through this gloomy earth.

There are times in our lives when we are confronted with overwhelmingly challenging situations and there appear not to be solutions in sight. At that point, where our human strength stops or we willingly hand over our struggles to God, God's intervention begins. When all options are exhausted, it is essential to acknowledge our human limitations and rely on God. Many of us make decisions based on our human understanding, and it is when we find ourselves stuck that we begin to seek God for direction. Some already have the path they desire to take; they just want God to endorse it. Men need guidance through life because their understanding and senses are unreliable. To trust in one's knowledge and understanding could be fatal. Who can genuinely lead us better than God, who sees the end from the beginning? When we rely on God, He will always direct us on the right path and approach to take. Proverbs 3:5–6 says, *"Trust in the LORD with all your heart, and do not lean on your own understanding. *In all your ways acknowledge him, and he will make your paths straight."* (NHEB.) One remarkable advantage of God's guidance is its accuracy. We can never make a mistake or make a wrong move if we rely on His guidance.

Another individual who benefited from God's direction was Isaac. Rather than him go down to Egypt as a result of famine, God appeared to him at Gerar and instructed him to stay in that land, that He was going to bless him there. God prospered him so much that his wealth began to intimidate the inhabitants of the land (Genesis 26:1–14).

There was also Peter. During the early days of Christianity, when the Jew–Gentile segregation was still in play, God showed Peter a vision, telling him to eat animals that were declared unclean in the laws of Moses. Afterwards, He told him that some men were coming to him and instructed him to go with them. Peter's obedience to this divine guidance led him to interact with the Gentiles, and that was a message that there is no segregation between Jews and Gentiles in Christ (Acts 10). If not for God's guidance, Peter would never have come to this realisation, because of his firm adherence to the Jewish traditions.

It is of the essence to note that sin hinders divine guidance. After Saul sinned and the presence of God left him, he was no longer a beneficiary of divine guidance. At a point in his life, when the Philistines gathered against him, he inquired of the Lord for guidance, but God did not respond. *"The Philistines gathered themselves together, and came and camped in Shunem: and Saul gathered all Israel together, and they camped in Gilboa. ⁵When Saul saw the army of the Philistines, he was afraid, and his heart trembled greatly. ⁶When Saul inquired of the LORD, The LORD did not answer him, neither by dreams, nor by Urim, nor by prophets."* (1 Samuel 28:4–6 NHEB.)

God does not intend to leave us to chance; He desires to reveal or guide us through the most appropriate path. Although there are several means by which God gives His children specific instructions such as angels, visions or leading of the Spirit, the general means by which God communicates with His children in this era is through His word – the Bible.

The credibility of instructions received from any other means of divine guidance can be ascertained when those instructions are compared with God's character and desires as revealed in the Bible. God's ultimate desire for mankind is that the whole world be saved and that we all live our lives by His word. When our minds are renewed and regularly refreshed by His word, we will be able to understand His good and perfect will for our lives. *"And do not be conformed to this world, but be transformed by the renewing of your mind, so that you may prove what is the good, well-pleasing, and perfect will of God."* (Romans 12:2 NHEB.)

Life is a journey and just like every other journey we need guidance. To get to heavenly glory we must be guided by the counsel of the Lord. Only by His counsel can we find eternal life. *"You will guide me with your counsel, and afterward receive me to glory."* (Psalm 73:24 NHEB.)

TOPIC 4: DOCUMENTATION OF AGREEMENT

GENESIS 21:22–32

There is a popular saying, "A faintest ink is sharper than the sharpest memory." This underpins the need to write things for recording purposes, retrieval when needed or evidence of people's rights and entitlements. When people agree on an issue the agreement should not be taken for granted. Documents with signatures and seals are proof of the legitimacy of transactions. It is advisable to register documents with appropriate agencies where necessary.

Every formal documentation of an agreement confirms that the agreement's contents are legally binding and can be validly used as indisputable proof of ownership or truthfulness of what has been agreed upon when the occasion demands. In documenting any form of agreement, it is imperative to have a vivid understanding of the agreement's terms before proceeding to seal it to prevent future denial or ambiguities of its interpretations. This was the nature of the agreement made between Abimelech and Abraham when Abraham dug a well in Beersheba. It must be said that this was an ancient way of formalising an agreement. Agreements were being sealed with human witnesses and, at times, with an oath. They knew there were tendencies for either people to forget or renege on what they agreed.

After Abimelech acknowledged God's proven presence with Abraham, he and Phicol, the commander of his army, came to Abraham, requesting him to swear by his God that he would reciprocate his goodness and kindness towards him since Abraham chose their territory as his dwelling place. Abraham concurred to do just as Abimelech demanded. Abraham took sheep and oxen and gave them to Abimelech and the two of them made a covenant. The reception of the seven ewe lambs by Abimelech represented his formal acknowledgement of Abraham as the well's owner.

The seal of agreement between Abraham and Abimelech exposes us to the significance of documenting any form of agreement. Abraham had mentioned a well of water Abimelech's servants had previously seized from him. Having an agreement was a sure way of preventing a repetition of such an incidence. The agreement contained mutual promises; there must be mutuality of commitments or obligations in any form of agreement involving two or more parties.

Many centuries after Abraham, Jeremiah bought a piece of land by the Lord's command and did proper documentation. *"I bought the field that was in Anathoth of Hanamel my uncle's son, and weighed him the money, even seventeen shekels of silver. ¹⁰I subscribed the deed, and sealed it, and called witnesses, and weighed him the money in the balances. ¹¹So I took the deed of the purchase, both that which was sealed, containing the terms and conditions, and that which was open; ¹²and I delivered the deed of the purchase to Baruch the son of Neriah, the son of Mahseiah, in the presence of Hanamel my uncle's son, and in the presence of the witnesses who subscribed the deed of the purchase, before all the Jews who sat in the court of the guard."* (Jeremiah 32:9–12 NHEB.)

Safekeeping of documents is essential; otherwise, the essence of the agreement could be lost if the document is lost or damaged. God instructed Jeremiah to keep the records safe in Jeremiah 32:13–14: *"I commanded Baruch before them, saying, ¹⁴'Thus says the LORD of hosts, the God of Israel: "Take these deeds, this deed of the purchase which is sealed, and this deed which is open, and put them in an earthen vessel; that they may continue many days."'"* (NHEB.)

In like manner, when you go into any transaction or agreement with another party, you are expected to document such transactions to prevent any future problems caused by the other party. Documentation helps prevent future issues that may have arisen if you had not documented them. We live in a world in which most people's words cannot be trusted. Therefore, it is imperative to document contracts or agreements so that the documents will show everyone your honesty and truthfulness if you are called upon. Any contract involving purchases – purchases of properties such as houses, lands and the like – should be documented and the documents carefully kept as proof of the contract for future reference. When parties make verbal agreements, there is a possibility of a breach of what was agreed; it becomes legally binding when the deal is formally documented in black and white.

Documenting an agreement is essential in a generation in which integrity has become scarce. In the case of violating the agreement, the written agreement may be presented as evidence to buttress the truthfulness of the transaction. This is not just about whether we trust the person. It is also about saving our successors from future conflicts. Wisdom is essential in dealing with others, especially when it has to do with material things. *"Wisdom is supreme. Get wisdom. Yes, though it costs all your possessions, get understanding."* (Proverbs 4:7 NHEB.) We are to be wise as serpents and harmless as doves.

CHAPTER 22

TOPIC 1: TEST AND TEMPTATION

GENESIS 22:1–2

How does a teacher know that his students are actually learning? He tests them! This test is not meant for the students to fail; it is to ascertain whether they have followed up with studies and are learning. Just as we are tested in our educational or career pursuits, the Christian life is saddled with various tests which serve to prove our knowledge and conviction in the word of God. These tests are not designed to make us fall, but to prove the genuineness of our conviction, faith in God and love for Him. 1 Peter 1:7 says: *"that the genuineness of your faith, which is more precious than gold that perishes even though it is tested by fire, may be found to result in praise, glory, and honor at the revelation of Jesus Christ"* (NHEB).

Genesis 22:1 says, *"It happened after these things, that God tested Abraham…"* (NHEB.) The Hebrew word from which the word "test" was translated is "nacah", which could be translated as "to tempt", "test", "try" or "prove". Some Bible versions translate the word as "tempt", which has caused arguments among people over whether God actually tempts people. Note that the word "tempt" in this context means the same thing as "test". The account of Abraham in Genesis 22 was a test and not a temptation, for God does not tempt anyone with evil. *"Let no one say when he is tempted, "I am tempted by God," for God cannot be tempted by evil, and he himself tempts no one."* (James 1:13 NHEB.)

To put something or someone to the test is to find out how good or true something or someone is. For Abraham, it was a test God used in appraising the level of his commitment.

The Lord is almighty and all-knowing, having nothing hidden from Him, seeing the end from the beginning. However, sometimes He relates with us at our level, not regarding His knowledge of the future. God tests us to prove what is in our hearts and how much regard we have for Him. He tests us to prove the innermost desires of our hearts. We might not know the nature of our hearts nor the disposition of our hearts towards God until He tries us. Tests reveal the strength of our faith and the depth of our love for God.

God tested Abraham by instructing him to take his only son, whom he loved, and sacrifice him as a burnt offering at the region of Moriah. God's intention was not to make him stumble or fall or even to kill Isaac but to prove the depth of Abraham's love for Him. God wanted to prove the disposition of the heart of Abraham towards Him. He set such a high standard for the test to reveal how far Abraham would be willing to go to obey Him. Not knowing why God had made such a demanding request, Abraham obeyed God promptly without questions. Abraham's obedience proved how much faith and reverence he had for God.

According to Deuteronomy 8:2, God did not only lead the Israelites through the wilderness for 40 years to humble them but also to test them to reveal the exact intent of their hearts – whether they would obey or disobey His commandments. *"You shall remember all the way which the LORD your God has led you these forty years in the wilderness, that he might humble you, to prove you, and to know what was in your heart, whether you would keep his commandments, or not."* (NHEB.)

When God tests His children, He expects us to make the right choice. Tests are not bad or evil; rather, they help to prove our level of commitment to God. Sometimes during our tests the devil introduces temptations to make us fall, and this God allows with one purpose in mind: to prove our genuineness and, in the process, solidify our character towards Him. In moments of tests or trials, Satan could make evil and enticing offers to us, suggestions that will involve us going against God's will to avoid the refining path ordained for us by God.

In the case of Job, Satan was an instrument in his test. Job was a righteous man. God even described him to the devil as a man who shuns evil. For Job to be described as a man who shuns evil implies that the devil would have tempted him countless times without success. Satan further requested permission from God for Job to be tested. He said to God: *""Does Job fear God for nothing? ¹⁰Haven't you made a hedge around him, and around his house, and around all that he has, on every side? You have blessed the work of his hands, and his substance is increased in the land. ¹¹But put forth your hand now, and touch all that he has, and he will renounce you to your face." ¹²The LORD said to Satan, "Look, all that he has is in your power. Only on himself do not put forth your hand." So Satan went forth from the presence of the LORD."* (Job 1:9–12 NHEB.)

Satan was telling God that Job's fear and reverence for Him was not for nothing; it was because God had blessed him and protected him on all sides. The way to prove that his love was true was for him to be afflicted. God permitted Satan to afflict Job severely, but Job remained committed to God. It is easy to praise God and be committed to Him when things are rosy, but it takes genuine faith and love for God to remain faithful and committed to Him when all things have fallen apart. The genuineness of Job's love for God was revealed in his trials. God tests us or permits trials to come our way to mould us and build us up to spiritual maturity. *"Count it all joy, my brothers, when you encounter various trials, ³knowing that the testing of your faith produces endurance. ⁴Let endurance have its perfect work, that you may be perfect and complete, lacking in nothing."* (James 1:2–4 NHEB.)

Temptation, on the other hand, is an enticement to sin. This enticement can either come from Satan or the desires of the carnal nature. Satan usually takes advantage of our carnal thoughts or desires to tempt us. James 1:14–15 says, *"But each one is tempted, when he is drawn away by his own lust, and enticed. [15] Then the lust, when it has conceived, bears sin; and the sin, when it is full grown, brings forth death."* (NHEB.)

God is never the author of temptation; neither will He lead us to sin. Tempting is part of Satan's ministry. Temptation aims to seduce or entice one to sin; it seeks to derail one from the will and purpose of God for his life. It is based on deception, and its sole aim is to alienate men from God, keep them spiritually dead and devoid of God's glory. An illustration that buttresses this truth is the story of Adam and Eve in the garden. Satan approached the woman as a friend and lured them into disobeying God, thereby bringing down God's judgement upon the entire human race.

It is imperative to note that, even though God permits His children to face temptations, He will not allow them to be tempted beyond what they can handle. 1 Corinthians 10:13 says: *"God is faithful, who will not allow you to be tempted above what you are able, but will with the temptation also make the way of escape, that you may be able to endure it."* (NHEB.) If we fail to overcome any temptation at any point in time, it is not because the temptation was too great for us but because we failed to exercise our dominion over sin, which was made available to us when we received Christ into our lives through faith in Him. A believer who overcomes a temptation gets strengthened in that aspect of temptation. A new believer who has just overcome a sinful habit becomes emboldened to believe that he can overcome it again. A Christian who fails repeatedly might begin to think victory is impossible. Backsliding is not far off if he is not careful. This is why we must be relentless and resolute in our pursuit of perfection.

Being tempted in itself is not a sin – Jesus Christ was tempted, and He was without sin. It is yielding to it that is a sin. We must recognise every temptation for what it truly is – a dangerous attempt to smear our relationship with the One who loves us the most and to rob us of eternal life.

It is important to note that though Satan is the root of temptations humans can sometimes be mediums through which temptations come. Therefore, in all our actions, we must be careful not to be a source of temptation to others. Let us ponder on these words of Christ; *"It is impossible that no occasions of stumbling should come, but woe to him through whom they come. ²It would be better for him if a millstone were hung around his neck, and he were thrown into the sea, rather than that he should cause one of these little ones to stumble."* (Luke 17:1–2 NHEB.)

Both tests and temptations are inevitable experiences in our Christian walk; however, they are not originated from the same source, nor do they have the same objective. Whether we are tempted or tested, our responses in each case should always be the same – to do God's will. Therefore, it is highly imperative to be profoundly conversant with God's word to help us respond to tests and temptations in absolute accordance with the will of God.

TOPIC 2: ABRAHAM'S OBEDIENCE

GENESIS 22:1–19

God jealously desires our hearts and He is unwilling to share them with anyone or anything else. Parts of our hearts will not suffice. Abraham's obedience was proof that God sat uncontestably on the throne of his heart, and nothing in his life was of more value to him than God.

Obedience from time past has been essential in the relationship between God and man. It is adjudged as even better than animal sacrifice in 1 Samuel 15:22: *"Samuel said, "Has the LORD as great delight in burnt offerings and sacrifices, as in obeying the voice of the LORD? Look, to obey is better than sacrifice, and to listen than the fat of rams.""* (NHEB.) Obedience is the only determining factor in our love for God as well as our relationship with Him. *"One who says, "I know him," and does not keep his commandments, is a liar, and the truth is not in him. ⁵But whoever keeps his word, God's love has truly been perfected in him. This is how we know that we are in him"* (1 John 2:4–5 NHEB).

Looking back at Abraham's life, we see the continuous obedience he displayed towards God's instructions. From when God had instructed him to leave his home to the place God was going to show him, down to this crucial point in his life, he had always been a man of obedience. But here is the greatest test of them all: God was asking him to take his son – someone he loved so dearly – to the region of Moriah, look him in the eyes and kill him as a sacrifice. What an enormous demand! There was no doubt that Abraham loved Isaac and would have willingly given up anything, including his own life, for the boy. Notice God's emphasis in His statement *"Now take your son, your only son, whom you love…"* (Genesis 22:2 NHEB.)

Let us also consider that Isaac was the promised child through whom God's promises to Abraham would be fulfilled, so this command would seem to hamper those promises. But what did Abraham do? The following morning, he took Isaac and headed out to the place God told him about in prompt obedience. God did not offer him a single clue as to why such a challenging request was made; nevertheless, he obeyed without hesitation. Abraham's faith is an example of the type of faith required for salvation, a kind of faith accompanied by works – an obedient faith. James 2:20–24 says, *"But do you want to know, foolish person, that faith apart from works is useless? ²¹Wasn't Abraham our father justified by works, in that he offered up Isaac his son on the altar? ²²You see that faith worked with his works, and by works faith was perfected; ²³and the Scripture was fulfilled which says, "And Abraham believed God, and it was credited to him as righteousness;" and he was called the friend of*

God. ²⁴You see that a person is justified by works and not by faith alone." (NHEB.)

This command of God makes sense when we read Abraham's story from our standpoint, but the command most likely did not make any sense from Abraham's standpoint. Isaac was not a menace to Abraham, neither was he a plague that needed to be cut off from his life. He was God's gift to him and his only heir. But the test was not about the boy; it was about Abraham, for God wanted Abraham to give up what he loved the most for His sake. The test was to prove how far Abraham was willing to go to please God. Abraham's obedience to God's request was an act of tremendous faith in the sovereignty of God, in that God reserves the right to make whatever demand He deems fit, and Abraham's responsibility was to obey.

Abraham understood that his happiness and fulfilment were not tied to having Isaac alive but living a life of obedience to God, so it should be for us today. Our satisfaction and happiness are not in what we keep and withhold from God, but in what we can let go of because God requires it or how much we are willing to yield to the instructions of God no matter how inconveniencing it is. Abraham valued obedience to God above his will and desires. He submitted himself to the will of God against his own will as Jesus did at Gethsemane; *"Father, if you are willing, remove this cup from me. Nevertheless, not my will, but yours, be done."* (Luke 22:42 NHEB.)

At times, God allows us to pass through some challenges to test our love for Him and our commitment to do His will – this is what differentiates His faithful followers from those who merely claim to follow Him. For Abraham, it was his son Isaac; for us today, it could be a job, career, relationship or bad habit. Note that the test of our obedience is not in obeying God when it is convenient or when it suits our desires; instead, the depth of our love for God is perfectly revealed when we obey God inconveniently or when we follow His will, even if it is against our will and desires; such obedience is genuinely selfless. We must be willing to obey God no matter the cost incurred in the process.

There are other saints of old whose acts of obedience are worthy of mention. Shadrach, Meshach and Abednego were willing to suffer the heinous death of being thrown into the fiery furnace rather than dishonour God. Also, Daniel was ready to be thrown into the lions' den rather than disregard his devotion to God. Let us ponder on the words of Hebrews 5:8 concerning Jesus Christ: *"Although he was a Son, he learnt obedience by the things which he suffered."* (NHEB.)

Abraham's obedience was also a personal act; he most likely did not inform his wife about it, for it would have been difficult for her to understand and the instruction was for him alone. He also asked his servants to wait at a given spot with the donkey while he and Isaac went yonder to worship. He most likely did this to prevent anyone from hindering him in obeying the Lord; thus, obedience to God in some issues may require a personal decision.

God has always been drawn to those who obey Him and tremble at His word down the ages. He takes delight in those who are willing to obey Him at all costs; those willing to surrender all to Him and hold nothing back, who are most concerned about pleasing Him and nothing more and who will not go against His commandments to satisfy themselves. Abraham was such a person; little wonder God called him His friend. When our relationship with God means more to us than anything else in our lives we will be willing to do anything to ensure the relationship continues unabated.

God said to Abraham through His angel, just as he was about to slay Isaac, *"For now I know that you fear God, seeing you have not withheld your son, your only son, from me."* (Genesis 22:12 NHEB.) By Abraham's act of obedience – not withholding his only son from God – he proved to God that he genuinely feared Him. God said to him further: *"I have sworn by myself, says the LORD, because you have done this thing, and have not withheld your son, your only son, [17]surely in blessing I will bless you, and in multiplying I will multiply your offspring like the stars of the heavens, and like the sand which is on the seashore; and your offspring will possess the gate of their enemies. [18] And in your offspring all the nations of the earth will be blessed, because you have obeyed my voice.* "(Genesis 22:16–18 NHEB.)

God did not leave Abraham without reward. As a result of his obedience God fulfilled His promise to him in making him a great nation, and through his Seed – Jesus the Messiah – all nations of the earth can receive the gift of salvation and become his spiritual descendants. *"If you are Christ's, then you are Abraham's offspring and heirs according to promise."* (Galatians 3:29 NHEB.)

Abraham's action of not withholding his son, and God's substitution of the ram for Isaac, was also a reflection of God's sacrifice for mankind. God gave His only Son, whom He loves, as a substitutionary sacrifice for the sins of the entire world.

Let the story of Abraham inspire us to be willing to obey God no matter what it will cost.

TOPIC 3: THE LORD PROVIDES

GENESIS 22:7-8; 13–14

As father and son trod on the lonely mountain road, their words were few but had the impact of a thousand. It was three days since they had left home and the mountain God spoke about was in view. The servants who came as escorts were told to wait at a point. Now, Abraham and his son Isaac had to make the remainder of the journey alone. The firewood, the fire and the knife were all available. Abraham's heart, motivated by obedience and strengthened by faith, was fixed on killing Isaac.

Isaac was used to seeing his father offer sacrifices to God; he knew the items used, but something seemed to be missing on this occasion – the sacrificial animal. His curiosity got the better of him, *"Isaac spoke to Abraham his father, and said, "My father?" He said, "Here I am, my son." He said, "Here is the fire and the wood, but where is the lamb for a burnt offering?"'* (Genesis 22:7 NHEB.) Abraham responded as if he was expecting the question: *"God will provide himself the lamb for a burnt offering, my son..."* (Genesis 22:8 NHEB.) Neither of them knew the impact their discourse would have on eternity. However, both trusted God. Isaac believed God would provide as his father had said, so he asked no further. None of them knew that God's provision would not just be for that day. Instead it would be a shadow of a once-and-for-all sacrifice for salvation. Abraham named the place "The Lord will Provide" because God miraculously provided a ram for the sacrifice. We should rest in that assurance that He is a God that sees a need and sees to its fulfilment.

God is a master provider; He provides long before the need arises. Whether plants for food or rain to water the plants, God provides. He is the God who feeds the hungry. He fed over 600,000 people daily – bread at sunrise and meat at sunset in the wilderness for 40 years (Exodus 12:37; 16:8, 35).

In comparing our earthly parents with our heavenly Father in Matthew 7:9–11, Jesus talks about the magnitude of God's love in comparison to the love of our parents in meeting our needs. *"Or who is there among you, who, if his son will ask him for bread, will give him a stone? ¹⁰Or if he will ask for a fish, who will give him a serpent? ¹¹If you then, being evil, know how to give good gifts to your children, how much more will your Father who is in heaven give good things to those who ask him."* (NHEB.) God does not only surpass our parents in love but also in abundance and ability.

The most common prayer points in a man's heart are his needs and the Lord is fully aware of all of them. Jesus admonished us in Matthew Chapter 6 not to worry about our needs. God clothes flowers whose existence might just be for days; He also makes sure that as the birds go out for food they do not wander without finding some. We are more valuable than the birds and the flowers; this means God always has us in His plans.

It is essential to note that there could be times when we are in need and it will seem as though there is no hope or sign that our needs will be met. At such times, we should not worry about the means or methods by which our needs will be met; instead, we are to do our own part and put our trust in God. If God denies or withholds supplies in His wisdom and sovereignty, it is for our good. God always provides for His children, though, often, not in the way we expect or hope. His provision may come differently and in a manner other than expected. In the account of Elijah, God met his need through strange means. Elijah drank from the brook and the ravens brought him food twice daily. When the brook dried up, God instructed him to go and meet a poor widow. The raven and the widow did not seem like mediums through which one could get provision during the famine, but these were the means God decided to use to provide for His servant. We should not restrict God to any particular method of provision. In whatever way it comes, He answers. He never ignores the needs of His children.

Having faith in God means trusting God whatever the outcome. He will always come through for us; sometimes, He does it in a way that we do not understand. If, after trying every humanly and godly means possible to meet our needs and if after asking for God's intervention, our needs are still not met, we should trust God's love and accept His sovereign will, that in the end everything works for our good.

Isaac later realised that he was the lamb the father had in mind. Although Abraham was willing to sacrifice Isaac, God had His plans: He provided a ram as a replacement. This was a foreshadow of the provision God made for mankind. The ram used as a substitute for Isaac symbolises the Lamb of God – Christ – who became the substitute for mankind. *"And he is the atoning sacrifice for our sins, and not for ours only, but also for the whole world."* (1 John 2:2 NHEB.)

Since God could sacrifice His only begotten Son for our redemption, He can also provide for all our needs through the same Jesus. *"He who did not spare his own Son, but delivered him up for us all, how would he not also with him freely give us all things?"* (Romans 8:32 NHEB.)

CHAPTER 23

TOPIC 1: STRANGER

GENESIS 23:1–20

Abraham lived in Hebron – in Canaan – like a stranger in the land God promised to give his descendants. When Sarah died Abraham needed a place for his wife's burial, so he asked the Hittites for a tomb he could purchase to bury his dead. Abraham started this request by stating the obvious, *"I am a stranger and a foreigner living with you. Give me a possession of a burying-place with you, that I may bury my dead out of my sight."* (Genesis 23:4 NHEB.) The reply of the Hittites should be noted: *"Hear us, my lord. You are a prince of God among us. Bury your dead in the best of our tombs. None of us will withhold from you his tomb to prevent you from burying your dead."* (Genesis 23:6 NHEB.) For a stranger to be accorded so much respect and even titled a "prince of God", he must have lived an exceptional lifestyle that made a significant impact on them.

It is worthy of note that the land Abraham lived in was adjudged by God as evil and awaiting God's wrath, so he was by no means living in a righteous environment. Yet, he conducted himself as a good ambassador and earned the Hittites' trust and respect. Abraham knew his God and did not deviate from His ways but reverenced God in the way he lived, evidenced by how they dealt with him. Abraham's exceptional lifestyle was not a reflection of his native land – which God took him from – but of the character of God, whom he obeyed.

In like manner, anyone who chooses to follow God forsakes the world; he is adopted into God's family through Jesus our Saviour as a co-heir of the Kingdom of God, our heavenly home, whose foundation is not made by human hands. Once adopted, we become strangers on earth because the kingdom we are adopted into is not of this world and does not accept dual citizenship. We live on earth like pilgrims passing through, aligning our ways with the constitution of the kingdom of God like good ambassadors. *"We are therefore ambassadors on behalf of Christ, as though God were making his appeal through us. We implore you on behalf of Christ, be reconciled to God."* (2 Corinthians 5:20 NHEB.)

Abraham would have earned the Hittites' respect because he earned his living through honourable work. Apostle Paul admonished us in 1 Thessalonians 4:11–12, saying: *"and that you make it your ambition to lead a quiet life, and to do your own business, and to work with your own hands, even as we instructed you; [12] that you may walk properly toward those who are outside, and may have need of nothing."* (NHEB.) Also, Abraham must have respected their culture but that did not mean he got entangled with them. Likewise, we should not live as though we are not concerned about the culture of the land we reside in. At the same time, we should not be intimidated into practising any culture contrary to God's word. We should be known for our good neighbourliness. A good relationship earned Abraham a good reputation.

As strangers in this world and ambassadors of the heavenly kingdom here on earth, just like Abraham in the pagan nation, we need to know about the kingdom we represent by diligently studying the constitution – the Bible – with emphasis on salvation. Our lifestyle speaks louder about us than what we tell people about ourselves. People may close their ears to hear us but open their eyes to see what we do and stand for. We are surrounded by witnesses as we travel as strangers in this world. We are expected to be living epistles of the gospel of salvation for the world to read. Though we are strangers, we are princes because we represent the King of all flesh.

As ambassadors of Christ, we should know that our relevance and respect does not come by our conforming to the ways of the world but by being different from the world. *"And do not be conformed to this world, but be transformed by the renewing of your mind, so that you may prove what is the good, well-pleasing, and perfect will of God."* (Romans 12:2 NHEB.) Our conduct and conversations should reflect the new life in Christ Jesus; hence, we should no longer live for self and sin.

People who visit a place for the first time are sometimes judged based on the behaviour of someone or some people who have visited those places from their native land in the past. Strangers have a duty to their hometown to leave a positive impression in the hearts of the inhabitants of the land in which they dwell. As Christians, we are obligated to be good representatives of the Kingdom everywhere we are; this will give the world a good image of the Christian faith, enabling people to welcome and trust other Christians they would later meet in life and accept the gospel.

Christians must live soberly and humbly as strangers and pilgrims on this earth. We must set our minds on things that will help our journey to heaven. We must have a transient view of everything we experience on this earth, whether good or bad, pleasant or unpleasant. The character of Christ must be evident in our lives and our relationship with others on this earth. We must mortify the deeds of the flesh and live an uncompromising life of holiness. We must live in fear of God and always remember that our days on earth will soon pass away like a shadow.

True pilgrims will never get attached to the country they are passing through. Their final destination will always be in their minds and they eagerly anticipate getting there. While going on the journey, they might use the available provisions they come across, but they will not settle down permanently. They have a mindset that affects how they conduct themselves on the journey as pilgrims.

Another outstanding example of godly living in a strange land is Joseph. He exemplified godly living in Potiphar's house, in prison and on the throne. He never lost focus through all these stages, whether in the face of persecution or in times of plenty. When he was coming to the end of his days he asked that his body be taken to the Promised Land when God visits the Israelites. Genesis 50:24–25 says, *"Joseph said to his brothers, "I am dying, but God will surely visit you, and bring you up out of this land to the land which he swore to Abraham, to Isaac, and to Jacob." 25 Joseph took an oath of the sons of Israel, saying, "God will surely visit you, and you shall carry up my bones from here.""* (NHEB.) What an unshaken expression of faith. Joseph knew his God, and this knowledge guided him through all that he did in life.

We are not to be unevenly yoked with the world. We should live in such a way that the world will behold and testify about our relationship with God. The evidence of our walk with God should be apparent to those around us. We are to shine as lights in a dark world, not living as hypocrites, doing everything for the applaud of men, but we are to be faithful to God in secret as well as before men. Apostle Peter wrote: *"Beloved, I urge you as foreigners and temporary residents, to abstain from fleshly lusts, which war against the soul"* (1 Peter 2:11 NHEB). We are strangers in this world, and we have to live in constant reminder that our Father will call us home one day.

CHAPTER 24

TOPIC 1: KNOWING GOD

GENESIS 24:1–7

There is a level of relationship you can have with another person which allows you to predict what that person will do. Your closeness to and understanding of that person make it achievable. This level of relationship does not just happen; it grows like a seed planted in fertile soil. You have to understand the person's strengths, weaknesses and reactions in different circumstances. When all these are put together, predicting what the person will do becomes quite realistic.

Abraham knew God to the extent that he could predict what God would do. In our text we see Abraham's intention to get a wife for his son – Isaac. He made his chief servant, Eliezer, swear that he would go to his kindred at Nahor to get a wife for his son. Abraham confidently told Eliezer that God would send his angel before him. God actually sent His angel to go and get Rebecca ready – although not known to her – even before Eliezer arrived at the well, just as Abraham had foretold. No one makes such bold predictions about a person's actions without trust and a clear understanding of how that person thinks and acts. Abraham knew God so closely that he could give his servant such an assurance. His promise was fulfilled exactly as he had foretold.

Abraham had walked with God for several years before this moment and had come to know God personally and intimately. After his call from his land of nativity, God revealed Himself to him in various dimensions. He had become a friend and confidant of God. It was on the strength of his intimate relationship and personal testimony of his dealings with God that he assured Eliezer not only of God's will to lead him but also the method – *"he will send his angel before you..."* (Genesis 24:7 NHEB) – in accomplishing this task.

The life of Abraham should be a challenge to us. How much can we say we know God? How much do we understand His plans for us? Can we confidently say God will do something and know that He will do it? Isaiah 43:10 says, *""You are my witnesses," says the LORD, "With my servant whom I have chosen; that you may know and believe me, and understand that I am he...""* (NHEB.) Isaiah uses three keywords, "know", "believe" and "understand". God wants us to know Him, believe in Him and understand Him.

Knowing God is not about knowing the scriptures alone. Someone can understand the scriptures, have them in memory and, yet, not know God. Such a person's knowledge of God is theoretical; he does not really know God. Theoretical knowledge is necessary but not enough for a deeper understanding of God.

Knowing God begins with having a relationship with Him, deciding to obey His word entirely and following Him in each step of your life. Two cannot walk together, relate or commune, unless they agree. A relationship with God begins when a person is born again and surrenders his heart and will to God, accepting God's way of life. Knowing God is like studying an object from afar: the closer you get, the clearer you see and understand. Or it is like ascending a height: the higher you go, the broader your view. We ought to draw close to God through His word to have an intimate relationship with Him. God has desires and dislikes; He has His will and purpose, and He can be pleased and displeased. In His word, we can learn all we need to know about Him to walk intimately with Him. We can learn His attributes and nature and learn more about Him from His dealings with men in the past. To us, the word of God should not just be a book of history but a lamp to our feet and a light to our path in this dark world. It must be a manual for our lives and the basis for making all our decisions. We ought to accept it as our constitution and have our lives governed by it. The more we walk in obedience to His word, the more He manifests Himself to us in different dimensions. *"The one who has my commandments and keeps them is the one who loves me. And the one who loves me will be loved by my Father, and I will love him, and will reveal myself to him."* (John 14:21 NHEB.)

Our relationship with God should not be theoretical or abstract in nature. Practically applying God's word leads to an experiential knowledge of Him – experiencing the reality of everything written about God in the scriptures. Abraham's knowledge of God was based on his experience with God over the years; he spent his life walking and communing with God as though two friends were communing together. His relationship with God should be a model for every Christian.

Spending quality time with God through the daily study of His word is one spiritual exercise that is indispensable to knowing God. We must hear the word, read the word, meditate on the word and live the word daily. This is necessary because it is through the word that God reveals Himself to us. Jesus is the word, and the word is God. John 1:1 says: *"In the beginning was the Word, and the Word was with God, and the Word was God."* (NHEB.) Therefore, to know God, we must highly esteem the word and be filled with it.

Saints who left marks in the sands of time knew God and could precisely predict what He would do; this is possible for us today also. Moses assured the Israelites saying, *"for the Egyptians whom you have seen today, you shall never, ever see again."* (Exodus 14:13 NHEB.) The Egyptians were drowned in the Red Sea and the Israelites never saw those armies again, just as Moses had said. Moses could predict what God would do because of his intimate relationship with God.

Apostle Paul wrote to Timothy in 2 Timothy 1:12, *"for I know him whom I have believed, and I am persuaded that he is able to guard that which I have committed to him against that day."* (NHEB.) That was a declaration of the knowledge he had of God, and his faith was based on that knowledge. The only limitation for us knowing God fully is an ineffective relationship with Him resulting from a lifestyle of disobedience and lack of zeal or desire to know Him.

Knowing God will require time and much of it. Let us invest our time on earth in studying His word with emphasis on salvation, in devotion and in prayer, to grow in the knowledge of God as did the saints of old. Knowing God is the secret to an extraordinary Christian life, *"but the people who know their God shall be strong, and take action."* (Daniel 11:32 NHEB.)

TOPIC 2: MARITAL GUIDANCE

GENESIS 24:1–7

Marriage is a sacred institution that brings a man and a woman together in companionship to be husband and wife. Since it is a lifelong union we must be properly guided to avoid the mistake that would bring regret in the future.

One of the hurdles of modern society is how young people go into marriages, negligent of their parents' guidance or advice. Young people nowadays feel the self-sufficiency of selecting a spouse without any involvement from parents. Some have this mindset that if parents are involved in their spousal choice problems will eventually arise, but what they forget is that, many times, "What an elder sees sitting down, a child will not see even if he climbs a tree." (An African adage.)

Marital guidance in choosing whom to marry is an essential part of parental responsibility. It involves guiding the marriageable children in a godly approach to marital decision making. In choosing a life partner, one must take the proper steps at the outset.

Abraham was aware that he would soon die and had one concern he needed to resolve before dying. Isaac was unmarried and Abraham knew that God's promise had to come to fulfilment in the life of the promised heir. He also knew that the blessings of God could only come to pass with the help of God. Abraham had always trusted God in everything and this concern was no exception. He did not sit and wait for God to bring a wife for Isaac; he needed to take steps. Abraham entrusted the delicate task of finding a wife for his son to Eliezer – his senior servant – who was in charge of all he had. Abraham made him swear that he would not take a wife for his son – Isaac – from the Canaanites but from Abraham's own country and relatives. There is a possible reason for Abraham making this decision: it could have been because of the iniquity and idolatry among the Canaanites – he did not want Isaac to be yoked with a Canaanite woman for his heart might be drawn away from God.

God later gave a commandment – similar to Abraham's instruction – to the Israelites not to inter-marry with the Canaanites lest their hearts be turned from Him and they begin to follow their gods. *"When the LORD your God shall bring you into the land where you go to possess it, and shall cast out many nations before you, the Hittite, and the Girgashite, and the Amorite, and the Canaanite, and the Perizzite, and the Hivite, and the Jebusite, seven nations greater and mightier than you; [2]and when the LORD your God shall deliver them up before you, and you shall strike them; then you shall utterly destroy them: you shall make no covenant with them, nor show mercy to them; [3]neither shall you make marriages with them; your daughter you shall not give to his son, nor shall you take his daughter for your son. For he will turn away your son from following me, that he may serve other gods; so the anger of the LORD would be kindled against you, and he would destroy you quickly."* (Deuteronomy 7:1–4 NHEB.) They were to marry from their tribe. The reason for the instruction is glaringly seen in the life of King Solomon. Solomon married from nations outside the tribes of Israel, which God had forbidden; the women turned his heart towards other gods so his heart was not entirely devoted to the Lord.

God warns us to avoid marrying outside the family of God – those who do not live according to His instructions. Our true family is the Christian fold, for we are all one body in Christ as it is written, *"For whoever does the will of my Father who is in heaven, he is my brother, and sister, and mother."* (Matthew 12:50 NHEB.) Christians and unbelievers are two different kinds of people with different values and priorities in life. The former seeks the righteousness of God; the latter is comfortable with a life of carnality. One has his affections set on things above, the other on the things of this world. One is living with eternity in view, the other is living for the glory and the pleasures of the world. *"Do not be unequally yoked with unbelievers, for what fellowship have righteousness and iniquity? Or what fellowship has light with darkness? [15] What agreement has Christ with Belial? Or what portion has a believer with an unbeliever? [17] Therefore, "'Go out from their midst, and be separate,' says the Lord, 'and touch no unclean thing,' and I will receive you."* (2 Corinthians 6:14–15, 17 NHEB.)

Christianity is a call to be separate from the world because friendship with the world is enmity with God. *"You adulterers and adulteresses, do you not know that friendship with the world is hostility toward God? Therefore whoever wants to be a friend of the world makes himself an enemy of God."* (James 4:4 NHEB.) A follower of Christ cannot be unevenly yoked with the people of this world. Christians should therefore not go into marriage with unbelievers, no matter how beautiful, handsome, intelligent or wealthy the person may be. Christians ought not to marry unbelievers. A Christian who marries an unbeliever risks their eternity with the Lord, for there is a high tendency that such a person will backslide, become lukewarm and have their affections removed subtly from the Lord and set on the very things that person renounced to follow Christ. It could trivialise their walk with Christ due to the unbelieving spouse's influence and the need to please the spouse.

Guidance is not always easy for humans to follow, especially when it comes to marriage. As Christians, we should allow God to guide us, walking in His dictates and direction. When we depend on His guidance we are sure to make the right choices, for He will guide us into His perfect will for our lives. Psalm 73:24 says: *"You will guide me with your counsel, and afterward receive me to glory."* (NHEB.)

Christian parents, then, should guide their children in choosing a life partner. Parenting is a responsibility entrusted to us by God; God gives children as a master gives his farm to servants to groom. Hence, parents must not fail God in this crucial aspect of their children's lives. Parents should not sit on the fence regarding the choice of whom their children should marry. Also, while guiding their children, they should not compel them; instead, they should get involved through prayers and godly counsel. Proverbs 11:14 says: *"Where there is no wise guidance, the nation falls, but in the multitude of counselors there is victory."* (NHEB.)

Every loving parent will want the best for their children. Children are expected to listen to their advice, ponder and pray over that that conflicts with their intentions. Proverbs 1:8–9 says, *"My son, listen to your father's instruction, and do not forsake your mother's teaching: ⁹ for they will be a garland to grace your head, and a necklace around your neck."* (NHEB.)

Note: a broken courtship is better than a wrong marriage.

Apart from godly parents being involved, we must depend on God earnestly through prayer for proper guidance. Just as Abraham's servant prayed to God, prayer for God to guide you in choosing your life partner is necessary to avoid making a mistake. God knows the heart of every man and knows the man or woman best for you. By seeking His face, you tell Him to guide you to make the right choice because you do not know who is best for you. Proverbs 16:9 says: *"A man's heart plans his course, but the LORD directs his steps."* (NHEB.) And Proverbs 3:5–6 says: *"Trust in the LORD with all your heart, and do not lean on your own understanding. ⁶In all your ways acknowledge him, and he will make your paths straight."* (NHEB.)

TOPIC 3: REALITY OF FAITH

GENESIS 24:1–9

Hebrews 11:1 defines faith as *"being confident of what we hope for, convinced about things we do not see."* (NHEB.) Faith is described as the confident affirmation of certainty about the occurrence of what one hopes for and the certainty that what one has not seen will happen. Faith in God enables us to face the unknown; it is essential in our walk with God. It is how we relate with God and, without it, we have no relationship with Him. Faith is believing in God's word, that God can do what He said He would do. It is that trust that compels us to take actions based on the word of God.

However, there is a misconception regarding faith among a good number of Christians in our contemporary times. Faith for a woman seeking the fruit of the womb could mean believing God, without a doubt, that she will definitely carry a child of her own. Faith for a university student who is diligent in studies and fears God could mean that they will come out with excellent grades. Faith for every Christian who wakes up in the morning and commits themselves to the hands of God through prayers could mean that they will tackle their daily endeavours and return home at the close of work safe and sound. All these are true about faith, but what happens when the woman believing that God will provide a child dies childless, the student falls short of the expected grade or something unpleasant happens to the Christian who had committed themself to God before leaving their house in the morning? Does it mean that they did not have faith enough? Or could it be that their relationship with God is faulty?

Faith is the fuel that drives our relationship with God; without faith, it is impossible to please Him: *"Now without faith it is impossible to be well pleasing to him, for he who comes to God must believe that he exists, and that he is a rewarder of those who seek him."* (Hebrews 11:6 NHEB.) Since faith is a tool of the spirit, its purpose is to aid us in our spiritual walk with God. Faith cannot be complete without trust. The misconception regarding faith among many Christians in our contemporary times results from an understanding of faith as an "unswerving expectation" from God for what we want, without giving thought to what God may want for us at that time, and also assuming that if we want it so much then it has to be the will of God. Trust is an essential element of our faith in God: it makes faith pleasing to God. "Trust" makes our faith steadfast even when our expectations are not met, because we believe that He is in control of whatever happens. When we trust in God, our faith in Him becomes unswerving even in the face of trying times.

When it was time for Isaac to find a wife, Abraham was not willing to leave such an important decision to chance. He called his servant, Eliezer, and made him swear that he would find Isaac's wife from his (Abraham's) home country and from among his relatives. He said to Eliezer, *"The LORD, the God of heaven, who took me from my father's house, and from the land of my birth, who spoke to me, and who swore to me, saying, 'I will give this land to your offspring.' He will send his angel before you, and you shall take a wife for my son from there. ⁸If the woman isn't willing to follow you, then you shall be clear from this my oath. Only you shall not bring my son there again."* (Genesis 24:7-8 NHEB.)

Abraham's statement was based on his understanding of the Sovereignty of God. Although he desired to find a wife for his son from among his relatives and believed that God would help his servant do so, he left the final decision to God and therefore did not hang the oath on his conviction but on God's sovereignty. He considered that if God chose not to help his servant achieve this, that would be fine by him, and his servant would be released from the oath.

Faith with an understanding of God's sovereignty is to trust that His will is not only superior to ours but far better for us. It is to be at peace with God even when it seems that our prayers are not being answered as we expect. We must understand that God has the right to change our plans, redirect the course of our lives and withhold from us answers to our requests if they do not align with His will for us. We must ask ourselves if the purpose of God or what He desires for us is against our desires, will we still accept it as best for our lives or will we be discouraged, lose hope in Him and turn our backs against Him? At Gethsemane, before His crucifixion, Jesus prayed, *"Father, if you are willing, remove this cup from me. Nevertheless, not my will, but yours, be done."* (Luke 22:42 NHEB.) He acknowledged the will of God over His life was supreme, no matter how inconveniencing that was for Him.

When Shadrach, Meshach and Abednego were told by King Nebuchadnezzar to choose between dishonouring God – by bowing to the image he had set up – and being thrown into the fiery furnace, they replied to the king that they knew the God they served was able to deliver them from the fiery furnace. However, they added that if God chose not to deliver them – letting them suffer the heinous fate of burning in the fire – they would still not dishonour God. They trusted God and were willing to accept His will as best for them no matter what it was (Daniel 3).

We must understand that everything God does is right, even if it may seem wrong to us. For the very reason that God does it, it is right. We are to remain committed to Him even when we do not fully comprehend His will for our lives.

Job is known in the Bible for the severe trials he faced in his lifetime, and although he did not understand at some point why God allowed such calamities to befall him, he never turned his back on God but remained committed to Him. He declared to his friends, *"Look, though he should kill me, I will hope in him. Nevertheless, I will argue my ways before him."* (Job 13:15 NHEB.) Sometimes we face troubles because God permitted some of the enemy's arrows to get to us; at other times we are the architect of our troubles. Whatever the case, if we turn to God or hold on to Him in faith, He will turn it all to our good in the end.

That said, what does the reality of faith mean to us as Christians? In simple terms the reality of faith is trusting God, even if the answer to our prayers does not conform to our expectations. It entails not doing anything against God's word to achieve our desired results.

In our walk of faith with God, let us recognise that we are all vessels in the hands of God and acknowledge the sovereignty and will of God. Because God is omniscient, knowing the end from the beginning, we should trust His will as being the best for us, for He loves us beyond what words can express and will always do what is best for us.

TOPIC 4: ELIEZER: GOOD STEWARDSHIP

GENESIS 24:1–67

As the oldest servant of Abraham, Eliezer can be appropriately regarded as a good steward who exhibited hallmarks of excellent stewardship in service to his master, Abraham. Transparent, honest and obedient, Eliezer, over the years, proved to be the kind of servant that Abraham could trust and depend on.

The extent of a task has a way of revealing levels of trust, no doubt. The higher the trust reposed in a person the higher the importance of an assignment handed to them. As a result of Eliezer's trustworthiness, Abraham chose him, and not anyone else, for the crucial task of getting a wife for his son, Isaac. This task was no easy one. Eliezer was required to find a wife for Isaac from Abraham's relatives and not from the Canaanite women. *"Abraham said to his servant, the elder of his house, who ruled over all that he had, "Please put your hand under my thigh. ³I will make you swear by the LORD, the God of heaven and the God of the earth, that you shall not take a wife for my son of the daughters of the Canaanites, among whom I live.""* (Genesis 24:2–3 NHEB.)

Despite the physical exertions the journey would require, Eliezer did not object, especially when it would have been easier to find a wife for

Isaac in their current vicinity. Even though Abraham had assured him of God's guidance in carrying out this task, his determination to ensure the mission's success led him to seek God's help in prayer – a prayer God answered even before he concluded (Genesis 24:12-15). His faithfulness in fulfilling Abraham's wish also made him secure the marital agreement between Rebekah and Isaac after carrying out every order he was given, giving every item he was asked to give and saying everything he had to say. Little wonder, then, that in one of Abraham's conversations with God, the very person he mentioned that would inherit his possessions, should he die childless, was no other person than Eliezer.

Though little was recorded about Eliezer's life and service to Abraham, many lessons could be gleaned from him concerning stewardship. If there is one quality that would make us excel in our service to God and stand out in our dealings with men, that quality is good stewardship. As a biblical principle, stewardship embodies a quality God desires us to demonstrate in every facet of our lives. Whether as an employee at a workplace or a domestic, God requires us to demonstrate faithfulness in whatever task we are entrusted with. In obedience, we are to carry out whatever task we are given without compromising or doing as we please. In all sincerity, we must discharge our duties with the right motive, as if it is to God, not with eye service. Colossians 3:22–23 says: *"Servants, obey in all things those who are your masters according to the flesh, not just when they are looking, as people pleasers, but in singleness of heart, fearing the Lord. ²³And whatever you do, work heartily, as for the Lord, and not for people"* (NHEB).

We can learn from and be encouraged by Eliezer's life to perform whatever task entrusted to us by giving it due attention, time and energy. Even when the people we serve maltreat us, as long as we choose to remain in their service we should still carry out our tasks diligently, just as we would for kindhearted superiors. 1 Peter 2:18–19 says: *"Servants, be in subjection to your masters with all fear; not only to the good and gentle, but also to the wicked. ¹⁹For it is commendable if someone endures pain, suffering unjustly, because of conscience toward God."* (NHEB.) We must also be spurred into giving our best regardless of the assignment's importance entrusted to us. A domestic who operates with a mentality that sees his duties as not requiring total commitment would undoubtedly be complacent and negligent about them. Luke 16:10 reveals that *"He who is faithful in a very little is faithful also in much. He who is dishonest in a very little is also dishonest in much."* (NHEB.) In point of fact, if we are unfaithful in managing other people's businesses and affairs simply because they do not belong to us, we would be laying for ourselves a foundation that would be detrimental to our future. Joseph's life should serve to teach us how to be good stewards wherever we find ourselves. Transformed from a favourite son to an ordinary servant, Joseph would have chosen to be slothful and sulky in his duties. But he was not. Despite his status as a slave, Joseph displayed exceptional faithfulness, diligence and management. These attributes propelled his master to put him in charge of his house, to the extent that Joseph's master did not bother about the status of his possessions. Not only that, his diligence and excellent stewardship continued even while in prison until he was appointed the second in command in Egypt.

Just as God desires us to show good stewardship towards others, He also requires us to exhibit stewardship in our service to Him for everything He has placed under our care. For every resource God has provided for us, every child He has given to us, and other things He has entrusted in our possession, none belongs to us but to God. As such, God expects us to demonstrate good stewardship by managing them faithfully and diligently. While it is a common sight to see people misconstrue God's provisions as personal possessions they can use as they please, God requires them to be utilised according to His will. And just like the two faithful stewards in the parable of the talent, when we are faithful and diligent with what God has given us, He will entrust us with more responsibilities.

Since we shall one day give an account to God of how we performed as stewards, it is binding on us to be faithful, diligent and transparent in our services to God and to others.

TOPIC 5: PARENTAL BLESSING IN MARRIAGE

GENESIS 24:1–67

Many young people allow the emotions of a romantic relationship to cloud their sense of reasoning. They want to leave their parents and cleave to their partners without getting their parents' blessing. But the truth is that if there is no proper leaving, that is, if an intending spouse leaves their parents in malice and with misunderstandings unresolved, an issue could be a foothold for the devil in causing harm to the marriage. As children of God, no intending spouse should rush into marrying a partner whose parents withhold their consent for any reason. Wisdom and patience are required in handling such issues amicably so that parents could be well pleased to give their blessing.

How Rebekah received her parents' blessings before leaving is instructive for us today. Eliezer, being divinely guided by God, encountered Rebekah at the well. Though Eliezer had met Rebekah and was sure at this point that she was the will of God for Isaac, he did not just take her away to his master. He followed her to her house, met her parents, disclosed his mission to Rebekah's family and recounted to them how he was divinely led to her. They were pleased with him and obliged his request to take Rebekah as a wife for his master's son, Isaac. When they were about to leave her parents poured blessings on her and her generations yet unborn – the promised descendants of Abraham. Her parents' blessings went with her and gave her peace, joy and fulfilment in her new home.

Parental blessings at that time and even in our society today are necessary for the peace, progress and stability of a new family about to begin. Parental blessings in marriage can be said to be positive words or goodwill from parents or those who have parental authority over the intending couple. These blessings accompany the intending couple on their journey of matrimony.

Getting parental blessings is necessary for a marital decision, but parents will generally withhold their blessings if they do not consent to the marriage. It can be frustrating when a person thinks they have found the right partner, only for their parents to disapprove of the choice. An obedient child would want their parents' blessing when taking this crucial step. You find yourself at a crossroads with two sets of people you care about. On one side, you have your parent(s). On the other, you have the person you desire to spend the rest of your life with. The best way to handle this conundrum is to obey God's word and never let emotions dictate your actions. The Bible says that children should honour their parents. ***"Children, obey your parents in the Lord, for this is right. ²"Honor your father and mother," which is the first commandment with a promise: ³"that it may be well with you, and that you may live long in the land.""*** (Ephesians 6:1–3 NHEB.) Adherence to this commandment by getting your parents' approval before entering into marriage is the right way to attract their blessings.

The importance of parental blessings in marriage can never be overemphasised. Therefore, as Christians, we must seek the consent and blessings of both parents involved. This is essential because marriage is the joining of two individuals and the unification of two families. Thus, blessings, the seal of parental approval of your intended marriage, are requisite. You are to pay close attention to your parents' opinions and carefully consider their judgements about your decision. For the very reason that they love you as parents, and because of their wealth of experience in the marital life you are about to begin, they should be able to guide you on what they sincerely perceive to be the best for you.

That said, perhaps, your parents refuse to give their blessings because they disapprove of your intending union; it is essential to try and understand the reason for their objection to address it adequately. In a situation where your parents' reason for disapproving the union is valid, it will be ultimately advantageous for you to obey them. You can further seek godly counsel from those with mature minds and get them involved when and where necessary. One thing is sure: if the person once disapproved by your parents is God's will for you, God will convince your parents to give you their seal of approval to marry each other.

It is often wise for intending couples to scripturally consider and carefully listen to any objection raised by their parents. They might be seeing what the young people might not see, especially when such an objection is made out of love and in line with the word of God.

There might be cases in which the parents refuse to consent to their child's marriage due to tribal preference or other unfounded sentiments. Such issues must be handled with wisdom. Intending couples are to employ several means to convince their parents. They should seek godly guidance on the most appropriate way to handle such cases without relenting in prayers. They can get others involved, especially those their parents are most likely to listen to. It will be wise to do everything within the confine of God's word to get their parents' consent and blessings before proceeding into marriage.

Someone may want to ask, what if parents still oppose their child's marriage after all is said and done? Can the child go ahead without the parents' blessings? Marriage is not a bed of roses; it is characterised by different hurdles. It would be good not to add the burden of parental grievance to that list. Hence, it is honourable and crucial to do all within the confine of God's word to seek one's parents' blessings.

As for the parents, the Bible says that parents should not provoke their children to anger. As long as children desire their parents' consent in marriage, parents should not reject their children's choices based on personal sentiments and prejudices. Their disapproval should be based on their children's spiritual and physical welfare – what they know will affect them severely in the long run. But their reasons should be communicated to their children to avoid every possibility of misunderstanding. Ephesians 6:4 says, *"And fathers, do not provoke your children to anger, but nurture them in the discipline and instruction of the Lord."* (NHEB.)

Over and above this, marriage is a holy institution that God loves. But before children walk down the aisle they need to receive their parents' blessings. Getting their full support will be of immense help and relief in building a marriage on a sound foundation, with your parents at peace with you and your choice.

TOPIC 6: DIVINE DIRECTION

GENESIS 24:12–20

Imagine a traveller going to an unfamiliar place. It would be helpful for the traveller on the journey if there was someone who understood the way to the traveller's destination to serve as a guide – giving them an accurate direction to ensure a hitch-free arrival at the destination. Generally, directions often specify the path to take to get somewhere, steps to take to achieve a set goal or what to do to fulfil a purpose. Indisputably, the best direction to any desired destination is obtained from the person who knows the way.

Today, independence is respected and dependency is seen as a weakness. We live in a world in which people feel confident enough to make decisions without being guided. It is worldly proof of strength if we execute things without being directed, but that should not be, since we have limited knowledge of life.

We can see how Eliezer depended on God and how God made his journey to the land of Nahor to find a wife for Isaac successful, as hoped for by Abraham. Long before Eliezer reached the well God had divinely arranged his meeting with Rebekah and guided him to this meeting as Abraham believed and assured him. *"The LORD, the God of heaven, who took me from my father's house, and from the land of my birth, who spoke to me, and who swore to me, saying, 'I will give this land to your offspring.' He will send his angel before you, and you shall take a wife for my son from there."* (Genesis 24:7 NHEB.) Eliezer believed in Abraham's statement and totally depended on God for proper guidance and direction to know the woman who would be a wife for Isaac, as evident in his prayer.

Before this time, Abraham had been receiving directions from God, from when God commanded him to leave his father's house and home country and on several other occasions in his walk with God. So, while sending Eliezer to his relatives in his home country to find a wife for Isaac, he was confident that God would guide Eliezer and make his assignment successful, and it was just as Abraham believed.

The need for God's direction in life's journey cannot be overemphasised. We have no idea what the future holds, nor can we see beyond the present. God made us, and He knows what is best for us. He called us and designed the way we are to follow; hence, being divinely directed is the only means to get it right in life. We can agree, there would have been no way Eliezer could have achieved the task of finding the right wife for his master's son without divine guidance. Eliezer was fully aware of the sensitivity of the task. He did not rely on looks – standing by the well and looking out for the most beautiful lady he could find. This would have been ill-advised, for beauty is not only fleeting, but it also does not reveal the heart's content. He did not rely on his understanding; he depended solely on God. He understood that only God could give the right wife to his master's son.

God does not leave us to grope hopelessly on the way to Him or in pursuit of assignments that are in line with His will. The way through this life, in general, is being given by God in His word – the Bible. We can only see and understand it when we align our lives according to His precepts.

A strong relationship with God is a prerequisite for Him to direct a man. Abraham had such a relationship with God, trusting and obeying God completely. This relationship is core in receiving divine direction from God. God faithfully directs the path of everyone who obeys and trusts in Him. *"The steps of a man are established by the LORD, and he delights in his way."* (Psalm 37:23 NHEB.)

Actually, God not only provides guidance in the manner He guided Eliezer but guides us in diverse ways, sometimes through angels, His audible voice, prophets, visions, circumstances and through His word. Hebrews 1:1–2 says: *"God, having in the past spoken to the fathers through the prophets at many times and in various ways, ²in these last days has spoken to us by a Son, whom he appointed heir of all things, through whom also he made the ages."* (NHEB.) One thing is sure: His leading is ever accurate, safe and tends to a blissful end. When we obediently relate with Him, He will guide us accurately through His word. Jesus is our Great Shepherd. When we choose to personally follow His instructions by becoming His sheep, as a shepherd guides the sheep, He will guide us, for He is the word of God.

The psalmist wrote: *"Your word is a lamp to my feet, and a light for my path."* (Psalm 119:105 NHEB.) The word of God as a lamp illuminates the path of life for a smooth journey, just like a lamp illuminates the way through the darkness. It guides and directs us, lighting our way towards fulfilling our purpose in life and eventually arriving at our eternal home. Many have failed in diverse aspects of their lives, such as seeking life partners, career choices, lines of businesses, and so on, because they failed to bring God into their affairs. We need proper guidance, which only God can provide. Proverbs 3:5–6 says: *"Trust in the LORD with all your heart, and do not lean on your own understanding. ⁶In all your ways acknowledge him, and he will make your paths straight."* (NHEB.)

When Eliezer got to the well, he called on God for help. Prayer is also essential for divine guidance. When we are at a crossroads and do not know what to do, we should not hesitate to call on God in prayer for guidance. A simple prayer is an acknowledgement of our reliance on God. Note that long before Eliezer got to the well or called on God in prayer, God had divinely orchestrated his meeting with Rebekah. She came to him before he had finished his prayer. This teaches that God is aware of our needs even before we ask in prayer. We need not worry; instead, trust Him wholeheartedly. Matthew 6:8 says: *"for your Father knows what things you need, before you ask him."* (NHEB.)

It is easier for us to experience divine guidance when God is our priority. But when our priority is material there is the risk that the devil might be leading and we would still be thinking it is God. If our pursuit is the salvation of our souls, we will not be misled by the devil if we focus on it. We need divine direction at every step of our way; it will save us time, heartbreaks and the loss associated with a lack of it.

TOPIC 7: ACKNOWLEDGING GOD

GENESIS 24:12–27

How often do we hear people fail to acknowledge God but instead credit things to luck? We often hear people use phrases like, "Today is my lucky day!" or "I am a lucky person!" Sadly, even Christians make the mistake of crediting favourable happenings to luck. It is often done unconsciously but that does not change the fact that we ignorantly undermine God's sovereignty and fail to give Him His due glory. To others, it is not luck, but they tend to acknowledge others as the source of their successes and growth. At other times, some of us are tempted to think that our strengths, intelligence and academic qualifications are the factors behind our achievements. This is giving human factors pre-eminence over the God factor. The truth is, without God, we can achieve nothing.

Stay long enough in perfumery and you will come out exuding the fragrance. Stay long enough in a foul-smelling environment and you could dispel people by the odour you exude. Moses stayed long enough in God's presence; he came out radiating God's glory. Abraham's servant stayed long enough with Abraham; he came out radiating Abraham's quality of acknowledging God in everything he did. Because of his long association with Abraham, the servant came to know and believe in the God of Abraham. The little he knew of

God was enough for him to display a kind of acknowledgement that might not be found among many Christians today. He said, *"Blessed be the LORD, the God of my master Abraham, who has not forsaken his loving kindness and his truth toward my master. As for me, the LORD has led me in the way to the house of my master's relatives."* (Genesis 24:27 NHEB.) Eliezer did not behave as careless men will do, as if the occurrence was fortuitous, but gave thanks to God, regarding it as God's providence and mercies. He did not boast of good luck or fortune but declared that God had dealt kindly and faithfully in fulfilling His promise to Abraham. He did not boast of his strength as a factor in his successful mission. He acknowledged God from the beginning to the end of his mission.

Acknowledging God is to recognise Him as the sole source behind whatever assignment we have done successfully, whatever good is bestowed on us, whatever blessing we are enjoying, whatever feat we have attained, the answers to prayers we have received, and, above all, the salvation of our souls. Paul understood this reality when he wrote, *"by the grace of God I am what I am…"* (1 Corinthians 15:10 NHEB.)

Christians are sometimes guilty of attributing happenings to luck or their abilities. The truth is that there is no such thing as luck. No cosmic force lines up to orchestrate events and nothing happens by chance or due to our power. Every single thing, from the weather to the most minor events, is controlled by the sovereignty of God, and for this we must acknowledge Him, giving honour to whom honour is due. *"You are the LORD, even you alone. You have made heaven, the heaven of heavens, with all their army, the earth and all things that are on it, the seas and all that is in them, and you preserve them all. The army of heaven worships you."* (Nehemiah 9:6 NHEB.)

Acknowledging God as the principal source behind our successful living should be non-debatable and permeate everything we do. We might be the ones people see acting on the scene, but God is the One working behind the curtains and the source behind whatever we are, and all glory must be given to Him alone. How true this is in light of Philippians 4:13: *"I can do all things through him who strengthens me."* (NHEB.) The young man Joseph fully demonstrated this admirable quality of acknowledging God when he responded to Pharaoh concerning the ability to interpret dreams. *"And Joseph answered Pharaoh, saying, "Apart from God an answer of peace shall not be given to Pharoah.""* (Genesis 41:16 NHEB.)

In contrast to Joseph, often we tow the path of Nebuchadnezzar, who attracted God's displeasure and wrath because he failed to acknowledge God as the source behind his greatness, and the consequence was him being driven to dwell among the beast for seven years. By this, we understand that God is never pleased when men's hearts are given to pride. As pride brought Nebuchadnezzar to disgrace, so did humility elevate Christ to glory. Christ is our standard, and He sets the tone we must follow. Though He was God in human form, He never failed in acknowledging the Father. In John 5:30, He had said: *"I can of myself do nothing. As I hear, I judge, and my judgment is righteous; because I do not seek my own will, but the will of the One who sent me."* (NHEB.)

People think that acknowledging God only centres on the spectacular and unique things that happen in their lives, but it goes much deeper than that. Acknowledging God also entails reverencing Him even if there seems to be nothing outstanding going on for us at the moment. For the fact that we pay nothing for the air we breathe it is more than enough reason to acknowledge the love of the Almighty; and for what it is worth, God is doing so much in the background that human senses are too limited to grasp. Acknowledging God goes beyond what God has done to what He has withheld from us. What many see as failures and react to them in that light could be God protecting them in the best possible way. We ought to spend our entire lives in reverence to Him. Even when we feel He has not done anything, even when surrounded by seemingly harsh conditions, we must still acknowledge and thank Him. It was to believers that Paul wrote: *"[16]Rejoice always. [18]In everything give thanks, for this is the will of God in Christ Jesus toward you."* (1 Thessalonians 5:16, 18 NHEB.)

Furthermore, when certain problems in our lives are being solved by God through our pastors, spiritual leaders or other brethren, it is appropriate to appreciate God's faithfulness in their lives. But often, we acknowledge the clay rather than the Potter, and this ought not to be. We must ensure we do not give God's glory to a mortal man, and, as such, the principal credit and glory must always be attributed to God for whatever He does for us through anybody. This goes farther than our spiritual leaders and cuts across all spheres of life. Whenever we find ourselves as beneficiaries of people's graciousness we are to be thankful to them, but never should we see them as our hope or portray them as the true source of our wellbeing. In all things, through all favours and through all help from men, we should be able to see the hand of God and acknowledge Him for His endless love and care.

Let us learn from now on to give God credit and acknowledge Him for His workings in our lives. Let us also teach our children the mistake of attributing what happens to them to luck or strength. We must teach them that both the good and seemingly bad things that happen in their lives are not detached from God's providential superintendence. Although some unpleasant things may sometimes happen because of our carelessness or evil cravings, some may result from evil people and the world's systems. Whatever the case may be, if we live our lives by the will of God, acknowledging Him in everything, He can turn every unfavourable or seemingly unfavourable situation to our good in the end. *"We know that all things work together for good for those who love God, to those who are called according to his purpose."* (Romans 8:28 NHEB.)

TOPIC 8: VIRGINITY

GENESIS 24:16

The world we live in gets more and more permissive by the day. Loss of virginity before marriage now seems normal. Sexual purity in our contemporary times is largely understood to be archaic.

Be that as it may, virginity has always been and will always be the will and expectation of God for His children before marriage.

The world had experienced sexual aberration, evident when God destroyed the world with a flood and Sodom and Gomorrah with fire. So, for Rebekah to be a virgin at a marriageable age is commendable. Considering that the world in the days of Noah and the cities of Sodom and Gomorrah were destroyed because of their sexual immorality, among other sins, it should not be assumed that Rebekah lived in a primitive world as far as sexual immorality is concerned. It was her determination to be virtuous that kept her.

Abraham had earlier charged his servant Eliezer to get a wife for his son Isaac from his country. He assured him that God would send His angel, who would guide him all the way. When Eliezer got to the well outside the town of Nahor he said a prayer, and before he had finished praying Rebekah had come out to meet him. The Bible records: *"The young lady was very beautiful to look at, a virgin, neither had any man known her. She went down to the spring, filled her pitcher, and came up."* (Genesis 24:16 NHEB.) The description of Rebekah is remarkable. She was not only beautiful but was also a virgin. Her beauty was not her doing; it was a gift from God. But her virginity, however, was her decision. She decided to keep her sexual purity until she got married.

The ancient culture placed a high value on the virginity of women. Virgins were regarded as more honourable than those who were non-virgins. Losing virginity before marriage was a grievous offence for any daughter in Israel. It was considered shameful and an act of dishonour to her family. Under the law, a newlywed who had lost her virginity before marriage was condemned to death after proof of her sexual impurity was provided. *"But if this thing be true, that the tokens of virginity were not found in the young lady; [21] then they shall bring out the young lady to the door of her father's house, and the men of her city shall stone her to death with stones, because she has done folly in Israel, to play the prostitute in her father's*

house: so you shall put away the evil from the midst of you."
(Deuteronomy 22:20–21 NHEB.) This emphasises the value God
places on sexual purity.

Sexual desire is created by God. Through sexual intimacy, man is to
procreate. It is an honourable act that must be guided by regulations.
The misuse of the gift God has given to us displeases Him. Sex should
be kept within the bounds of marriage. Like most gifts given to us by
God, sex can be honoured or abused. But most times in life, people
choose to abuse it. The Bible from the Old Testament to the New
Testament condemns sexual immorality.

In the centre of increasing moral and societal degradation, we must
ensure that we maintain our sexual purity as children of God.
Remaining a virgin until marriage is a choice that requires a significant
level of discipline and determination. It is a choice, and we must
purpose in our hearts not to give in to the pressures and temptations
that surround us every day. Our reaction to sexual temptations
should be marked by self-control, which is possible through the Holy
Spirit's help.

Fornication is borne out of a carnal and selfish desire, a sensual lust
often mistaken for love. This was the kind of affection Amnon had for
Tamar, and it made him send for her and sleep with her against her
will. He thought not of God or Tamar but only of himself, satisfying
his carnal desires. Little wonder that after he raped her he hated her
much more than he had loved her (2 Samuel 13).

The love of God considers God and the good of the other party. True
love is when a man is willing to follow the proper procedure to make a
woman his wife first and not defile her before marriage. From time
immemorial, God has been against fornication. This is contained in
His word: *"Flee sexual immorality. "Every sin that a person does is
outside the body," but he who commits sexual immorality sins
against his own body. ¹⁹Or do you not know that your body is a
temple of the Holy Spirit which is in you, which you have from*

God? You are not your own, ^{20}*for you were bought with a price. Therefore glorify God in your body."* (1 Corinthians 6:18–20 NHEB.)

Christians must be wary of the devices of the evil one. We must have control over our eyes and our desires. We must endeavour to avoid situations that would tempt us to sin. Virginity is marked by courage, self-control and the guidance of the Holy Spirit. Every day, many pray to God to keep them from temptation, yet they seek temptations themselves more often than not. Jesus warns us in Matthew 5:28, *"but I tell you that everyone who looks at a woman to lust after her has committed adultery with her already in his heart."* (NHEB.) Today, we find ourselves in a worse environment than the earthly days of Jesus. Why? With the advent of media technology and the internet we find ourselves in situations in which we are easily fed sexually immoral content. If we are exposed to sexual messages and images that we choose to watch on the television or surf on the internet, we will reap increasingly stronger erotic thoughts, desires and possible urges to put them into action.

Our bodies are the temple of the Lord, and our most reasonable and holy service to God is to present our bodies as living sacrifices, holy and acceptable to Him. Not only is premarital sex an offence to God, it can also make a person susceptible to sexually transmitted diseases and demonic possession or unwanted pregnancy that could lead to abortion.

Preserving one's virginity has a way of bestowing honour and dignity on the virgin. Though civilisation has bastardised the significance of maintaining one's virginity in this generation by making it an unpopular virtue, it does not, however, change the unbendable standard of God regarding sexual purity and abstinence. No matter how unpopular virginity is, premarital sex is a sin with attendant grievous consequences. Hebrews 13:4 says: *"Let marriage be held in honor among all, and let the bed be undefiled: for God will judge the sexually immoral and adulterers."* (NHEB.)

Peradventure you have lost your virginity in the past; you need not run away from Christ. Do not feast on your state and continue in sexual immorality. You can come just as you are and with a repentant heart, pray for forgiveness, make a decision to submit to Him as Lord, and serve Him faithfully for the remaining days of your life. With your newfound faith in Christ old things are passed away and all things are new. 1 John 1:9 says: *"If we confess our sins, he is faithful and righteous to forgive us the sins, and to cleanse us from all unrighteousness."* (NHEB.) God is willing to receive you, and He can open a new chapter of favour for you and bless you with a blissful marital union.

In reality, virginity is good but is not entirely equivalent to salvation. As good as being a virgin is admirable and pleasing to God and a mark of a high standard of morality, being a virgin without the salvation of one's soul will not guarantee you eternity with God. Therefore, as a virgin or non-virgin you must surrender your life to Jesus and live a life of holiness by total obedience to God's word. 1 Thessalonians 4:7-8 says: *"For God called us not for uncleanness, but in sanctification. ⁸ Therefore he who rejects this does not reject man, but God, who has also given his Holy Spirit to you."* (NHEB.)

For a Christian, entering marriage as a virgin shows the strength of one's moral character and love towards God. It promotes trust between spouses and engenders deep love. Followers of Christ must maintain a high moral standard within a perverse environment of permissiveness. God brought about sex, and He made it a sacred gift reserved only for within marriage. Sex was not designed to be a fleeting passion but for intimacy, an essential element of companionship in a marital union. God's standard on total abstinence from sexual intercourse until marriage remains immutable. Hence, whoever disregards this instruction dishonours God.

CHAPTER 25

TOPIC 1: PUTTING YOUR HOUSE IN ORDER

GENESIS 25:5-6

Death constitutes an inevitable reality that every mortal must confront. It is a reality that entails the mortality of our existence and could affect the fate of those we leave behind.

When it comes to matters related to death, most people often refrain from entertaining any thought or discussion on it. The thought of death often poses an emotional obstacle and puts a thread of restraint on people from planning for their loved ones before their earthly departure. Letting the thought of death prevent us from preparing for our family comes with many pitfalls that may not bode well for their future. Since death would not show us the courtesy of notifying us before visiting, choosing to defer preparations for our loved ones or failing to prepare for them all together may prove to be disadvantageous to their wellbeing in the event of our demise. While we may not fancy thoughts on matters that relate to death, the reality is that death is inevitable; we can at least make life easier for those we would leave behind by making adequate preparations for their wellbeing.

Abraham represents a classic example of a father who made the wise decision to prepare for his family's welfare before death. Judging by the decisions he made, it can be said that Abraham understood the necessity of putting his household in order before departing this world. First, after Sarah's death Abraham made funeral preparations for her, himself, and his descendants by buying land to serve as a cemetery. Also, he provided marital guidance to his son, Isaac, by ensuring he married from the right family. Further, he ensured his possessions were distributed among his children accordingly before his death. Without a shred of doubt, these actions were acts of wisdom. Each of his children was given their share of the inheritance. By that action, a potential future dispute was averted.

Putting our house in order before our demise is an act that God approves of, as seen in the story of King Hezekiah. One remark that stood out when God informed Hezekiah of his impending death was: *"Set your house in order..."* (Isaiah 38:1 NHEB.) It can be said that if God saw wisdom and importance in making preparations for our household we must rest assured that we would be making a prudent decision by making preparations for our loved ones before our demise. While everyone may not have the opportunity Hezekiah had in being notified of the day of their death, we can, in our capacity, influence the impacts our death will have on loved ones after our departure.

One of the most unique ways to demonstrate love for our families as parents is to put our houses in order by making adequate preparations for them in every way possible. Regardless of our financial status we owe it to our family to make the necessary preparations and provisions for them before our departure. Many challenges could rear their ugly heads when the family's breadwinner neglects to prepare before his demise. Struggle for properties among families and family members killing each other over inheritance are not strange occurrences; they are tales as old as time. As a parent still drawing breath, you can play a vital role in averting unpleasant experiences by taking necessary measures where needed. For those who possess properties, own businesses and have possessions of worth, there is always the option of having a will drafted before your death. As a legally binding document, a will goes a long way to averting strife and ensuring that family members get what their deceased loved one wished to bequeath to them.

It is worth noting that while a written will is good, we can support it with video technology. With video technology, we have a means by which we can back up our will and put our house in order. In recent times, people have pre-recorded videos explaining how they intend their properties to be shared among those they leave behind. Copies are made and entrusted to individuals to ensure that the will's execution is according to the recorded information. After the individual's death, the video is played to the concerned persons, letting each party know what belongs to them.

Despite the assurance that comes with the video, the fate of the will could still be tampered with by human shenanigans, just as a written will is liable to human manipulations. Many are the stories that have been recounted of well-documented wills being contested and cases of lawyers and executors compromising and disrespecting the testator's wishes.

Those who desire to avert any potential conflict and dispel any lingering worries on what happens after they are gone can consider the Abraham template. While still very much alive, Abraham allocated his possessions as he deemed fit. This shows that putting your house in order is not limited to carrying out actions when you think you are close to death; it is also necessary when you are still very much alive. It would be prudent for those who have properties to allocate them to those they wish should possess them, while those who own businesses can assign them to their children or those they want to manage them. With such a succession plan happening during our lifetime, we can guide our successors on how to run the business, correct them where necessary and ensure they are familiar with the operations. Any issue concerning business partners or friends should be addressed to clarify what is rightfully theirs between the partners and the successors.

Another aspect we must put in order before our departure from this world is our relationship with family members. Departing this world while there is still division in your home or while you are still at odds with a family member could leave your house in disorder. Setting your house in order also involves settling all grievances within the household. Whether it is grievances directly with a family member or among the children or siblings, you must attempt to find an amicable resolution to it.

Beyond the allocation of properties and resolution of grievances, our family members' relationship with God must also be put in order before our demise. It is not good enough for us to be saved while our family members wallow in the miry pit of sin. It is not good enough for us to make heaven while they are heading headlong into hell due to our negligence in leading them in the way of the Lord. Leaving the spiritual state of our home in disorder does not bode well for them. Deuteronomy 6:6–9 admonishes us on what to do: ***"These words, which I command you this day, shall be on your heart; [7]and you shall teach them diligently to your children, and shall talk of them when you sit in your house, and when you walk by the way, and when you lie down, and when you rise up. [8]You shall bind them for a sign on your hand, and they shall be for symbols between your eyes. [9]You shall write them on the door posts of your house, and on your gates."*** (NHEB.)

By teaching and nurturing our family members through the word of God while we are still alive and not on our death bed, we can leave them a legacy that would not only see them through the course of their lives but also ensure the salvation of their souls.

TOPIC 2: FULFILMENT OF GOD'S PROMISE

GENESIS 25:12–16

We live in a world in which it is easy for some people to make promises they never intend to keep, where marital vows are breached at the slightest provocation, where public-office holders make empty promises they are not committed to fulfilling with impunity. Beyond all doubt, we live in a world in which most people's words are no longer their bonds.

But to our God, unfaithfulness cannot be named with Him. He is a faithful God and He ever remains committed to His promises, even to His promise to save the world through His Son, Jesus. The fulfilment of His promises is immutable. He is a promise-keeping God – He always fulfils His promises to the exact details of His word. He is omniscient, omnipotent and upright. The implication of these attributes of God concerning His promises is that God, being omniscient, makes His promises with full knowledge of the future – knowing the end from the beginning; God, being omnipotent, makes His promises with confidence in His ability to do all things; and God, being upright, cannot lie. These attributes of God make it impossible for Him to make a promise He does not intend to fulfil. Numbers 23:19 says, *"God is not a man, that he should lie, nor the son of man, that he should repent. Has he said, and will he not do it? Or has he spoken, and will he not make it good?"* (NHEB.)

Let us consider how God fulfilled the promises made to Abraham concerning Ishmael. It should be recalled, while God was reaffirming His commitment to give Abraham a son through Sarah, that Abraham responded: *"Oh that Ishmael might live before you."* (Genesis 17:18 NHEB.) The Almighty God made promises to him regarding the lad. Obviously, Ishmael was not the child of promise nor did God intend to establish His covenant with Abraham in him. Yet, for the sake of Abraham, God promised to bless him and make 12 princes out of him. The verses in context, Genesis 25:12–16, show how God implemented His promises concerning Ishmael as He promised his father – Abraham.

(For more on the Fulfilment of God's Promise, see Chapter 21, Topic 1)

TOPIC 3: PARENTAL LOVE

GENESIS 25:28

Ask parents about their love for their children; the response will be: "We love all our children equally." Let us give it to most parents, deep down in their hearts they love all their children, as much as is within their powers, equally. But the equitable demonstration of affection from parents to their children is challenged by the children's personalities or other factors. Parents may consciously or unconsciously display the love for one child more intensely than the way they show for another child. This can lead to problems for the whole family while the children grow and become adults.

In court, a young man was asked why he murdered his brother; he replied: "Daniel was always the loved one, right from when we were young. I always felt like an outsider in my own home; Daniel always gets the best gifts, and all the applauds were usually on him. He was mom's and dad's favourite, 'precious little Dan'", he scoffed sarcastically. He said further, "We grew up, and then I thought this might change, but it was the same old story. Daniel kept being the person taken to the company and shown the ropes in management while I played second fiddle, always playing catch up. It was even more hurtful considering I was the first child, but that didn't do any good; my parents' love always swayed to Daniel's side. I grew so angry at both my parents and Daniel that I did not even give it a second thought when someone suggested I take Daniel out of the picture." (Johnny, 2022.)

Let us take a look at Isaac's family in our passage: two parents, two children, and two different directions of love: How did it get to that level? They were twins, same gender, so one would not say it was gender preference. Genesis 25:28 says, **"Now Isaac loved Esau, because he ate his venison. Rebekah loved Jacob."** (NHEB.) The scripture clearly mentioned why Isaac loved Esau; Esau was a hunter and Isaac loved his game. The passage did not directly say why Rebekah loved Jacob but we can deduce the reason from the scriptures. First, Jacob was a quiet man, dwelling in tents. Secondly, Rebekah had a knowledge of the prophecy concerning Jacob: **"The LORD said to her, Two nations are in your womb. Two peoples will be separated from your body. The one people will be stronger than the other people. The elder will serve the younger."** (Genesis 25:23 NHEB.)

Whether unconsciously or deliberately Rebekah aligned herself with the one she thought would be the master over the other. This preference would later cause Rebekah to manipulate her husband to bless Jacob over Esau. She loved Jacob more than Esau and worked to ensure that Jacob took the blessings of the firstborn. Isaac loved Esau because he ate his game, but Rebekah loved Jacob, showing that each parent's preferential love for one child means less love for the other child. It might not have been outright hatred, but one child would always be favoured over the other. As always, in cases of preferential love from parents, there were consequences. At a point, Esau was plotting to kill Jacob because Jacob had deceived their father into blessing him instead of Esau; and both brothers could not see each other for over 20 years after their mother had arranged for Jacob to flee to her brother in Padan Aram.

A good number of parents exhibit favouritism towards a child consciously or unconsciously. This is usually displayed by consistently favouring, spending more time with, paying more attention to, giving more privileges to, and exerting less discipline on the preferred child. Most parents do not start out intending to love one child more than the other. Inherent in most parents is love for all their children. Unequal parental love for children often manifests due to an assortment of factors. Some of these factors are qualities exhibited by the children. For some parents, their preference for one child over another could be due to different factors such as intellectual or physical abilities, birth position, gender, resemblance or unique talents. For others, the degree of love expressed towards their children is conditional on how successful a child is.

Parental favouritism is a serious issue that has been tearing homes apart. It is like cancer: it eats deep into the core of the family, destroying it little by little, till it grows to a stage that it becomes disastrous. Parents are often oblivious to its effects on both the more favoured and the less favoured children. Regardless of the reason for favouring one child over the other, the consequences can be far-reaching. Proverbs 28:21 rightly puts it: ***"To show partiality is not*** *good...*" (NHEB.) Jealousy and unhealthy rivalry tend to manifest when one child is loved more than another. Rather than supporting their siblings, unequally loved children will see each other as competitors rather than collaborators. Children who feel less loved often exhibit envious resentment for siblings who are more loved than them, and dislike their parents. The story of Joseph and his brothers illustrates the effect of favouritism in the family. Genesis 37:3–4 records how Jacob loved Joseph more than his brothers: *"Now Israel loved Joseph more than all his children, because he was the son of his old age, and he made him a coat of many colors. [4]His brothers saw that their father loved him more than all his brothers, and they hated him, and couldn't speak peaceably to him."* (NHEB.) It is pretty apparent that Jacob's preferential love for Joseph, evidenced by presenting him with a beautiful clothing gift, as well as Joseph's dreams, elicited envy, conspiracy to murder, and finally, human trafficking by the other brothers.

Another effect of favouritism on the family is that in the long run, unfavoured children may find it difficult to accept who they are because they do not feel loved and accepted by their parents. Lack of acceptance can affect emotional wellbeing, the ability to believe in oneself and the ability to withstand criticism from others.

In raising children, parents should avoid generating conflict in the family by preferring one child over another, which may eventually result in permanent hatred between family members.

A parent may have reason(s) for preferring one child over another but should not allow it to escalate into strife. Instead, parents should learn to carry all their children along. Even if they prefer a particular child for whatever reason, they should learn not to make it obvious to prevent the other children feeling neglected or unloved. Parents should understand that children may not all be the same in their actions, reactions and approaches. To fully thrive, every child must be made to feel loved and special. Every child has potential that we need to discover and nurture. Parents should provide a conducive environment for their children to express themselves but with a guiding love.

Furthermore, regardless of how wayward or ill-behaved a child is, parents must not diminish their love for such a child. Instead, they should exhibit the love of Christ. They should pray for the child and lovingly lead them to Christ through the word of God.

That said, this does not exonerate children from taking responsibility for their actions or give children the leeway to conduct themselves in whatever manner they choose. Children should try to be in their parents' good books by exhibiting behaviours that honour their parents according to biblical instructions.

In conclusion, children need affection, warmth and time from their parents and parents should bring up their children in the way of the Lord with love, devoid of favouritism and division, so that the devil may not gain entrance and tear the family apart. The word of God and prayer should have a central place in the family and should not be pushed aside.

TOPIC 4: BIRTHRIGHT

GENESIS 25:29–34

Esau had a test of value presented to him in the form of food versus birthright. He had just returned home exhausted and famished and was greeted by the smell of his brother's stew. He immediately engaged his brother in dialogue so that the brother would offer him some. But Jacob, seeing his brother's desperate need, pitched him a deal which would see a transfer of birthright in return for the stew, and Esau, who was consumed by hunger, immediately agreed to this deal, swapping his birthright for a bowl of stew. At that moment Esau failed a crucial life test of the value of things.

This is a vital lesson for all of us, for *"Like a city that is broken down and without walls is a man whose spirit is without restraint."*

(Proverbs 25:28 NHEB.) A man without self-control is given to his desires, having no restraint over his appetite. He is willing to satisfy himself, not minding the consequences of his action in the long run. He is always liable to do something fatal or unfavourable to himself. Such a person is described as a city whose walls are broken down. A city with broken-down walls is a defenceless city, exposed to many woes and mischiefs. Esau simply displayed a lack of self-control in the face of hunger, leading to his birthright's loss.

Some special privileges and advantages belonged to the firstborn son among the Hebrews. By birthright, the first son inherited the family's leadership and the judicial authority of the father. In Deuteronomy 21:16–17 it is stated that the first son was also entitled to a double portion of what other children were having. *"then it shall be, in the day that he causes his sons to inherit that which he has, that he may not make the son of the loved the firstborn before the son of the unloved, who is the firstborn: ¹⁷but he shall acknowledge the firstborn, the son of the unloved, by giving him a double portion of all that he has; for he is the beginning of his strength; the right of the firstborn is his."* (NHEB.)

Esau was highly privileged as the firstborn. He exchanged all of that for food, having more regard for his appetite than his rights as the firstborn son. He was not too concerned about the consequences of his action in satisfying his hunger. His attention was on momentary relief at the expense of his birthright. His unbridled appetite cost him his inheritance. Hebrews 12:16–17 says: *"that there be no... profane person like Esau, who sold his own birthright for one meal. ¹⁷For you know that even when he afterward desired to inherit the blessing, he was rejected, for he found no place for a change of mind though he sought it diligently with tears."* (NHEB.)

Although natural birthright comes with its attendant benefits in many cultures, there is a birthright of far greater value – the spiritual birthright. As natural birthright accompanies natural birth, the spiritual birthright is bestowed on us through spiritual birth, and it is the most valuable thing to us as Christians. John 1:12–13 says: *"But as many as received him, to them he gave the right to become God's children, to those who believe in his name, ¹³who were born not of blood, nor of the will of the flesh, nor of the will of man, but of God."* (NHEB.) We are privileged to become sons of God and co-heirs with Christ by our spiritual birth. Through Jesus, that birthright in God enables us to come to God as sons, and we can call Him Abba, Father. But regrettably, because of obsessive desire to satisfy the flesh, mundane pleasures and inordinate cravings for wealth and position, we sell our spiritual birthright by compromising our faith.

We should be mindful as Christians of our decisions in every circumstance of life. Circumstances should not control us to the extent that we compromise our faith and lose our identity. Usually, out of carelessness, we trade our lives for less valuable and temporary pleasures instead of living for God's kingdom and righteousness. Let us learn from Esau's mistake of not recognising the value of what he had.

We find ourselves behaving like Esau when the world offers pleasures of far lesser value than the kingdom of heaven. The world offers you sexual immorality to satisfy your fleeting passion, and you choose it over your salvation. The world offers you the fear of physical consequences, and you choose it over the fear of the Lord. The world offers you sinful means of obtaining treasures on earth that moths and thieves can destroy, and you prefer it over the treasures in heaven. This ought not to be.

Our soul's salvation should be more important to us than anything this world could offer. Mark 8:36–37 says: *"For what does it profit a person to gain the whole world, and forfeit his soul? ³⁷For what will a person give in exchange for his soul?"* (NHEB.) We must stop looking at life shortsightedly. There is something in store for us of far greater value than whatsoever the world may offer us – that is, our sonship and right to the kingdom of God.

Esau made the mistake of not recognising the value of what he had and later regretted it. His action is a lesson for us. After he lost his birthright he sought the blessing with tears but all to no avail. Likewise, no amount of tears on Judgement Day will help us if we lose our salvation for a morsel of bread offered by the world. All we need to do to secure our heavenly birthright and inheritance is to be done now while we are alive, that is, living by the word of God. We should place our life as vessels in complete surrender in God's hands; then our birth inheritance will be guaranteed.

TOPIC 5: UNDUE ADVANTAGE

GENESIS 25:29–34

We may have come across someone who needed our help at some stage in our lives. The question then is: how did we react? Was our reaction borne out of love, assisting the person with their burden? Or did we see the person's situation as a fertile ground to be ploughed to our advantage? Life will always throw us situations like these and how we react to them helps show the kind of person we are.

As every passing second ticked, the growling in his stomach increased. Like an oppressed person, his stomach protested vehemently; his ravenous appetite craved to devour the delicacy prepared by his brother. Just when he thought his craving would be gratified there and then, Jacob stopped him in his famished tracks. *This is the opportunity, my opportunity,* Jacob might have thought to himself. "Hurry! Let me have some of that red stew, Jacob," Esau requested desperately. "Sell me your birthright first," Jacob demanded in response. Like a man who felt the hourglass of his life trickling down, Esau, who felt the piercing claws of hunger grazing the walls of his belly, caved into Jacob's demand.

When a person's weakness is discovered, he can be easily manipulated or taken advantage of, making such a person give up something he would never have given up in a normal scenario. Con artists make a fortune from this: they capitalise on people's needs and desperation and use it to convince them to give away things that are quite dear or essential to them. With this, we can say that undue advantage is the act of a person preying on others' weaknesses to achieve a selfish goal to the detriment of those others.

The act of taking advantage of people's situations contravenes the instruction of God. Exploiting people who need assistance demonstrates un-Christ-like behaviour and contrasts with the believer's attitude of love expected towards neighbours.

There are many scenarios in which people have used others' situations to gain something that usually the victim would be unwilling to give up. There are cases in which one person needs financial assistance from another, only to be greeted with the option of giving up something essential, or in which a trusted person takes in someone with the promise of help and instead traffics that person for monetary gain. The list of examples of such opportunism is endless. It is a plague that destroys our society. Some Christians who are supposed to be the light of the world are also involved in this self-centred lifestyle. They have become so conformed to the world's lifestyle of opportunism that the ones meant to be sheep have joined the pack of wolves, exploiting the needs of others to satisfy themselves. We often only think "If I help this person what do I gain?" rather than "If I don't help this person what would happen to them?" Usually we are only interested in the material things we stand to gain and forget the more important issue: what the other person will lose. We have become so self-centred that all we care about is ourselves; after all, "my happiness is all that matters".

If we have genuinely given our lives to Christ in repentance the Holy Spirit will flood our hearts with love for God, which will be reflected in our love towards our fellow human beings. Love is pure and does not take advantage of others; it is not selfish but gives. Love is the mark of a yielded life in Christ Jesus. If we say we love the Saviour and believe in His word we must prove it by how we live. By our new nature in Christ, we would not use a person's condition or circumstance as a field to harvest, a field to satisfy our selfish nature at others' expense. God expects us to show an attitude devoid of exploitation and ulterior motives towards those needing assistance. We are not to take advantage of others simply because we are in a position in which we can do so. It is essential to follow the instruction contained in Philippians 2:3–4: *"doing nothing through rivalry or through conceit, but in humility, each counting others better than himself; ⁴ each of you not just looking to his own things, but each of you also to the things of others."* (NHEB.)

As Christians, if we are in the habit of taking undue advantage of someone else's situation, we must stop doing this. It is an issue in our lives that needs addressing. The flesh will always subscribe to the gains of the flesh but the Holy Spirit-driven person will always consider the effect their action will have on others, and ultimately on their salvation. Because the fruit of the Spirit is love, kindness and goodness, we are to walk in love just like Christ taught us. Ephesians 5:2 says, *"And walk in love, even as Christ also loved us, and gave himself up for us, an offering and a sacrifice to God for a sweet-smelling fragrance."* (NHEB.)

Only when we start putting ourselves in other people's shoes and looking at our actions through their eyes can we say that we are believers or children of God. If we know our actions will hurt others and do not want something similar to happen to ourselves, love entails that we do not do it. And if we know that our actions towards others will be good for them because we know they will be good for us, love requires that we carry out those actions. Matthew 7:12 says: *"Therefore whatever you desire for people to do to you, do also to them; for this is the Law and the Prophets."* (NHEB.) When our idea of life is always putting ourselves first and always wanting to be number one, taking advantage of others is relatively easy. Jacob took advantage of Esau's condition because he wanted to be first, and this we should not emulate because love entails doing to others what you would have them do to you.

On the flip side, as Christians, people may try to take advantage of us because of our nature. Some people are selfish, lovers of money or simply greedy. When they meet an easy-going person they try to employ the exploitation strategy by taking advantage. The Bible says we should be as innocent as doves and as wise as serpents. We are to be discerning and not to easily give in to such schemes orchestrated by others. We are to put ourselves in a position in which we do not have to do anything under tension or pressure. Many people are victims because they let their desires control their reasoning. For instance, a person who has a strong desire for money can be easily taken advantage of. Just like Esau, we all have some natural appetites and desires that should be restrained and curbed. Unless this is done, those desires will take us to unwelcome places, making us lose things we wanted to keep. To this end, we should never let our desires control us, for in so doing we are making it a weakness that people can exploit. Ignorance is also a significant factor in why people are taken advantage of. We must try not to be blinded by the clouds of ignorance and yearn for enlightenment. In so doing, we reduce the chances of being exploited.

Those who have been victims can learn from it, save others from similar pitfalls using their experience, and be shrewder in the future, for it is said, "Once beaten, twice shy." Forgive the person who took advantage of you and pray for God to forgive the person also. Your experience should be a springboard of learning in your dealings with people in the future.

REFERENCES

Campbell, M. (1996) *Behind The Name*. Available at: www.behindthename.com (Assessed: 18 March, 2022).

dictionary.com (2022) Available at: https://www.dictionary.com (Assessed: 18th March, 2022).

Oxford Learners Dictionary (2022) Available at: https://www.oxfordlearnersdictionaries.com (Assessed: 18 March, 2022).

Strong, J. *Strong's Hebrew and Greek Dictionaries*. e-Sword app version 13.0.0. Meyers, M. 2000-2021. Available at: https://downloads.digitaltrends.com/esword/windows/post-download (Assessed: 18 March, 2022).

Lightning Source UK Ltd.
Milton Keynes UK
UKHW010713150922
408910UK00002B/341

9 781803 810461